TEACHING LANDSCAPE:
THE STUDIO EXPERIENCE

Teaching Landscape: The Studio Experience gathers a range of expert contributions from across the world to collect best-practice examples of teaching landscape architecture studios. This is the companion volume to *The Routledge Handbook of Teaching Landscape* in the two-part set initiated by the European Council of Landscape Architecture Schools (ECLAS).

Design and planning studio as a form of teaching lies at the core of landscape architecture education. They can simulate a professional situation and promote the development of creative solutions based on gaining an understanding of a specific project site or planning area; address existing challenges in urban and rural landscapes; and often involve interaction with real stakeholders, such as municipality representatives, residents or activist groups. In this way, studio-based planning and design teaching brings students closer to everyday practice, helping to prepare them to create real-world, problem-solving designs.

This book provides fully illustrated examples of studios from over twenty different schools of landscape architecture worldwide. With over 250 full colour images, it is an essential resource for instructors and academics across the landscape discipline, for the continuously evolving process of discussing and generating improved teaching modes in landscape architecture.

Karsten Jørgensen is Professor of Landscape Architecture in the School of Landscape Architecture at the Norwegian University of Life Sciences, Norway. He was Founding Editor of *JoLA*, the *Journal of Landscape Architecture*, 2006–2016.

Nilgül Karadeniz is Professor of Landscape Architecture at Ankara University, Turkey. She is a founding member of the LE:NOTRE Institute and she chaired the Institute between 2016 and 2018.

Elke Mertens is Professor of Landscape Architecture and Open Space Management at the Hochschule Neubrandenburg – University of Applied Sciences, Germany. She has been active in the LE:NOTRE Thematic Network as well as in ECLAS as a member of the executive boards.

Richard Stiles is Professor of Landscape Architecture in the Faculty of Architecture and Planning at Vienna University of Technology, Austria. He is a past President of the European Council of Landscape Architecture Schools and was Coordinator of the European Union co-funded LE:NOTRE Thematic Network in Landscape Architecture for 11 years.

Recognizing how landscape architects employ knowledge from a wide range of disciplines, the editors of *Teaching Landscape: The Studio Experience* present examples where educators create learning environments that resemble real-world situations in which students learn how to synthesize case-specific information. Authors from around the world pass on inspiring experience where, by addressing a variety of challenges at different scales, students work in groups to develop design and planning approaches, to apply different theories, methods, techniques and technologies, and to train in communication and management skills.

Diedrich Bruns
Professor Emeritus of Landscape Planning,
University of Kassel, Germany

Edited by Karsten Jørgensen | Nilgül Karadeniz | Elke Mertens | Richard Stiles

TEACHING LANDSCAPE:
THE STUDIO EXPERIENCE

LONDON AND NEW YORK

First published 2020
by Routledge
2 Park Square, Milton Park, Abingdon, Oxon OX14 4RN

and by Routledge
52 Vanderbilt Avenue, New York, NY 10017

*Routledge is an imprint of the Taylor & Francis Group,
an informa business*

© 2020 selection and editorial matter, Karsten Jørgensen,
Nilgül Karadeniz, Elke Mertens and Richard Stiles;
individual chapters, the contributors

The right of Karsten Jørgensen, Nilgül Karadeniz,
Elke Mertens and Richard Stiles to be identified as the
authors of the editorial material, and of the authors for
their individual chapters, has been asserted in accordance
with sections 77 and 78 of the Copyright, Designs and
Patents Act 1988.

All rights reserved. No part of this book may be reprinted
or reproduced or utilised in any form or by any electronic,
mechanical, or other means, now known or hereafter
invented, including photocopying and recording, or in
any information storage or retrieval system, without
permission in writing from the publishers.

Trademark notice: Product or corporate names may be
trademarks or registered trademarks, and are used only for
identification and explanation without intent to infringe.

British Library Cataloguing-in-Publication Data
A catalog record for this book is available from
the British Library

Library of Congress Cataloging-in-Publication Data
Names: Jørgensen, Karsten, editor. | Karadeniz, Nilgül,
editor. | Mertens, Elke, editor. | Stiles, Richard, editor.
Title: Teaching landscape : the studio experience /
edited by Karsten Jørgensen, Nilgül Karadeniz,
Elke Mertens and Richard Stiles.
Description: Milton Park, Abingdon, Oxon ;
New York, NY : Routledge, 2019. |
Includes bibliographical references and index.
Identifiers: LCCN 2019017638 (print) | LCCN
2019021632 (ebook) | ISBN 9781351212915 (eBook) |
ISBN 9780815380542 (hbk) | ISBN 9780815380559
(pbk) | ISBN 9781351212915 (ebk)
Subjects: LCSH: Landscape architecture--Study and
teaching. | Landscape design--Study and teaching.
Classification: LCC SB469.4 (ebook) |
LCC SB469.4 .T43 2019 (print) | DDC 712.076--dc23
LC record available at https://lccn.loc.gov/2019017638

ISBN: 978-0-8153-8054-2 (hbk)
ISBN: 978-0-8153-8055-9 (pbk)
ISBN: 978-1-351-21291-5 (ebk)

Typeset in Joanna MT and DIN Schrift
Cover and graphic design: Oliver Kleinschmidt, Berlin

Cover images:
Front cover – top left: Roxy Thoren;
top right: Marie Andersson;
bottom left: Chelsea Schmitke, Heather Scott
bottom right: SMAK Ghent; drawing: Carl Steinitz
Back cover – left: John S. Webb; right: Marie Andersson

Publisher's Note
This book has been prepared from camera-ready copy
provided by the editors.

CONTENT

INTRODUCTION

VI Foreword
Attila Tóth

VIII Beaux-Arts to Bauhaus and beyond...
Karsten Jørgensen, Nilgül Karadeniz,
Elke Mertens, Richard Stiles

DESIGN STUDIOS

2 Introduction

4 From urban acupuncture to the third generation city—alternative studio narratives
Marco Casagrande

16 Walk and dance through landscape
in design studio teaching:
reflective movement as an initial
and explorative design tool
Carola Wingren

30 Overlook: art and materiality in the
landscape architectural curriculum
Roxi Thoren

42 Creative landscape inhabitance:
the ReGenerate Studio
Shannon Satherley

56 Urban Intervention Studio
being site specific: temporary design
installations in transforming urban areas
Bettina Lamm, Anne Margrethe Wagner

68 Digital design: opportunities and
challenges for design studios
Jillian Walliss, Heike Rahmann

80 A phenomenological method
for the landscape studio
Susan Herrington

LANDSCAPE CONSTRUCTION CLASSES

95 Introduction

96 Rainwater management as part of
the HRS site engineering education
Peter Petschek

104 Teaching environmental technological
design: fostering meaningful learning
integrating green infrastructure into
architectural and urban design
Maria-Beatrice Andreucci

LANDSCAPE PLANNING STUDIOS

120 Introduction

122 Teaching in a collaborative studio
context: on educating conductors
and "getting started"
Carl Steinitz

136 Teaching a regional landscape project
studio in the interdisciplinary setting
Adnan Kaplan, Koray Velibeyoğlu

150 Landscape science in studio
Joan Iverson Nassauer

162 Toward a second coast:
speculating on coastal values
through landscape design studio
Maria Goula, Ioanna Spanau,
Patricia Pérez Rumpler

176 Teaching landscape urbanism
in the French context
Karin Helms, Pierre Donadieu

186 Teaching the unpredictable:
critically engaging with urban landscapes
Lisa Diedrich, Mads Farsø

LANDSCAPE HISTORY AND THEORY

201 Introduction

202 Recollecting Landscapes: teaching and
making landscape biographies
Bruno Notteboom, Pieter Uyttenhove

214 Learning from history: integrating an
archive in landscape teaching
Ulrike Krippner, Lilli Lička, Roland Wück

226 Teaching the history of urban open space
using a multi-scale approach
Bernadette Blanchon

APPENDIX

247 Biographies
252 Index

Foreword

Attila Tóth

Chair of the LE:NOTRE Institute
Assistant Professor of Landscape Architecture
at the Slovak University of Agriculture in Nitra

Over the last thirty years, the European Council of Landscape Architecture Schools (ECLAS) together with, the LE:NOTRE Institute, its successful project that aims to link landscape education, research and innovative practice—has created and developed a fruitful platform for sharing experiences in landscape education across Europe. This book is one of the valuable outcomes of this international networking and cooperation, and its publication marks the centenary of the first university programme in Landscape Architecture in Europe that was established by the Agricultural University of Norway in 1919. It also marks three decades of pan-European networking in the discipline that started at an event hosted by the Technical University in Berlin in 1989. One of the beautiful features of landscape architecture teaching in Europe is its diversity, which builds upon rich traditions and histories. In some countries, landscape architecture was established in agricultural and horticultural schools, in some others it was in forestry schools, and in many countries landscape architecture has been taught at architectural and urban-design faculties. This creates an interesting and colourful patchwork of approaches that is nicely reflected in this book.

Design studio as a form of teaching is the highlight in landscape architecture education, in that it gets very close to the future professional practice of students. It simulates to a certain extent a professional design studio environment. Students have the chance to learn from existing problems, challenges and assignments in the landscape and to get into interaction with real stakeholders, such as municipality representatives or residents. Studio-based design teaching brings students closer to everyday practice and enhances their motivation, while at the same time, it offers a great opportunity for teachers to stay in a vivid touch with professional design as studio supervisors and mentors. Besides the professional experience such as field mapping, site analysis and design, students can also acquire very important and relevant soft skills and social competences such as team work, division of tasks, time management, design communication, presentation and argumentation of their projects.

Teaching landscape is a complex task. It builds upon three main knowledge and skill pillars—a natural, a technical and a creative one. Studio teaching can be seen as a tympanon supported by these three pillars that integrates knowledge of natural sciences and plants, applied technical and drawing skills and creative capability of students. This complex knowledge and skill set then interacts with society in the context of participatory planning and landscape democracy processes, as landscape architects have to deal with a wide range of landscapes ranging from everyday to outstanding, from degraded to high-quality, as well as their perception by people. Today, landscape architects are much more likely to play the role of innovative co-designers than conventional designers. Thanks to studio teaching, as students they are able to acquire the professional capacity and conceptual understanding for taking up leading roles in landscape projects from urban to rural settings.

Design studios provide a great opportunity to introduce and test novel experimental methods. In many cases, they can be combined with research—following the idea of research for / by / on design and leading to research-guided teaching. This approach brings science to studios and stimulates critical and scientific thinking of students. Design studios can vary thematically—from small-scale private gardens through more complex public open spaces, up to large-scale landscape planning projects. Studios can also vary in design detail and the level of project documentation—from sketches and landscape studies to construction details and implementation projects for building permit. This way, students can test their ability and creativity to develop different design philosophies, ideas and concepts, as well as their technical skills to create diverse construction details and planting-design solutions.

As a teacher, I have been involved in semester design studios, as well as short-term summer schools and workshops in Landscape Architecture for the last seven years in my role as Assistant Professor at the Slovak University of Agriculture in Nitra, and more recently as Visiting Professor at the University of Novi Sad in Serbia. During this period, I have had the opportunity to assist with the co-design of many unique, yet challenging urban and rural spaces with engaged and motivated students. This has been a great opportunity to learn, not only for students but also for me as a teacher. Most of these design studios have been taught in co-operation with stakeholders such as local governments and involving mainly mayors, municipal representatives and local residents. It was thus a great opportunity not only to teach and learn, but also to promote landscape architecture as a profession and raise the awareness of the public on the importance of landscape issues. During the current academic year I have had the experience of starting to develop a brand new bachelor design studio at the Department of Landscape Architecture in Nitra—the Park Design Studio. It is the first landscape design studio at the bachelor level of studies, building upon natural-science and society subjects, plant knowledge as well as technical and drawing skills. It has been a truly impressive and inspiring experience for me as a teacher, to follow how students have profited from fieldwork, mapping and designing tangible, yet relatively small and graspable open spaces between the university pavilions. This bachelor design studio has confirmed my positive experience from master design studios and has shown that teaching through studio design is the most efficient and effective way in landscape architecture education, be it bachelor or master level of studies.

In studio teaching, the teacher becomes part of the design team in the role of a mentor or a more experienced lead colleague. This is quite different from the conventional understanding of a teacher's role and brings more interaction, knowledge sharing, co-operation and exchange into education. This book provides a colourful bouquet of manifold teaching approaches to design studios, landscape construction classes, landscape planning studios, and landscape history and theory teaching. It can be seen as a fruit of 100 years of landscape education experience and three decades of pan-European exchange between landscape schools. I am sure that this publication will inspire landscape teachers and students across and beyond Europe and I truly hope that the exchange of teaching and learning experiences will continue in thematic workshops at future ECLAS Conferences and LE:NOTRE Landscape Forums.

Beaux-Arts to Bauhaus and beyond...

Karsten Jørgensen | Nilgül Karadeniz | Elke Mertens | Richard Stiles

This book both builds on and complements its companion volume: *The Routledge Handbook of Teaching Landscape*. Whereas in looking at approaches to 'Teaching Landscape' in the Routledge Handbook, the processes were, in most cases, broken down into separate activities, ranging from reading the landscape, through to its representation and transformation, 'The Studio Experience' focusses on teaching in an integrated manner, building on and bringing together these parts of the learning process. Whereas lectures, seminars and workshops primarily focus on acquiring competences related to knowledge and skills, studio-based projects could be said to have the main task of building an overall understanding, the most important competence in the education process.

As a mainstream paradigm for teaching in most, if not all, design disciplines—primarily architecture and the fine arts—the Studio represents an holistic approach to problem solving and has long been accepted as the conventional way to do things. It is one in which the various other aspects of teaching—such as those addressed individually in the Routledge Handbook—are brought together, subsumed and integrated—it is about learning to 'see the wood for the trees', as the saying goes.

As this book will bear witness to, studio teaching is anything but a homogeneous activity, but if there is any common characteristic, it perhaps is its open-ended nature. Its origins can be traced back to the beginnings of Modernism and its rejection of the Beaux-Arts traditions, in which the pedagogic approaches focussed primarily on learning to reproduce pre-determined end-products through repeated copying of revered exemplars from the accepted classical canon.

The Bauhaus, which celebrates the 100th anniversary of its founding in 2019, by contrast, formalised a new paradigm. This emphasised, amongst other things, exploring the characteristics of different materials with the aim of finding novel approaches to combining the Arts and industrial production technology, with the expressed intention of not repeating the accepted, tried and tested design solutions to pre-defined problems ...

Although its name and the iconic Dessau campus designed by Walter Gropius suggest that the Bauhaus was primarily an architecture school, in fact it did not acquire a dedicated department for architecture until eight years after its foundation and only five years before it was closed down by the Nazi authorities. If architecture came relatively late to the Bauhaus, the treatment of landscape and open space passed it by altogether.

It may just have been chance that the founding of the Bauhaus in 1919 coincided with the establishment of Europe's first academic landscape architecture programme in Oslo, but more likely a shared post-First World War mood of optimism and renewal lay behind both developments. Whether or not this was the case, over the subsequent decades, and even more so during recent years, the developing traditions of landscape architecture education have embraced much of the inspiration and the didactic principles which the Bauhaus embodied. Especially the ideas employed in its foundation course and materials workshops can be said to have subsequently been integrated into today's landscape studio teaching, to the extent that instead of being aimed at the generation of known products as in the days Beaux-Arts, the design studio—in the field of landscape as in other design fields—is fundamentally about teaching process: it is about 'how?' rather than 'what?'.

Despite its one hundred year history, academic landscape architecture is still a relatively young discipline by historic standards. As such, it is still experimenting with ways of teaching and learning, and this book can both be seen as part of this process as well as a documentation of it. Landscape too presents a challenge in that it is also a very complex object of study and a multifaceted concept in itself and one which is still in evolution. This is something that has always made it difficult to borrow wholesale from the teaching traditions of neighbouring design disciplines. Added to this, traditions of teaching about approaches to interventions in the landscape are also very varied and diverse, coming as they do from different academic traditions across the arts and humanities—natural sciences divide.

Whereas natural sciences-based approaches lend themselves to investigating and under-standing the physical aspects of landscape, the emphasis on its perception by people, which has been codified in the European Landscape Convention, has meant that the balance of landscape teaching has shifted in the direction of the arts and humanities, and this is very much reflected in many of the examples of studio teaching and learning which are presented here.

But neither the arts and humanities, nor the natural sciences, have traditions of employ-ing studio-based teaching and learning methods, hence the lack of models for landscape architecture which can easily be borrowed, and thus the imperative of the *de novo* develop-ment of studio models which are appropriate for addressing the multifarious challenges of the discipline.

While this absence of easily transferable studio teaching models—with the possible excep-tion of architecture and some of the fine arts—might be thought of as a disadvantage, it also represents a challenge and an opportunity, as is borne witness to by the richness and variety of approaches presented in this volume.

One of the things which could be said to distinguish studio teaching in landscape architec-ture is the way in which it is always associated with place. Originally, at least, the 'Studio' was itself also a physical place—and one which stands in spatial opposition to the lecture theatre. This contrast between the two locations of teaching is also reflected in the modes of teaching and learning involved and in the pedagogic philosophy of the studio.

The layout of the lecture theatre underlines the stark distinction between the role of the student and that of the teacher. In lecture-based teaching, students sit passively—as it were 'at the feet', of the teacher—who in turn stands on a raised platform to impart his or her knowledge to the students 'from a distance'. The studio, on the other hand, is a space in which everyone is on the same physical, and thus metaphorical level. For much of the time students tend to be 'left alone' in the studio to work things out for themselves, the 'teacher' only visiting them from time to time in the role of mentor—not in order to im-part some pre-determined knowledge, but to help and encourage them to find their own solutions. In this way, student-centred learning largely replaces teaching—thus the studio 'place' reflects the studio 'process'.

IX

In most other disciplines which use the studio process, the studio place is also a workshop where things get made—such as paintings, sculptures, buildings, or at least models of them, in the case of the fine arts or architecture. The subject matter of the landscape studio, on the other hand, is rarely if ever to be found in the studio. Landscape students therefore have physically to leave the studio in order to participate in it. To this extent the studio process predominates over the place in the case of the landscape studio.

The process is also something which not only requires the right space, but also takes time. Searching for solutions cannot be compressed into a limited time scale, it is a process which requires growth and unfolding. It also requires a degree of discomfort: thus being required to leave the familiar, and hopefully comfortable, physical environment of the studio is also an essential metaphorical characteristic of the studio method. It always involves having to move out of one's familiar 'comfort zone' and into the unknown in order to investigate, explore and conquer 'new territory' in search of solutions—which brings us back to the essentially 'open-ended' nature of the studio experience as its main common characteristic. In the case of landscape studios, the complexity of landscape as a subject matter involves more variables, and consequently their open-ended nature is as a rule likely to be still greater than in the case of other studio-based disciplines.

As this volume illustrates, this common characteristic of landscape studios is also geographically widely accepted and practised. The studio case studies presented here are drawn from different continents: as well as Europe, North America, Southeast Asia and Australia are all represented. The 'studio experience' which the book as a whole aims to convey is composed of what might be called a 'collage' of different individual studios which are described in the various chapters. Some of these focus on just one specific example, while others relate the experience of running studio programmes which have been taught over many years with a similar basic approach and subject matter.

Broadly speaking, the studio experience presented here is also predominantly the experience of studio teaching rather than studio learning, although there are a few cases where the experiences of some of the participants in the studio are expressed in their own words, but generally it is their work prepared in the course of the studio which is left to speak for itself.

Beyond this, matters such as (landscape) scale and particular substance, influence the form of the studio experience. These distinctions have provided the basis for organising the book, which ranges from design studios through studios for teaching particular more specialised aspects such as construction or history and theory, through to topics that certainly cannot fit within the four walls of the physical studio such as landscape urbanism and landscape planning.

The fact that landscape is such a complex phenomenon, both in terms of its physical nature and environmental characteristics as well as its rich cultural meanings and values, means that over the decades since the establishment of the field as an academic discipline, the modes of studio teaching and learning in particular have continually evolved and developed. While the inspiration of the Bauhaus approach has done much to influence the pattern of the landscape studio, as this volume demonstrates it has long since moved beyond the Bauhaus, and will need to continue to change to keep in step with the future needs for transformation of tomorrow's landscapes.

DESIGN STUDIOS

Landscape design studios aim to foster creativity and to help students to generate original design solutions. Here design as a process takes precedent over design as a product, even if the product is the concrete output of teaching and learning situation being provided by the studio. According to the underlying philosophy: it is unlikely that the design product will be able to be used again in another context, but the process—in some form at least—should be able to be adapted to new situations that will be encountered in the future.

In each of the examples presented in the following chapters the processes are often very different, but the common feature is the way in which they aim to place students in novel situations as a means of stimulating the creative process. They range from expecting students to confront 'real life' situations in real time and at 1:1 scale (Casagrande, and Lamm and Wagner), through to working with digital models in the virtual world (Walliss and Rahmann). The use of arts-based techniques (Wingren, Thoren and Satherley) to stimulate cross-media approaches can be thought to work on the assumption that creativity is a sort of generic, transferable, skill which is independent of the media in which it is practised, and that indeed it is perhaps more likely to be found when working in a medium that is not the one familiar to the students concerned. Finally, the application of a more theoretical approach emphasising direct experience, rather than analysis from a distance, is taken to shaping the design studio as a whole (Herrington).

All case studies build in some way on the aim of confronting students with the new and unfamiliar within the context of the studio process as a key to opening up creativity in order to come up with novel and unexpected design solutions.

The setting for the first chapter is urban Taiwan and involves two 'real life' if highly unconventional urban intervention projects where large groups of students played a central role transforming neglected city districts at scales not often attempted within the scope of most design studios. Marco Casagrande presents his dramatic examples of 'urban acupuncture' as cases of student-led 'guerrilla landscape urbanism'.

A specific design studio is also the focus of Carola Wingren's chapter, but this explicitly places it in the context of longer term experience in teaching in a similar mode and making and representing a transect across the landscape using a range of media and techniques, in particular dance, in order to communicate ideas to a lay public.

Work undertaken at a residential 'field school' provides the central feature for the studio process described by Roxi Thoren in her chapter on the role of art in landscape architectural education. This production of site-based art works has taken place as part of a developing programme over several years and in each case represents the culmination of a process which starts in a more conventional academic context with keynote lectures and research seminars.

The way in which academia has been forced to embrace society's current obsession with measurement of success in terms of defined learning outcomes lies at the heart of Shannon Satherley's chapter on higher education's need to balance the teaching of 'bankable' skills with the importance of personal creative artistic development on the part of students. The chapter aims to demonstrate that a compromise between skills teaching and the learning of artistic creativity is indeed possible.

As with the case of urban Taiwan, Bettina Lamm and Anne Wagner's contribution is also devoted to teaching through the medium of 1:1 interventions in the urban environment and makes specific reference to Casagrande's work, although their emphasis is on the role of temporary interventions. These are part of a long-term teaching and learning programme and are allied with a more conventional design studio component to provide a bridge between a range of different didactic modes.

In contrast to the participative arts-based approaches that form the predominant inspiration of the teaching strategies expounded in the previous chapters, Jillian Walliss and Heike Rahmann focus on digital techniques as a means of unlocking student creativity rather than just as a means of presenting design outcomes. Specifically, the educational potentials which parametric design offers with regard to the interactivity of the design process and the challenges it presents to traditional design thinking are explored in this chapter.

The last contribution in this section, by Susan Herrington, explains how Christoph Girot's theoretical approach of 'Four Trace Concepts' was operationalised into a specific design studio to address the issues associated with the landscape of a former railway corridor in Vancouver. Here, acquiring an experiential understanding of the 11-kilometre-long project site played a central role in the studio and provided the basis for the development of the various design solutions which are presented in the chapter.

From urban acupuncture to the third generation city— alternative studio narratives

Marco Casagrande

My works and teaching are moving freely in between architecture, landscape architecture, urban and environmental design and science, environmental art and circus, adding up into crossover architectural thinking of 'commedia dell'architettura'. This chapter explains two projects where students have played a major role, and where the projects have contributed significantly to the students' understanding of how punctual manipulation of the urban energy flows can create an ecologically sustainable urban development towards what I call the Third Generation City.

It is good to work with students. It suits the nature of our works. Our construction sites are in different countries, and we require high presence and ability to make changes and developments during the construction period. Living together is an important quality of running a student workshop in the urban laboratory. We breathe the same air and form a collective mind. New knowledge building comes from this collective consciousness. This requires sensitivity, focus and courage from the participants. This is the kind of construction site I would like to offer to the students.

Treasure Hill

In 2003 the Taipei City Government asked me to come over for a period of three weeks in order to make plans for urban ecological restoration. I ended up working with the un-official settlement of Treasure Hill, which had originally been a Japanese Imperial Army anti-aircraft position, which was then taken over by the Kuomintang Army in the end of the 1940's, whose soldiers turned the bunkers into more comfortable housing and had been living there with their families ever since. The same City Government, but a different Bureau, had decided to demolish the Treasure Hill settlement. Around 400 households were supposed to leave. The demolition project seems poorly planned. Treasure Hill is built terraced on a hillside rising from the flood-bank of the Xindian River, and the heavy machines of the City Government only managed to reach to the first three layers of the housing, which they ripped apart, but the rest of the settlement was just left to rot, to die slowly, cut away from its life sources. They also destroyed the farms and irrigation systems of the urban farming settlement and the connections between the different houses: small bridges, steps and ramps, and they stopped collecting trash from Treasure Hill, and there were lots of garbage bags in the alleys. One cannot drive a car inside Treasure Hill, which probably saved it from further demolition.

Some houses were abandoned and I entered them. The interiors and the atmospheres were as if the owners had left all of a sudden. Even photo albums were there and tiny altars with small gods with long beards. In one of the houses, I could not help looking at the photo album. The small tinted black and white photos started in Mainland China, and all the guys wore Kuomintang military uniforms. Different landscapes in different parts of China and then at some point the photos turned to color prints. The same guys were in Taiwan. Then there was a woman and an elderly gentleman posed with her in civil clothes by a fountain. Photos of children and young people. Civil clothes, but the Kuomintang flag of Taiwan everywhere. A similar flag was inside the room. Behind me, somebody enters the house, which is only one room with the altar on one end and a bed on the other. The old man is looking at me. He is calm and observant, somehow sad. He speaks and points with his hand to the altar. Do not touch—I understand. I look at the old man in the eyes and he looks into mine. I feel like looking at the photo album. The owner of the house must have been his friend. They have travelled together a long way from the civil war of China to Taiwan. They have literally built their houses on top of Japanese concrete bunkers and made their life in Treasure Hill. His friend has passed away. There is a suitcase and I pack inside the absent owner's trousers and his shirt, both in khaki colour.

I started to collect the garbage bags, carried them down the hill and made them into a pile close to a point which you could reach with a truck. The residents did not speak to me, but instead they hid inside their houses. One could feel their eyes on one's back, though. As I walked around the ruins of Treasure Hill, I found out that this unofficial settlement is actually presenting many of the values which I was supposed to suggest for the City Government. They were collecting and composting all their organic waste and used the topsoil as fertilizer on their farms. They were stealing water from the official grid, but not too much to actually annoy the city. The pipes are leaking anyway. They carefully used the water and then filtered the grey waters descending by gravity through patches of jungle until it reached the bottom platform, where they had their farms, as relatively clean water for the plants. They were also stealing electricity, but not too much. The community had a common outdoor movie theatre, a couple of alley lights and a speaker system operated from the house of Missis Chen, the Matriarch of Treasure Hill. The population was mainly old KMT veterans and illegal migrant workers. The farms were designed to accommodate the annual flooding of the river. There was no 12-meter-high flood wall like there was in other parts of the city.

The day after I met the old man in the house, the residents start helping me with collecting the garbage. Professor Kang Min-Jay organizes a truck to take the bags away. After a couple of days we organize a public ceremony together with some volunteer students and Treasure Hill veterans and declare a war on the official city: Treasure Hill will fight back and it is here to stay. I'm wearing the dead man's clothes.

I thus decided to change my program in Taipei and try to stop the official demolition of the organic urban farming and urban nomad settlement of Treasure Hill. I wanted to rebuild the connections between the houses, the nervous network of the built human organism and I wanted to restart the farms. There was less than three weeks to do all this, and no construction material nor manpower. The only solution I knew that could work was the students. I started a tour in the local universities and tried to recruit students to work in Treasure Hill. In the end, we had around 200 students with professors as team-leaders. Most of the students came from the Tamkang University Department of Architecture, Chinese Culture University Department of Architecture and National Taiwan University Department of Social Building. A big help came from the Nantou County, where Architect Hsieh Ying-chun brought a team of construction workers to strengthen our forces. Professor Roan Ching-Yueh facilitated this.

Figure 1 Architecture students from Tamkang University helping in construction work at Treasure Hill.

Figures 2 & 3 Treasure Hill was a formally illegal settlement of urban farmers in Taipei, Taiwan. A workshop of Casagrande Studio and local students supported the farmers' resistance towards the authorities attempts to demolish the settlement. The settlement is saved and today it is one of Taipei's tourist attractions.

Figure 3 New steps at Treasure Hill after the demolition was stopped.

Figures 4 Gardening at Treasure Hill.

Figure 5
Treasure Hill community garden.

We sent a team of beautiful girl students to the nearby bridge construction site to explain what we were trying to do in Treasure Hill. As a result, the construction workers started to offload construction materials for us. Rumors started to spread around the city that something is cooking up in Treasure Hill. More people volunteered for the reconstruction and soon media started to show up. After the media came the politicians to pose with Treasure Hill. Soon the City Government was explaining that this was exactly why they invited me from Finland; the same City Government, which was demolishing Treasure Hill just three weeks earlier.

We have a long talk with Professor Roan about Treasure Hill and how to stop the destruction. He suggested that Hsieh Ying-Chun (from Atelier 3) should join us with his Thao tribe crew of self-learned construction workers. With the manpower and simple construction material we start reconstructing the connections between the houses of the settlement, but most importantly, we also restart the farms. The nearby bridge construction workers even help us with a caterpillar. The local community advised us about the farming and offered us food and Chinese medicine. Children from somewhere come to share our dinners as well. Hsieh Ying-Chun's house is the heart of the community.

Working in Treasure Hill had pressed an acupuncture point of the industrial Taipei City. Our humble construction work was the needle which had penetrated through the thin layer of official control and touched the original ground of Taipei—collective topsoil where Local Knowledge is rooting. Treasure Hill is an urban compost, which was considered a smelly corner of the city, but after some turning is now providing the most fertile topsoil for future development. The Taiwanese would refer to this organic energy as 'Chi'.

What happened in Treasure Hill, what made the power-shift from demolition to construction? I think the answer is students. The purity of their energy is so respected in Taiwan that students are actually regarded as kind of a social power. The students could also jump into the situation in Treasure Hill and start working, instead of negotiating their salaries and benefits. The students had the networks to spread out the rumors and to use Treasure Hill as an urban acupuncture point for the whole of Taipei. Whole cities can be designed by rumors. For me, the students were working as some kind of Special Forces, and I think the city regarded them that way too. Maybe even the students felt of bit of that as well. Treasure Hill was a lucky, constructivist accident and a showcase of the local knowledge and hidden organic powers that lie under the thin layers of concrete, asphalt and industrial control. The students of Treasure Hill were able get in dialog with this local knowledge. Treasure Hill was a big step for us in understanding the possibilities of Urban Acupuncture.

Ruin Academy—Urban Acupuncture

After Treasure Hill we continued to develop the research, teaching and design methodology of Urban Acupuncture in the architecture department of Tamkang University (2004-2009), at the time the leading architecture school in Taiwan. My professorship was focused on crossover architecture and urban acupuncture as a tool for biourban restoration. My works before the teaching were as much landscape architecture and environmental art as architecture or urban planning. We were studying ruins, how nature reads the man-made structures and spaces and how local knowledge emerges in the city. We developed the idea of the Third Generation City, the organic ruin of the industrial city, an organic urban machine—city as part of nature.

The multidisciplinary research was then continued in the SGT Sustainable Global Technologies research center in Aalto University, Finland (2009-2012) though real-life assignments, but still with Taipei as our case study. Our research & design groups consisted of landscape architecture, futures studies, civil engineering, environmental engineering, environmental art and architecture students. The multidisciplinary groups were able to reach the level of new knowledge building, something that is harder within the fixed academic disciplines. We produced a Third Generation City plan for the Guandu flood plains of Taipei with 150,000 new inhabitants, an Urban Acupuncture plan opening up the covered rivers and irrigation channels under Taipei, especially the Leo-Kong Channel, and worked in cooperation with the local universities on River Urbanism, the reconnection of the Taipei City and the river systems.

As the academic disciplines within the university have become harder and stronger, the universal idea of multidisciplinary knowledge building has been corrupted. The academic disciplines are very territorial and protective; real cross-disciplinary dialog is hard to find or to initiate. This is also not only the case between the different disciplines, but also between different universities or schools. University thinking has become very industrial.

In order to create a freer and more open platform for cross-disciplinary academic dialog, we set up the Ruin Academy in Taipei (2010) in cooperation with the JUT Foundation for Arts and Architecture, Aalto University SGT center and International Society of Biourbanism. The participating Taiwanese universities included the Tamkang University department of architecture and National Taiwan University departments of sociology and anthropology. Other individuals were accepted to Ruin Academy from various backgrounds including horticulture, biology, journalism, landscape architecture and cultural studies. The JUT Foundation managed to organize an abandoned five-story apartment building in the Urban Core area of Taipei for us to use as the platform for our academic squatting.

As the first task, we ripped off all the windows and interior walls from the building and left only the primary structure. Then we drilled 15 cm holes through the whole building from the roof to the basement, so that it can rain inside. We carried in tons of topsoil. With these conditions we could establish vegetable gardens and other plantations inside the Ruin Academy. The students were working and sleeping among the vegetation, in some dry corners away from the rain. Instead of windows, we had bamboo growing out from the window holes. We had open fires inside and a public sauna on the fifth floor.

Ruin Academy was organizing local knowledge-based research and design for the Taipei City Government. Our work was totally unofficial, but the City Government was very supportive. They could send officers to negotiate with us and to suggest issues that we could focus on, because they couldn't. They even asked us to say things that they could not say. All the City Government departments claimed that it was impossible to work with the other departments and that we should do a bit of this cross-department / cross-disciplinary work which they themselves could not do. The City Government wanted to get in dialog with local knowledge, but officially this was impossible.

Ruin Academy was working toward the ecological restoration of the urbanized Taipei Basin. This work is still far from being accomplished. In Taipei, possibly also in other Asian cities, it is in many ways easier to operate as a foreigner, especially as a foreign professor. The local professors are tied up with the Confucian hierarchy and even the students can find it hard to work openly. The situation changes when foreign teachers and students are present, the rules loosen up, and of course, the foreigners can always be blamed if things go bad. It has been very fruitful to organize multidisciplinary research & design teams with mixed Taiwanese and foreign students and researchers.

Landscape architecture is a discipline that touches more the other disciplines within the general framework of built human environment than any other: architecture, urban planning, civil engineering, environmental engineering, sociology, anthropology, cultural studies, futures studies, biology and ecology. As a discipline of constructive biology, landscape architecture has potentially the best tools to take further the thinking of Biourbanism and the methodology of Urban Acupuncture. This new multidisciplinary knowledge building

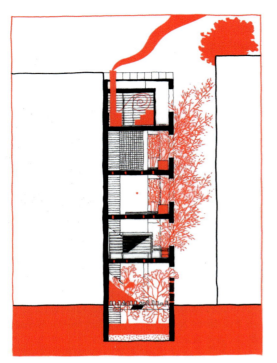 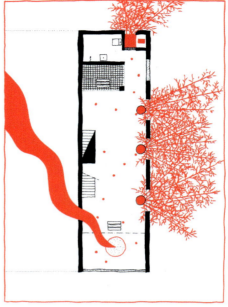

Figure 7 **Plan of fourth floor at Ruin Academy.**

Figure 6 **Cross Section Ruin Academy.**

Figure 8 The Ruin Academy set up in an abandoned Japanese-Taiwanese sugar factory (closed down in 1996) in Taitung, Taiwan, to make research on the Third Generation City.

Figure 9 Ruin Academy Study Corner.

Figures 10
Academy Archive in Ruin Academy.

Figure 11 Fireplace at Ruin Academy.

Figures 12 Paracity Rooftop.

Figure 13 Architecture students from Tamkang University taking part in the Casagrande Paracity workshop in Taipei.

Figures15 Marco Casagrande with Paracity Model.

Figures14 The basic building block of the Paracity.

12

Figures 16 **The basic building block of the Paracity.**

Figures 17 **Paracity render. Flood situation.**

can only happen with students. Of course, experts and researchers can be involved, but the main responsibility is on university students and their teachers. From my part the work with Taipei for example is not ready and it will not proceed with local developers, officials or politicians. It can only proceed with freedom of thinking, with students.

After the initial discovery in Treasure Hill, the research of Urban Acupuncture continued at the Tamkang University Department of Architecture, where Chairman Chen Cheng-Chen under my professorship added it into the curriculum in the autumn of 2004. In 2009, the Finnish Aalto University's Sustainable Global Technologies research center with Professor Olli Varis joined in to further develop the multi-disciplinary working methods of Urban Acupuncture in Taipei, with focus on urban ecological restoration through punctual interventions. In 2010, the Ruin Academy was launched in Taipei with the help of the JUT Foundation. The Academy operated as an independent multidisciplinary research center moving freely in-between the different disciplines of art and science within the general framework of built human environment. The focus was on Urban Acupuncture and the theory of the Third Generation City. Ruin Academy collaborated with the Tamkang University Department of Architecture, the National Taiwan University Department of Sociology, Aalto University SGT, the Taipei City Government Department of Urban development and the International Society of Biourbanism.

Urban Acupuncture is a biourban theory, which combines sociology and urban design with the traditional Chinese medical theory of acupuncture. As a design methodology, it is focused on tactical, small scale interventions on the urban fabric, aiming at ripple effects and transformation in the larger urban organism. Through the acupuncture points, Urban Acupuncture seeks to be in contact with the site-specific Local Knowledge. By its nature, Urban Acupuncture is pliant, organic and relieves stress and industrial tension in the urban environment—thus directing the city towards the organic: urban nature as part of nature. Urban Acupuncture produces small-scale, but ecologically and socially catalytic development on the built human environment.

Urban Acupuncture is not an academic innovation. It refers to common collective Local Knowledge practices that already exist in Taipei and other cities. Self-organized practices which are tuning the industrial city towards the organic machine, the Third Generation City.

In Taipei, the citizens ruin the centrally governed, official mechanical city with unofficial networks of urban farms and community gardens. They occupy streets for night markets and second hand markets, and activate idle urban spaces for karaoke, gambling and collective exercises (dancing, Tai-Chi, Chi-Gong etc.). They build illegal extensions to apartment buildings, and dominate the urban no man's land by self-organized, unofficial settlements such as Treasure Hill. The official city is the source of pollution, while the self-organized activities are more humble in terms of material energy-flows and more tied with nature through the traditions of Local Knowledge. There is a natural resistance towards the official city. It is viewed as an abstract entity that seems to threaten the community sense of people and separates them from the biological circulations. Urban Acupuncture is Local Knowledge in Taipei, which in larger scale is keeping the official city alive. The unofficial is the biological tissue of the mechanic city. Urban Acupuncture is a biourban healing and development process connecting the modern man with nature.

Conclusion—third generation city and paracity

The first generation cities were the human settlements in straight connection with nature and dependent on nature. The fertile and rich Taipei Basin provided a fruitful environment for such a settlement. The rivers were full of fish and good for transportation, with the mountains protecting the farmed plains from the straightest hits of the frequent typhoons.

The second generation city is the industrial city. Industrialism granted the citizens independence from nature—a mechanical environment could provide everything humans needed. Nature was seen as something unnecessary or as something hostile—it was walled away from the mechanical reality.

The Third Generation City is the organic ruin of the industrial city, an open form, organic machine tied with Local Knowledge and self-organized community actions. The community gardens of Taipei are fragments of third generation urbanism when they exist together with the industrial surroundings. Local Knowledge is present in the city, and this is where Urban Acupuncture is rooting. Among the anarchist gardeners are the local knowledge professors of Taipei.

The Third Generation City is a city of cracks. The thin mechanical surface of the industrial city is shattered, and from these cracks emerge the new biourban growth which will ruin the second generation city. Human-industrial control is opened up in order for nature to step in. A ruin is when manmade has become part of nature. In the Third Generation City, we are designing ruins. Third Generation City is true when the city recognizes its local knowledge and allows itself to be part of nature.

The Paracity is a biourban organism that is growing on the principles of Open Form: individual design-built actions generating spontaneous communicative reactions on the surrounding built human environment. This organic constructivist dialog leads to self-organized community structures, sustainable development and knowledge building. Open Form is close to the original Taiwanese ways of developing the self-organized and often 'illegal' communities. These micro-urban settlements contain a high volume of Local Knowledge, which we believe will start composting in Paracity, once the development of the community is in the hands of the citizens.

REFERENCES

Casagrande Laboratory. (2010). *Anarchist Gardener.*
Taipei: Ruin Academy. Web: http://issuu.com/
ruin-academy/docs/anarchist_gardener_issue_one

Casagrande, M. (2013). *Biourban Acupuncture –
From Treasure Hill of Taipei to Artena.* ISBN 8890892315.
Rome: International Society of Biourbanism.

Casagrande, M. (2015). *Paracity: Urban Acupuncture.*
ISBN 9788894139402. Netherlands: Oil Forest League.

Walk and dance through landscape in design studio teaching: reflective movement as an initial and explorative design tool

Carola Wingren

Practicing landscape architecture through design is complex. It involves different kinds of (landscape) challenges, representational expressions, and design processes (Wingren, 2009). Teaching landscape architecture through design can be seen as even more complex, as it also involves pedagogic aims for the students. In this chapter, I discuss how different ways of moving through the landscape can enhance landscape understanding and design ability among students in the initial phases of their design process. I do this by describing and analyzing part of my own teaching practice in a design studio at Master's level.

Moving/walking through the landscape is a common method within landscape architecture to understand scale, space, materiality, topography, etc. The examples discussed here are based on intuitive explorations in the pedagogic environment of the studio course and on examples in literature of different disciplinary fields, e.g., landscape architecture (Foxley & Vogt, 2010; Schultz & van Etteger, 2017; de Wit, 2016), geography (Ryan, 2012), and art, choreography, and site-specific performance (Pearson, 2010). An interdisciplinary collaboration in the 1960s by choreographer Anna Halprin and her landscape architect husband Lawrence was especially interesting, involving architects and local residents in explorative processes followed by diagrammatic work (notations) based on the relations between space and movement (Halprin, 1986; cf. Hirsch, 2016; Merriman, 2010).

The studio course described here has taken place once a year for the past ten years. It runs in winter and always involves a 'moving through the landscape' exercise with other initial exploratory exercises or tools (sectional drawing, model making, etc.). This provides a quick, thorough understanding of the landscape selected for a subsequent design task and promotes an experiential, experimental, and exploring attitude in future design. The design task has differed over the years, e.g., 'Green in a densified city', 'Coastal design in relation to rising sea levels', 'Design in relation to urban inundations', and 'Memorial sites close to the sea'. As the theme often arises in a parallel exploration or research project, the teaching aim is two-fold: to explore the theme and find better teaching tools.

Aim and method

While 'movement through the landscape' is an established learning method in landscape architecture, HOW to move through the landscape and THE RESULTS (depending on different ways of moving, analyzing, and representing) vary between cases. The examples presented here concern the studio course taught in 2012-15, when a clear change in methodology took place. In 2012-13, the 'movement through the landscape' exercise was formulated and organized in relation to physical aspects of an existing landscape, while in 2014-15 it considered specific processes within landscape change over time. In parallel, the methodology changed from 'walking through the landscape' and representing these experiences in 'diagrams' (Svensson & Wingren, 2012; Wingren, 2015) to choreography-based 'dancing through the landscape' and representing actual and future processes in the landscape in 'physical movement' (Wingren, 2018). All exercises in 2012-15 were based on experiencing landscapes (inner and outer) and interpreting them through visualizations for communication purposes.

The results from the workshops are discussed here from two perspectives: students' and teachers'. The student perspective is determined annually in digital course evaluations involving numerical ratings and individual reflections on teaching strategies and methods. Students are asked 20 or more questions at the end of the course, some standard and some individually prepared by the teachers. The questions of relevance for this chapter are variations on the following: 'Which "themes" were the most valuable for you (list three)?' and 'Which themes could be taken away or added?' Two additional questions about whether the movement workshop enhanced group dynamics and landscape process understanding are also relevant in the present case: 'Do you agree that the overall feeling and togetherness in the whole group has been special and positive, and if not, why not?' and 'Do you agree that the body/forces and movement workshop gave you a greater understanding for issues that may be difficult to understand otherwise, such as the strength of moving water [also erosion in 2015] and what it can do to human constructions and life?'.

As the explorations have been part of a tentative early phase of studio teaching developed intuitively from the teachers' prior understanding of practice and in relation to an imagined need among students, the teacher perspective is also important. As in former work (Wingren, 2009), the problem of reflecting over one's own practice is handled partly by transparency in the present discussion, so that the reader can draw their own conclusions. Transparency for the 2014 workshop is enabled by an initial fictive diary extract where I, as main teacher, recapture experiences from the 2014 course by earlier inner reflections and by looking at the film *Rising Waters* (Varhegyi, 2016). The results from both perspectives are addressed in the concluding discussion.

Four categories emerged clearly when analyzing the material from the teachers' perspective: a) time frame used, b) aim and level of abstraction, c) methods and tools for investigation and liberty to elaborate them, and d) representations used for communication. Other conclusions related to e) how the involvement of artistic methods promotes design abilities and individual positioning and f) how they might affect and promote development of landscape research and a common discourse of landscape architecture in relation to new contemporary design methods and challenges. The workshops are presented below and the results are summarized in a concluding discussion drawn based on categories a) to f).

Movement exercises or workshops—an overview

In the first years (2012-13), students were asked to explore an existing landscape feature, e.g., density or humidity of a site, amount of greenery, intensity of sounds or smells, etc. Representations were made using tools such as pens, pencils, and, to some extent, sound recorder and camera, and a format of paper (A3) to exhibit results in a hall where

February 2014, extract from C:s (fictive) diary

Sunday night Febryary 16th – the movement workshop will soon start: "Anxiety….about organizing this week's movement workshop….. excited, but so nervous….

Wednesday February 19th – the performance is approaching: After the first day in Höganäs, searching for the specific landscape and movements for the performance, we have spent three days in the temporary dance studio at school, where the happy atmosphere of the first days has gone and everyone is getting increasingly serious about the task. The physical challenge involved in practicing dance and movement six hours a day for a whole week has been difficult for many students. The most challenging time was in the middle of the week, when the students started to question the meaning of everything, with comments such as: 'I didn't choose to study dance when applying for landscape architecture' and 'This seems too political'. The choreographer R called for me on Wednesday and we were both determined that it would end there. A meeting with all the students and one-to-one talks with the most hesitant, who were given the offer to leave (no one did), calmed the situation and gave me the chance to reformulate and clarify the aim and method. The work went on with more convinced students and I could relax.

Thursday February 20th: Oh I am so tired, but at the same time happy about all these people helping in this work. I do not really know what I have started. The team has been developed through need and, in addition to the choreographer and myself, consists now of a film maker, two PhD students, and one course assistant who encircle the rehearsal, working on documentation, sound, advertising, permission, and props. We work intuitively and new things turn up the whole time. G has chosen a palette of sounds, representing rainfall, storms, and thunder, but also life by the sea, like birds or children at play, to dramatize the story. Props have been chosen step-by-step, in relation to the story developing from the students' and choreographer's work; six geese representing the wildlife, swimming hats representing a future bathing culture developed in relation to an historical context, snow sticks in fluorescent colors representing danger and forces from waves and storms. The sticks are also used to show other kinds of forces or actions, such as rowing with oars. To represent water, all students use bright blue hats and gloves, glowing against their dark jackets and trousers. I am exhausted, but there is no way back. I need to trust myself!

Friday February 21st: A 'run through' on site was performed today, with visitors from the media, to announce the show. We are spending tonight in the youth hostel on-site, singing, watching ourselves on television, laughing, and restoring the team, because tomorrow is the show….here we come!

Saturday February 22nd: After a final dress rehearsal in the morning, the performance began at midday, starting at the beach, where both choreographer and film-man went into the icy water to challenge the students to do their best. By midday an audience of 50-100 people had gathered by the harbor. The students seemed to feel the responsibility to move the audience emotionally by their imagined story. For half an hour they walked, ran, danced, and moved for more than one kilometer along a stretch from the harbor and the sea through streets and by houses to the plaza in front of the library. Here, a final scene representing the slow rate at which people understand, accept and act took place, ending with one person falling down on the ground; drowned because of refusing to listen to warnings from others. Young and old seemed to understand the very direct communication of risks, fears, and possibilities for action. Tears were shed and comments were given during this half-hour performance, which for me culminated in hearing a ten-year-old boy saying to his friend: 'Now she died, drowned!' People were then invited to the library, where there was an open discussion about how to handle sea level rise in the local situation of Höganäs. People discussed what to believe, what to do, and especially which responsibilities individuals, municipalities, and politicians should bear. Experts' (our) answers were precise but mentioned different strategies and students found that they were now responsible for testing different solutions. The shared responsibility for dealing with future challenges became obvious.

Saturday February 22nd, later: I am so tired….. but also touched, by the collective work of the student group. And so convinced that the way we worked has influenced their design process, by a specific understanding that would have been difficult to gain without this work, and the understanding of local citizens. The situation in the library will affect their understanding of their own responsibilities in relation to the municipality's strategic work with new housing and sea level rise. Next time I will also allocate resources to follow up the experiences of the locals – it wasn't possible this time. Why wasn't the Mayor there. Didn't he dare?

Figure 1 **Extract from a fictive diary of the teacher/researcher C (author of the chapter), describing feelings and experiences during the dance movement workshop in 2014.**

Figure 2 Poster announcing the public performance of the dance movement workshop in 2014. Design Karolina Alvaker.

Figure 3 Passage under the railway north from the housing area Rosengård during the density walk in Malmö in 2012. This point proved to be one of the most important 'breakpoints' in the individual representational drawings by students.

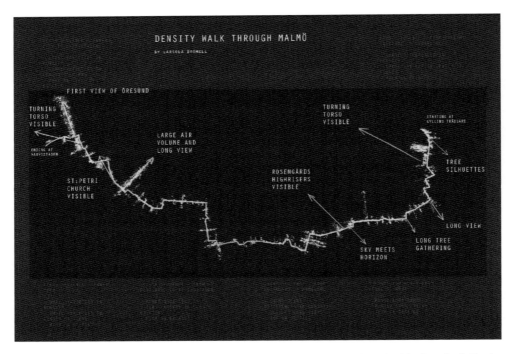

Figure 4 Larsola Bromell examined density at detailed level and length in views on his walk, and described the distance from Gyllins trädgårdar to Varvsstaden through six sequences (2012).

discussions took place. Students had one field day of walking, one studio day of transforming experiences to communication, and finally one day for presentations and discussions to develop the concepts (density, green, or other). In 2012, students were asked to walk from periphery (agricultural area where half the students had their design project) to periphery (harbor area where the other half of the students had their design project), along a specified line through Malmö city center, to investigate density (Fig. 3). The exercise, to visualize an open and abstract question about density, initially raised many questions and insecurities, but finally developed into personal ways of describing density of different kinds (buildings, vegetation, wind, sky, light, human activity, etc.), with breakpoints and intensity as important factors expressed by amplitude of lines, colors, or other means (Svensson & Wingren, 2012) (Fig. 4). In 2013, students walked across the city of Helsingborg from south to north (their individual design task on 'green acupuncture' was located along this stretch) and asked to visualize a specific sensory or physical aspect of the city environment; green, humidity, sound, smell, etc. (Fig. 5). There were fewer questions, probably as the task was more concrete, and several students continued the investigations in their individual design project.

In 2014-15, the challenge was abstract: to understand the influence sea level rise can have on the landscape in future and the design actions needed. Thus we introduced dance and choreography as an important explorative tool to make the subject concrete and un-

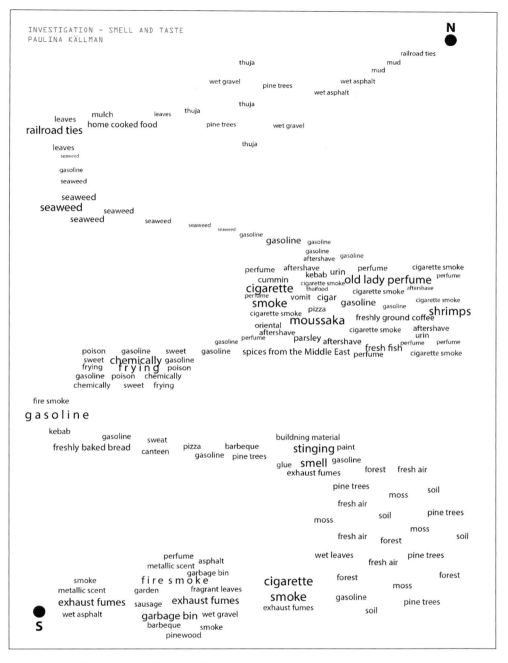

Figure 5 Paulina Källman expressed different smells she encountered on her walk from south to north in Helsingborg. She denoted the perceived strength of the smell by the size of the letters (2013).

Figure 6 In 2014, the movement dance workshop was reported and debated in newspapers and on television, as it was a public performance. In 2015, when the performance was not public, the media came to the beach to photograph and write about the beach dance in an article entitled: 'Beach dance gives a sense for sand'.

Figure 7 Student project by Fanny Linnros in 2015, inspired by the sand grains in her representational techniques.

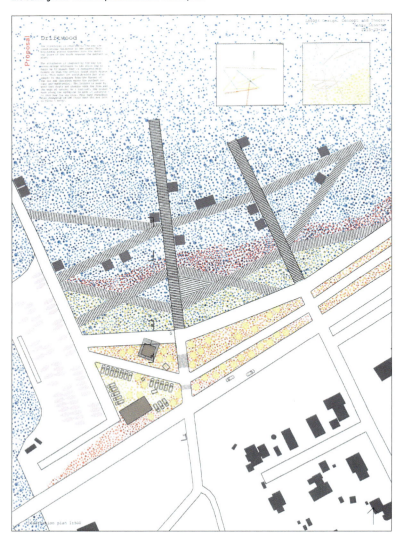

derstandable through bodily experience (Thrift, 2007). These movement exercises were longer than the earlier workshops and were divided into two parts, one involving a field excursion with preparation of sketches, materials, photos, and sounds, and the other consisting of several days of moving and dancing outside on the actual coastal site and inside a provisional dance studio, elaborating different moves for a performance (in 2014 in public). In these studios based on choreography, the students' bodies acted as tools under the lead of a choreographer, facilitating and framing a collaborative group work where individual ideas needed to be processed by the group and accepted, transformed, or rejected. In the 2015 workshop (in Vellinge), which included a 'movement and experience podcast', an engineering PhD student was involved in the work. Her expertise had a decisive role for the direction of the explorations, which finally focused on coastal erosion (Figs. 6 and 7). In the longest and most physically and psychologically demanding workshop, ending with a public performance (Höganäs in 2014), as teacher and researcher I set the topic by asking the choreographer: 'Can you make the students walk the line and dance the waves, so that they understand what it is all about?' A technical team supported the work, searching for props, working on sounds, and documenting through photo and film (Varhegyi, 2016) (Figs. 8-19).

Results from student's course evaluations

A voluntary digital course evaluation was held at the end of the studio course. Approximately 80-90% of students completed the evaluation each year (30 out of 37 students in 2012, 29/33 in 2013, 25/31 in 2014, and 31/34 in 2015). In 2012 and 2013, seven students (23-24% of respondents) cited the movement workshop (density week) as the most valuable of their seven exercises in the first year and five students (16-17% of respondents) said it was the most valuable of their 10 exercises in the second year. Several students mentioned the importance of the sequence of initial exercises before entering the final project. Only a few students wanted the exercise to be taken away (2013). One student in 2012 described its importance thus: 'Density week [is one of the most valuable exercises] because I think it is important for us to experience the landscape the way we did that day…'

When the exercise changed to 'movement/dance', seven (2014) and 10 (2015) students (32-35% of respondents) mentioned the movement workshop as one of the most valuable exercises. Only two students wanted the exercise removed and two proposed small changes (2015). One of the comments from 2015 emphasizes how the exercise gives a spatial and atmospheric understanding and liberates the student's thoughts: 'Podcast on the beach and dancing on the beach helped to understand the atmosphere and the space around me. It was very liberating to use this as a tool to understand the landscape and the needs of people and nature.'

There was a positive group dynamic in the studio courses in 2014 and 2015, with students giving 'togetherness' an average rating of 4.5 and a median of 5 on a scale of 1-5 (1 = not at all, 5 = totally agree). Several students made positive comments, such as 'we feel', 'to come together', and 'being part of the class'. One comment from 2014 was: 'I have really enjoyed being part of this class. Especially in the dance week, we really came together and it felt like I got to know the staff and students very well.'

The question about how the movement workshop improved understanding of difficult issues (relating to a research question about communications about rising sea levels) was probably posed too early, since the choreographer believed that it takes at least nine months to make 'body experience' become cognitive knowledge (Varhegyi, 2016). It still received a positive evaluation from the students, who gave this an average rating (and median) of 4 (scale 1-5 as above). Several comments were also positive (none was negative) (Fig. 20).

Figure 8

Figure 9

Figures 8 and 9 Monday 17 February 2014 in Höganäs. Students' first confrontation with the sea and the site. Discussions with the choreographer Rionach Ní Neíll. Photos: John S Webb.

Figure 10 Working in the studio back at school, Tuesday to Thursday, finding out how different moves can express feelings and forces (2014).
Photo: John S Webb.

Figures 11-13 Friday 21 February, the students' final day of work on-site, adapting what was prepared in the studio to the site of Höganäs before the final 'run-through' on the following morning. The film-maker and choreographer challenged the students by entering the icy water before the students began the performance with the 'hakka', running down the dunes and challenging the sea (2014).
Photos: John S Webb.

Figure 11

Figure 12

Figure 13

Figure 14

Figure 15

Figure 16

Figures 14-18 An audience arrived for a half-hour performance along a stretch from the harbor to the main street and the library a kilometer away. Using only blue hats, gloves, and red fluorescent sticks, the students represented future challenges from the sea at different places, but they also visualized possibilities for Höganäs to become an even better seaside resort; waves are striking, walls are falling, but citizens are also collaborating and helping each other in the images portrayed by the students bodies (2014).
Photos: John S Webb.

Figure 17   Figure 18

Figure 19 Everybody was invited for discussions in the library: researchers, students, politicians, and the public (2014).

Figure 20 Two quotes from students in 2014 and 2015 when asked about how the movement workshop improved understanding of difficult issues, such as the strength of moving water and what it can do to human constructions and life.

Student from 2014

"As Rionach [choreographer] told us, it might take some time to understand what we have experienced during the movement week. I trust that this process will take place and I agree [that exercise give great understanding for …the strength of the water…] because of that… For me the week gave me insight about how you can use alternative methods to change negative images of a site together with locals, in the way that Anna and Lawrence Halprin worked in some projects, very interesting."

Students from 2015

"Very good week. Gave a thorough understanding of the forces in nature and that we shouldn't think that we have it all under control in our maps, sections, pictures, models etc. We need more forms to express movements and forces in nature."

"I was skeptical about this exercise after having viewed the film from the last year. I didn't think I would participate in a public display of dance/movement. However, this exercise did end up being the most eye-opening experience of the whole course and I think that it was necessary for me as a designer to let go of certain inhibitions and also allow myself to be more conscious about experiencing place or landscape. Super excited about this exercise!"

Concluding discussion

a) Time frame used

The time input is usually seen as an important ingredient for good reflective work, and was probably important in the workshops, but not proven by them. There was a difference in time allocated between the first, less complex workshops (2012-13) and those in 2014-15, where bringing in more people, competencies, and professional discourses took more time. It would be interesting to study the importance of time frame more closely.

b) Aim and level of abstraction

The level of abstraction initially seemed to complicate understanding of the task and the work for the students, but by the end the results were equally interesting. The complexity of the dance movement was introduced in an intuitive way, inspired by experiences from a European conference in art and geography, answering a need to find methodologies to approach landscape processes. This influenced the choice of bringing in 'artistic help' when professional landscape methodology was not found. The 2012-13 workshops used methodology closer to landscape architecture methods. All workshops involved making the landscape experience into a concrete visualization, but those in 2014-15 also involved the challenge of working with 'the uncertain'.

c) Methods and tools for investigation and liberty to elaborate them

Simple rules for using methods and tools (walk, record, present using pen, color, and paper) gave freedom to the students in the 2012-13 workshops, where individuality was possibly related to this simplicity in visualization/communication. This freedom was partly lost in the 2014-15 workshops, where the choice of bringing in other professionals and working collectively gave little possibility for individual decisions. Every visualization had to be processed by the collective/group, with the choreographer and the teacher (me) agreeing on the importance of an aim (performance) for making the work progress.

d) Representations used for communication

In the 2012-13 workshops, students were encouraged to come up with new and appropriate graphical communication methods, which resulted in a number of different representational techniques, but with similarities, which had pedagogic value when discussed later in the presentation phase. Many students used lines and dots for communication and it was important for them to use some kind of amplitude to show relative density or intensity (Svensson & Wingren, 2012). The introduction of the dance workshops gave instant results when presenting to other students or a public, and that ending with a public performance gave additional results that could perhaps be used within a collaborative design or planning process. These were: a public discussion about sea level rise, a 30-minute film for research purposes, and major interest outside the university in newspapers, television, lectures at other institutions, and two exhibitions, where the movement workshop could be seen as one of the important levers (Germundsson & Wingren, 2017).

e) Artistic methods – design abilities and individual positioning

The observations from the movement workshops described and analyzed in this chapter indicate a possibility to use bodily experience and artistic explorative methods based on movement and choreography in initial phases of landscape design for understanding the complexity within the landscape, and landscape challenges and changes. The value of bodily experience (Thrift, 2007) especially in relation to societal and landscape changes and landscape architecture, has been mentioned by others (Hirsch, 2016; Merriman, 2010). It can be argued that the involvement of artistic methods promotes individual positioning in relation to a future design work and also adaptation of general design abilities to involvement with society.

f) Artistic methods – development of landscape research and a common discourse of landscape architecture in relation to new contemporary design methods and challenges

The value of explorative artistic methods for interdisciplinary research has already been pointed out (Rust, 2007). The observations from our workshops and from former work by Lawrence Halprin support this, and it would be highly valuable to continue such work to promote a common discourse of landscape architecture and a 'common language of environment awareness' in relation to new contemporary design challenges and development of landscape research (Hirsch, 2016; Wingren, 2018). In such work, it is important to be aware of the challenge for both teachers and students. Thorough preparations and agreement on what will be involved and on future use of images or other material would be useful in such work. It could also be valuable to allocate time for a follow-up study at least a year after a movement workshop has taken place, to allow the embodied knowledge to become cognitive.

Acknowledgements

I would especially like to thank my colleague and landscape architect Jitka Svensson, with whom I have developed the walking exercises throughout the years and who has been a continual support and idea maker for the movement workshops. Special thanks also to choreographer Rionach Ní Neíll, who ran the dance movement workshops in 2014-15. Other important contributors to this work were the head of the planning office at Höganäs municipality, Kerstin Nilermark, PhD students Gunnar Cerwén and Kani Ava Lind, co-researcher Tomas Germundsson, and of course the Swedish Contingencies Agency, whose research funding was helpful in implementing the movement workshop in 2014. I am also very grateful to photographer John S Webb and film-maker Lajos Varhegyi, who made possible the extensive documentation of the dance movement workshop in 2014. Key personnel throughout the period were the course assistants: Merle Talviste, Hanne Nilsson, Karolina Alvaker, and Larsola Bromell. Finally, a big thank you to the Master's students in Landscape Design who have participated in the movement workshops over the years, especially those involved in 2012-15!

REFERENCES

de Wit, S.I. (2016). Let's walk urban landscapes. New pathways in design research. *Journal of Landscape Architecture* 11:1. 96-97. DOI:10.1080/18626033.201 6.1144695

Foxley, A. & Vogt, G. (2010). *Distance & engagement: walking, thinking and making landscape.* Baden, Switzerland: Lars Muller Publishers.

Germundsson, T. & Wingren, C. (2017). Kampen om kusten – en ekologisk, ekonomisk och politisk utmaning. In *Politisk ekologi – om makt och miljöer.* Eds. Jönsson, E. & Andersson, E. Studentlitteratur. Lund.

Halprin, L. (1986) *Lawrence Halprin: Changing Places* (exhibition), San Francisco Museum of Modern Art from 3 July to 24 August 1986, San Francisco, CA: The Museum.

Hirsch, A. (2016) *The Collective Creativity of Anna and Lawrence Halprin.* GIA Reader.

Merriman. P. (2010). Architecture/dance: choreo-graphing and inhabiting spaces with Anna and Lawrence Halprin. *Cultural Geographies* 17:427.

Pearson, M. (2010). *Site-specific Performance.* Houndmills, Basingstoke, Hampshire: Palgrave Macmillan.

Rust. C. (2007). Unstated contributions: How artistic inquiry can inform inter-disciplinary research. *International Journal of Design* 1(3):69-76.

Ryan, A. (2012). *Where Land Meets Sea: Coastal Explorations of Landscape, Representation and Spatial Experience.* Farnham: Ashgate

Schultz, H. & van Etteger, R. (2017). Walking. In *Research in Landscape Architecture: Methods and Methodology.* Eds. Van den Brink, A., Bruns, D., Tobi, H. and Bell, S. London: Taylor & Francis Ltd, 179-193.

Svensson, J. & Wingren, C. (2012). *Investigation of design tools for urban green in a densified city.* https://ign.ku.dk/ english/research/landscape-architecture-planning/ landscape-architecture-urbanism/world-in-denmark/ world-denmark-2012/papers/

Thrift, N.J. (2007). *Non-representational Theory: Space, Politics, Affect.* Milton Park, Abingdon, Oxon: Routledge.

Varhegyi, L. (2016). The film *Rising waters:* https://vimeo.com/193333694

Wingren, C. (2018). The human body as a sensory tool for designing—in order to understand, express and propose changes in coastal landscapes. A time for designing. *Landscape Review* 18:1.

Wingren, C. (2016). New strategies to act within the uncertain. http://conferences.chalmers.se/index. php/Transvaluation/Transvaluation/schedConf/ presentation

Wingren, C. (2015). Urbana nyanser av grönt. *Stad & Land* nr 187. SLU, Alnarp.

Wingren, C. (2009). En landskapsarkitekts konstnärli-ga praktik – kunskapsutveckling via en självbiografisk studie. *Acta Universitatis agriculturae Sueciae* nr 2009:27, Alnarp.

Overlook: art and materiality in the landscape architectural curriculum

Roxi Thoren

Material inquiry in landscape architecture

Gaston Bachelard, in *L'eau et les rêves*, described two types of imagination: the formal and the material. Formal imagination, he said, is based in novelty and appearance, surface and light, while material imagination is based in essence and substance (Bachelard 1942: 1). This difference, between the shape of things perceived by the eye and the materiality of things perceived by the hand, is critical in maintaining a landscape architectural pedagogy centered on design thinking and *poiesis*.

Bachelard called for the incorporation of both formal and material imagination within 'poetic creation,' but lamented the contemporary 'neglect of the *material cause* in aesthetic philosophy.' (Bachelard 1942: 2) Seventy-five years later, the situation has not improved, and the tendency towards formal imagination is visible in many landscape architecture programs. Digital media make it easy for instructors to light the spark of formal imagination and to encourage students' creativity in innovations and appearance. This form of creativity is valuable and vital; it 'works where there is joy...produced either by forms and colors, variety and metamorphosis, or by what surfaces become' (Bachelard 1942: 2). But equally important is Bachelard's concept of material imagination, which explores the 'stable, dense, slow and fertile,' seeking not the new, but the eternal. Bachelard's essay is a call to a material epistemology, where knowledge is generated through physical manipulation of matter rather than visual manipulation of form.

Where in our landscape architectural curricula do we place this 'stable, dense, slow and fertile' learning? This chapter describes one model of a material-based pedagogy, in which landscape architect students learn through experimentation, prototyping, and installation in a 'turn once again *toward* the world for what it has to teach us' (Ingold 2013: 6). Over the course of a month-long field school, students use the methods of situated art, as defined by Claire Doherty, to explore and problematize ideas in contemporary landscape architecture. The students create art installations, using a material epistemology outside of the typical landscape studio practice, which forces the students to engage, in Bachelard's terms, the 'particular rules and poetics' of the materials they choose to work with, and those rules and poetics guide the students to insights they would not have had otherwise. Each art installation is an example of the essential value of material inquiry to the discipline of landscape architecture.

Fieldwork in the curriculum

Two courses compose the Overlook Field School: a spring research seminar and a month-long summer field school. The two courses seek to reclaim second nature—the productive landscape—as a central inquiry within the discipline of landscape architecture, and reposition landscape architects as central in the team of experts making large-scale land use decisions. And the two courses also seek to centralize praxis, *poiesis*, and material experimentation within the landscape curriculum. In both the seminar and the field school, students work with a team of faculty members that includes landscape architects, artists, and designers. Both in the seminar and at the field school, students are asked to generate rapid iterations of their artworks, learning through making both the potential and the limitations of physical sites.

Each year, faculty select an annual theme within the inquiry of productive landscapes, including agriculture, forestry, and waste. Through readings, field visits, and guest lectures, the spring seminar provides the theoretical basis to explore the annual topic. The seminar also provides a practical basis for the students, as they prototype methods of field research and create initial designs for artworks that they will further develop at the field school. During the field school, students live for a month on a 400-acre farm, using the fields, lake, and forests at the property as the site for field research that culminates in an exhibition of site-based art installations that test and implement both theory and practical knowledge in an art praxis. Depending on the annual theme and the student's own research inquiry, the artworks variously reveal or engage site systems, monitor and record natural and ecological processes and changes, or are co-created over time with the animals and processes on site.

While each module is quick, ideas develop slowly as students revisit and refine ideas over a six-month period, through different fora, with different experts, through different lenses and media. At the field school, students live, study, and make art at a farm for four weeks in the summer. The residential experience provides an unusual immersive opportunity. Students advance their work rapidly from site documentation and critique models to prototypes for final projects, while their ideas slowly unfold over the days, as participants return to questions or topics over a meal, a car ride, or a swim.

Field research

Students use the landscape as text, studying the annual theme through field research. When studying agriculture, the field school visited large-scale industrial tomato farms and small-scale biodynamic farms, regional food distribution centers and local farmers' markets, gathering data on land use, crop and animal rotation, financial models, and markets to understand the role design can play in returning *culture* into agriculture, sustaining food systems, ecosystems, and beauty (Fig. 1). Similarly, when studying power, the field school toured hydroelectric turbine halls, methane reclamation projects, fracking rigs and natural gas wells, wind and solar arrays, and coal mines, interviewing industry representatives to explore the systems behind the industries, and revealing points where design interventions could improve ecological function of a pipeline or educate the public on resource extraction and use. (Fig. 2).

Art as a research inquiry

Drawing on the work of Beardsley (1984), Bye (1983), Dee (2012), Howett (1985), Krog (1981), and many others, the field school positions artistic methods as a critical mode of landscape architectural practice. Working with internationally recognized artists and designers, the students create material responses to the field research sessions, culminating in installations on the field school landscape. Artist James Turrell has said that 'the

Figure 1 **Beds and hoop houses.**

Figure 2 **Natural gas well drilling.**

Figure 3 **Acid mine drainage coats many regional streams and lakes in dissolved iron.**

media of art are perception,' and the student works frequently seek to reflect or clarify the student's own changed or heightened perception of the landscape, or to create sites that frame the visitor's perception of the place. The projects often reveal points of conflict and unintended consequences in natural resource use. During the year in which power was the annual theme, several of the student installations highlighted the problem of acid mine drainage—the acidification and iron deposits that occur in rivers when groundwater filters through abandoned mines (Fig. 3). And projects also often reveal non-visual aspects of the site; several artworks in the power field school revealed the potential for wind or solar energy production on site by harnessing the natural resource within the artwork.

Sited art and situations

In *Being and Circumstance*, sculptor Robert Irwin sought to clarify the relationship between exterior sculptures and their sites, characterizing these sited works as 'phenomenal art,' engaged in the act of place-making. He described phenomenal art as a way that both artists and viewers perceive the world, order the world, and are embodied in the world (Irwin 1985: 23, 26), goals shared with landscape architecture. He discussed four categories of sited art, ranging in their relationship to their sites from what he termed a 'transcendent' relationship, art that through its placement creates a situation out of an 'ordinary' circumstance, to works where the art-making process begins with a phenomenological reading of the site, through 'sitting, watching, and walking' (Irwin 1985: 26-7). This latter category —site-conditioned sculpture—'crosses the conventional boundaries of art vis-à-vis architecture, landscape, city planning,' and positions the viewer on equal footing with the artist in creating the meaning of the sculpture, creating a 'social implication of a phenomenal art' (Irwin 1985: 28). This proposition of Irwin's forces us to view the relationship between art and landscape architecture not as an either-or condition but rather both-and. Most contemporary landscape architectural practice falls in Irwin's site-conditioned category, using artistic methods that begin with site analysis, observing site systems, natural events, extant ordering systems, and sensual experiences, and lead to an artistic expression that is a 'quiet distillation' of the site (Irwin 1985: 27). Irwin describes site-determined work as an art practice where the artist is secondary to 'being and circumstance', i.e. the subjective experience of both artist and observer, and the temporal and physical conditions of the place itself.

Such works create *situations* for the viewer—moments in space and time that allow exploration, reflection, and insight. These works are potentially powerful opportunities for understanding landscapes and their edaphic, biologic, and climatic systems, as 'situation-producing works contest a literal reading of the specifics of place as fixed and stable' (Doherty 2009: 23). This perspective, contesting the idea of landscapes as visual or fixed and understanding instead the mutability and subjectivity of landscapes, is vital in any pedagogy of landscape architecture. Making sited art and situations asks students to grapple with these complex, conflicting, and contested interpretations of landscapes they will design on and for during their professional careers.

Art historian Claire Doherty categorizes situated art as exploring four key themes: the specifics of site and location, contemporaneity, engagement and interruption, and place as an event-in-progress. Doherty's framework provides an analytical scaffold for analyzing the student work from the field school and critiquing its significance within the discipline of landscape architecture. The student work described and illustrated below is selected from four summers of the field school, while students were studying forestry (2013), power (2014), water (2015), and co-creating with animals (2016). Doherty's model allows us to find connections between student works across a variety of research inquiries, and highlights the pedagogic value of teaching students to use art methods in their research and design process.

Specifics of site and location

These are artworks that explore the contingent details of a site, the ecological trajectories of specific species of trees and animals, the cultural history and past uses of a site, or the regional geomorphology. These works often reveal the need for landscape architecture to be deeply rooted in the specific biotic and edaphic conditions of a place, which are frequently hidden from sight and difficult for clients or visitors to comprehend. These pieces ask the viewer to see the site beyond the brief duration of a single visit.

The Overlook property is home to a fragile population of newts. The animals are typically nearly invisible, hidden in the leaf duff of the forest floor, emerging after rains. Justin Kau's *3 Newts, 180 Minutes* (2016) tracked the movements of the red eft, a juvenile stage of the newt with a striking orange color (Fig. 4). Kau monitored a population of the efts for three hours, then built small stone walls, painted eft-orange, that traced the movements of the animals after they left the forest floor. The walls highlighted the ephemeral action of the newts, their color, their pace, and their meandering path, revealing to observers the specific character of this charismatic neighbor.

Mine, Midden, Artifact, by Kate Tromp van Holst (2014) explored the cycles of material culture from extraction through production to waste, mining small landfills on the property for discarded artifacts from the early twentieth century and juxtaposing them with items related to the region's wealth-generating coal mining industry (Fig. 5). The piece used the material specificity of local landfills to connect the site to the extractive regional landscape, and in doing so, problematized the economic and material systems that can lead to the degradation of landscapes.

Figure 4
3 Newts, 180 Minutes (2016), Justin Kau.

Figure 5 *Mine, Midden, Artifact* (2014), Kate Tromp van Holst.

Figure 6 *Sing Canary* (2013), Emma Froh.

Figure 7 *In Transition* (2016), Rachel Spencer and Jillian Stone.

Contemporaneity

Doherty (2009) describes contemporaneity as artworks that acknowledge temporal conditions of the site, highlighting the present condition as an evolution from past conditions. In some of the field school projects, students revealed this diachronic site to engage the past as it relates to and informs the present, and through that construct, also conceive of present interventions as they will shape the future. These types of projects often reflect the geologic and cultural history of the 400-acre property, explore its current social and ecological conditions and challenges, and speculate on the various futures that might occupy this landscape. Many of these pieces explored current challenges to the property, including a voracious regional population of deer that eliminates a viable shrub layer through browsing, challenges with invasive plant species, or the destruction of the ash forest by invasive borer beetles.

In *Sing Canary* (2013), Emma Froh explored the tension between the oneiric history of cultural landscapes, their apparent stasis preserved in the present, and the invisible processes and agents at work shaping the future landscape. The work was inspired by deer blinds on the property, but rather than hiding the viewer to look out and observe deer, the piece focused inwards, using form, color, and video installations to highlight the invisible presence of deer, browsing and destroying the future forest (Fig. 6).

Similarly, *In Transition* (2016) inserted itself into the long processes of forest transition, highlighting the landscape-forming agency of non-human species. Through subtractive and additive design, Rachel Spencer and Jillian Stone transformed six dying ash trees into Janus-like markers of forest transitions. One side of the tree was peeled back and painted to reveal the trails of the emerald ash borer, an invasive species that had eaten the cambium and girdled the tree. On the opposite face, as if emerging through the tree from the carved back, feeders full of native tree species seeds encouraged squirrels to remove the seeds and cache them locally, replanting the future forest (Fig. 7).

Engagement and interruption

All landscapes are a nexus of processes in motion. Artworks that use engagement and interruption as a tactic identify those site systems, and either heighten or disrupt them to render them perceptible for viewers. At the field school, students identified local flows of materials, energy, people, or nutrients on the site, and used those within their works, interrupting or gathering, filtering and collecting the identified system. Gini Piercy's *Canopy* (2013) engaged and enhanced the light-filtering phenomena of the forest canopy, using canvas strips to create a dappled shelter that distilled the essence of the forest as light filter (Fig. 8). The structure highlighted the quality of light in the broadleaf forest, where even the shadows are bright and holes in the canopy let through dancing spots and splotches. *Water Rite* by Shelby Meyers, Kyle Pollack, and Colin Poranski (2015) explored the movement of water across the site and the region; the piece comprised physical elements that structured a performance, a mimetic ritual where participants engaged in the fouling of a reservoir through the cleansing of objects. The piece pondered our place within the water cycle, and our role in the concentration and dispersal, contamination and cleansing of water (Fig. 9).

Place as an event-in-progress

Many landscape processes are slow, taking place over decades. Their actions are invisible yet very powerful. Artworks that engage these events-in-progress reveal the seeds of a future condition already planted, a future form already in creation. At Overlook, these events-in-progress include the emerald ash borer beetle killing the current forest and deer browsing seedlings and shrubs, both processes that will transform large swaths of the forest into meadow.

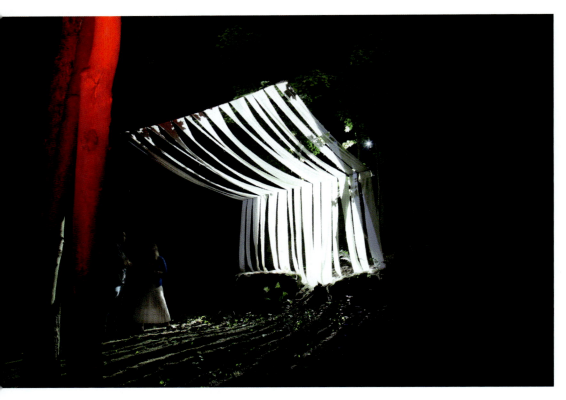

Figure 8 *Canopy* (2013), Gini Piercy.

Figure 9 *Water Rite* (2015), Shelby Meyers, Kyle Pollack, and Colin Poranski.

Figure 10 *Preview* (2013), Patty Hines.

Figure 11 *Electric Fescue* (2014), Andrew Jepson-Sullivan.

Figure 12 *White* (2015).
Audrey Charman and Bryn Davis.

In *Preview* (2013), Patty Hines wrapped black armbands on the ash trees in a small copse (Fig. 10). The bands seem uncomposed, but at two points they aligned into a single, solid void through forest. They presaged the death of the ash from the inevitable arrival of the emerald ash borer which will kill all the ash trees that compose 70% of the forest at Overlook.

Electric Fescue by Andrew Jepson-Sullivan (2014) playfully investigated the regeneration of old farm fields, as plants convert solar energy into biomass, and species colonize and rebuild depleted soils (Fig. 11). It took inspiration from the undulating meadows at Overlook, and explored the use of renewable energy in art and landscape architectural design. The brightly colored tubes formed a thicket of grass-like stems, with solar panel inflorescences at the end of each stalk, reflected light animating the forest clearing as they sway in the wind.

White (2015), by Audrey Charman and Bryn Davis, critiqued the assumptions of endless natural resources, and the risks to culture when those in power value the status quo over proactive environmental agendas. The piece drew on the coal mining history of northeastern Pennsylvania; when the mining industry collapsed, so too did the economy and the cultural and domestic institutions of many towns. Seemingly solid cultural assumptions—livelihood, home, health—were revealed as fragile and endangered. In the art piece, white domestic furnishings hang suspended from the tree canopy, held fast by blocks of ice. As the day warmed, and the ice melted, the trappings of civilization slowly fell. The natural resource depleted, the furniture sat askew in a dry creek bed (Fig. 12).

The value of material practice to the discipline

In his 'Dialectics of Site and Nonsite', Robert Smithson critiqued the studio or gallery as a *nonsite*, as abstract, singular, closed, and internally directed. He opposed this to the *site* as a locus of art, as an open and indeterminate milieu, where subtractive design methods were appropriate (Smithson 1972: 143). A similar discussion can, and should, be held on the pedagogy of studio-based design. Landscape architecture instructors teach students, future designers of sites, both deep, internally directed design ethics through the *nonsite* of studio, and also receptivity to the open and indeterminate *site* itself. Bachelard's formal and material imaginations provide a framework for the tactics of each pedagogic realm, the formal imagination suited to the studio and the material imagination suited to site-based design. Both types of imagination, and both types of pedagogy, are vital to landscape architectural education, as students learn to sculpt the land, its edaphic features and biotic inhabitants, into a desired future condition. The Overlook Field School challenges students to expand their preconception of the profession of landscape architecture to include site-based art practices, to accommodate making as a mode of inquiry and expression. Through art practices, students engage in what anthropologist Tim Ingold terms 'an art of inquiry,' where knowledge is generated through practice and material engagement (Ingold 2013: 6). The students' artistic works reveal the diachronic site. They explore the past that has created the present, and the present in action that is forming the future. They manifest a way of perceiving, of seeing objects—hills, trees, buildings—as temporary physical arrangements of geological, ecological, and social processes always in action. These works, neither objects nor landscapes, reveal the everyday richness of the forests and fields of Overlook.

Material praxis and artistic investigation enables a poetic understanding of place. It requires artistry to design places that are thoughtful and clear, imbued with meaning in subtle ways. This can be learned through the art of seeing, the experience of being, and the work of doing—through material imagination. If our students in landscape architecture are to join a profession of place-makers, then studying the artist's perception of space creation and material knowledge should be seen as a necessity, not a luxury.

Doreen Massey wrote, 'This is an era, it is often said, when things are speeding up, and spreading out…Much of what has been written about space, place, and postmodern times emphasizes a new phase in what Marx once called "the annihilation of space by time."' (Massey 1994: 152) While Massey has critiqued and problematized this 'space-time compression,' the art made at Overlook suggests that fieldwork can, possibly, reverse that annihilation to build space over time, through situated exploration, and meditation on matter.

REFERENCES

Bachelard, G. (1942), *Water and Dreams: An Essay on the Imagination of Matter*, E. R. Farrell (trans.) 1983 (Dallas: Pegasus Foundation).

Beardsley, J. (1984), *Earthworks and Beyond: Contemporary art in the Landscape* (New York: Abbeville Press).

Bye, A. E. (1983), *Art into Landscape: Landscape into Art* (Mesa, AZ: PDA Publishers).

Dee, C. (2012), *To Design Landscape: Art, Nature & Utility* (London, New York: Routledge).

Doherty, C, ed. (2009), *Situation* (Cambridge: MIT Press).

Howett, C. (1985), 'Landscape Architecture: Making a place for art', *Places: A Quarterly Journal of Environmental Design* 2/4: 52–60.

Ingold, T. (2013), *Making: Anthropology, Archaeology, Art and Architecture* (London, UK, New York, NY: Routledge).

Irwin, R. (1985), *Being and Circumstance: Notes Toward a Conditional Art* (Culver City, CA: Lapis Press).

Krog, S, (1981), 'Is It Art?' *Landscape Architecture* 71/3: 373–376.

Massey, D. (1994) *Space, Place, and Gender* (Minneapolis, MN: University of Minnesota Press).

Smithson, R. (1972), 'Dialectics of Site and Nonsite' in J. Flam (ed) *Robert Smithson: The Collected Writings* (Oakland, CA: University of California Press).

Creative landscape inhabitance: the ReGenerate Studio

Shannon Satherley

Introduction

'There is a tension in contemporary design studio teaching between the prevailing instrumentality of the "learning outcomes" approach, and the facilitation of student learning through creative experience' (Satherley 2017: 2). This 'tension' is notable in those universities which prioritise the preparation of students for employment over their holistic development as designers. It mirrors the challenges faced by many design practices in an environment increasingly governed by economic rationalist imperatives to focus on practical problem-solving, devaluing design speculation and experimentation (Buchanan 2007). In the context of tertiary education, Doughty describes how an emphasis on quantitively assessable learning 'outcomes' can diminish student engagement with their own 'curiosity' and 'imagination' (2006). Lyon echoes this, identifying a growing mistrust of 'magic' and 'mystery' within design education (2011: 117). This is not to say that practical problem-solving is devoid of creativity; rather, the identified tension is a question of balance. If we accept the notion of landscape architecture as a hybrid of 'art and science' (Weller 2006: 71), then a challenge of landscape architecture studio teaching in this environment is to invite students to experience the 'art' of landscape, to creatively experiment with design process, as well as to acquire the practical skills required of a pre-professional graduate.

In an effort to address this challenge, the Queensland University of Technology undergraduate landscape architecture ReGenerate Studio has experimented with combining creative arts methods with the teaching of practical site planning skills. The studio occurs midway through a four-year degree, and its prescribed learning outcomes prioritise consolidation of these practical skills, making limited reference to students' creative design development, and are oriented to the assessment of outcomes, not processes. As this studio is positioned prior to the degree's more challenging, increasingly speculative senior design studios, the author considers it important to also encourage student capacities for creative, i.e. 'inventive, imaginative' (OED 2010) landscape interpretation and design processes.

Since 2014, this studio has been based in a contemporary performing and visual arts venue, Brisbane Powerhouse, which has also acted as the studio 'client'. The Powerhouse opened in the 1930s as a major electricity supplier for the city, and was decommissioned in 1971. Its buildings and grounds were then abandoned until its rebirth in 2000 as Brisbane Powerhouse Centre for Live Arts (Brisbane Powerhouse). Drawing on this history, the semester-long studio brief is to create a site plan to 'ReGenerate the whole Powerhouse landscape as an open system generating creative energy' (Satherley 2014-16: 2).

This brief, and the studio teaching strategy, are philosophically premised upon Ingold's concept of 'creative inhabitance', in which landscape is continuously re/created through a process of 'incorporation, not of inscription' (1993: 162). Students are encouraged to explore how landscapes are created more through what we do within them, than by what we put upon them: i.e. to design from within rather than without, and to prioritise design process as much as outcomes. Ingold's 'creative inhabitance' is also enacted in a very literal sense, taking a lead from the creative processes inherent in Brisbane Powerhouse's vibrant arts program. Students are asked to initially explore—or 'inhabit'—its landscape through their own development of artistic narratives, performances and installations. This process directly informs their more traditional design development right through to the final site plans they present to Powerhouse management at semester's end.

As will be illustrated, the student response to this process of creative landscape inhabitance has been largely enthusiastic. Studio teaching staff and visiting design practitioners have also informally observed that the degree of creativity and landscape-specific responsiveness of student work has increased by comparison with the same studio in previous years, while still meeting the practical skills consolidation required by the prescribed learning outcomes. This chapter further outlines the ReGenerate Studio teaching strategy, and discusses a small sample of student experiences and projects to illustrate how it has encouraged significant creative studio learning.

Creative landscape inhabitance: a teaching strategy
Introducing creative arts methods
Buchanan argues that designers share with artists a capacity to approach the new with 'wonder', something which then fades with familiarity (2007: 44-5). Thus, in the first third of the ReGenerate Studio semester, before students become too familiar with the Powerhouse landscape, we invite them to experience it both materially and through their imaginations, using creative arts methods such as storytelling, performance and visual art-making. These methods offer students the means to begin germinating design concepts at the earliest possible stage of the semester, while many still retain a fresh sense of landscape 'wonder' or 'magic', and thus an openness to creative design ideas. They also experience first-hand the artistic processes at the heart of this arts venue, and thus begin to inhabit the landscape: they work within its spaces and places, but also within its program.

Brisbane Powerhouse occupies a visibly post-industrial landscape (Fig. 1). Students are therefore first introduced to Latz + Partner's approach of using fantasy and storytelling to create 'imaginative landscapes out of industrial dereliction' (Latz and Latz 2001: 73). Peter Latz began the design process for Landschaftspark Duisburg-Nord by writing stories about its blast furnace as a mountain with an encircling dragon or ravens (Weilacher 1996; Latz 2001). This precedent from design practice is intended to give students confidence in the legitimacy of such an approach. They are invited to adopt this precedent, or another method—or process—of creative landscape inhabitance, selected from a wide range of sources including the V2_Institute for Unstable Media (V2) and Red Earth (Red Earth), or to propose their own process. This guides them through three weeks of free creative exploration and experimentation within the landscape (Fig. 2). As Nussbaum describes, a state of uncertainty invites the discovery of new opportunities (2013), and students are urged to treat the entire process as a creative experiment in which there is no 'right' or 'wrong', only 'interesting'.

Figure 1 Student group visiting Brisbane Powerhouse (Job 2014).

Figure 2 A student experiment drawing the path of the sun (Job 2014).

Figure 3 A student uses historic framing conventions to highlight the material history and sensory qualities of the landscape (Satherley 2015).

Figure 4 **A student choreographs a performance** (Satherley 2016).

Figure 5 **A student's performance of poetry, music (and bubbles) highlights the uncanny atmosphere of Brisbane Powerhouse's post-industrial landscape** (Satherley 2015).

Figure 6 **Testing and revising design ideas within the Powerhouse landscape** (Satherley 2015).

Differentiating creative process and outcomes

Echoing the aforementioned concern with the prioritisation of 'learning outcomes', Wilson and Zamberlain argue that definitions of creativity used in design education tend to focus on the 'novelty and originality' of 'creative products', rather than of 'the variety of modes in which creativity is being practiced, driven, harnessed and implemented' (2017: 115). In the ReGenerate Studio, students are required to select an artistic process rather than a form to emulate or adapt as a guide for their own creative landscape inhabitance, rather than placing someone else's formalised ideas upon the landscape.

The first studio phase of experimental landscape exploration culminates in the fourth week with the presentation by each student of an artistic 'intervention' within a space in the Powerhouse landscape which has captured their imagination (Fig. 3). This intervention can be a storytelling, a performance, an installation, or a participant experience such as a guided walk (Fig. 4). The aim is to express to the class, guests and passers-by the distinctive qualities the student perceives in, and visions they have of, this landscape (Fig. 5). The experience of public performance or display differs from traditional design studio presentations in being much more personal in content, yet much more public in context. It gives students a real experience of the program occurring within the Powerhouse arts venue, as well as drawing the class together as a mutually supportive audience. As will be described, this has facilitated many students' ease with, and confidence in, their own creativity and its role in landscape design development.

There is of necessity a formal assessment made of these landscape interventions. Each student submits a short text explaining the critical reasoning behind their choice of creative arts process, and their application of it as a response to this particular landscape. They must also reflect on what they can—or cannot—learn from both process and final intervention, to inform their Powerhouse landscape design development. It is the criticality and creativity of the thinking revealed in these texts that is primarily assessed. This is made clear to the students at the outset, to encourage creative risk-taking, drawing on Ellsworth's 'pedagogies of sensation', which echo Ingold in understanding bodily movements and sensations as critical to informing knowledge. This sets up conditions for 'possible experiences of thinking … as experimentation in thought rather than representation of knowledge as a thing already made' (Ellsworth 2005: 27).

Site planning through creative landscape inhabitance

To ensure students meet the practical learning outcome requirements of this studio, these first four weeks also include the consolidation of their previously learnt site-planning skills in design brief analysis, client meeting and investigation of the landscape's materiality, functionality, history and politics. Students submit a site opportunities and constraints appraisal on the same day they present their interventions. They complete this largely in their own time, with in-class feedback available, and the assurance that this familiar activity will be assessed alongside the less familiar activity of the landscape intervention. The intent is to provide a sense of security, freeing students to immerse themselves in the desired creative experimentation. The process of developing design concepts and site plans then follows a traditional trajectory through the remainder of the semester, but with constant reference back to each student's landscape intervention experience. Many studio classes are held within the Powerhouse landscape itself, enabling students to test and rework ideas within the landscape (Fig. 6). In these ways, some of their initial 'wonder' and creative landscape imaginings are carried through into their site plan development.

Figure 7 Student a. tree-dressing ritual (Satherley 2015).

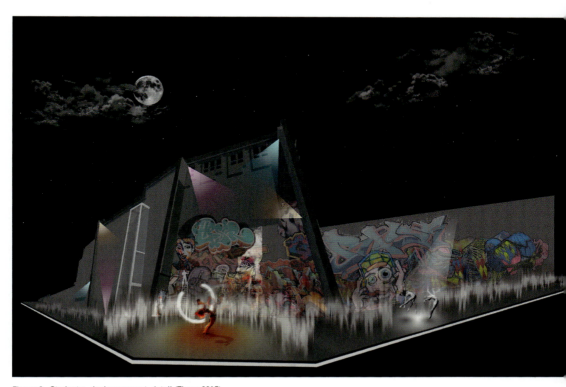

Figure 8 Student a. design concept, detail (Thorp 2015).

Figure 9 **Student a. site plan. detail (Thorp 2015).**

Learning creative landscape inhabitance: student experiences

The success of the ReGenerate Studio teaching strategy in encouraging creative design experimentation naturally varies amongst students, but has demonstrably succeeded with all but a small minority. For some students the methods of creative arts are familiar, and the landscape intervention process comes easily to them. Regardless, anecdotally, most students find themselves to some degree creatively 'inhabiting' the Powerhouse landscape, and feel they are designing from within, rather than placing ideas upon it from the outside.

An example of this creative landscape inhabitance is the work of a student whose landscape intervention required the class to come together after dark to participate in a theatrically lit tree-dressing ritual (Fig. 7). Drawing on several precedents of ritualised performance, his aim was to 'distil and celebrate the rituals present' in the landscape. Although the ritual itself was somewhat anti-climactic, the student found the process of developing it 'enriched my understanding of the [P]owerhouse landscape'. He then developed a design concept (Fig. 8) and site plan (Fig. 9) called Intervention, 'an abstraction of the performance task' (Student a. 2016). He describes his work as a 'spatialised depiction of ritual amplified', drawing on the period when Brisbane Powerhouse sat abandoned, and became a site for 'underground' arts such as graffiti and experimental performance (Student a. 2015). Intervention is a formally sophisticated physical incision through the Powerhouse landscape, dug down to reveal former coal bunkers, and rising to arc out over the Brisbane River. It creates an interstitial space between historic and new spaces, facilitating old and new artistic and social rituals within the Powerhouse landscape.

Another student's intervention comprised the delicate insertion of small pieces of found driftwood from the site's riverbanks into a topiary garden, inspired by the British artist Anthony Goldsworthy's creative process. The driftwood was arranged to lead visitors through the garden (Fig. 10), until at the last moment a hidden space was revealed, containing a forgotten piece of the site's heritage fabric (Fig. 11). The student carried

this logic into her design concept (Fig. 12) and site plan (Fig. 13), proposing a journey revealing five distinctively different aspects of the Powerhouse landscape to visitors in turn. Although she adopted her creative process easily, this student had previously found the articulation of design concepts challenging. The intervention process opened to her a new way to 'communicate a direction at a time when it can be hard to concisely express ideas'. Her landscape exploration and intervention became 'a resource I used throughout the rest of the studio as it captured and retold early inspiration and understanding of the site' (Student b. 2016).

However, for some students, being asked to adopt creative arts methods is a significant challenge to their image of landscape architecture. A mature student with a prior career in engineering identified that, to his surprise, his final Powerhouse site plan could clearly be traced back to his intervention process, and that 'without this seed being planted my ideation and design generation process would have been less creative and a more technical response to the brief' (Student c. 2016). His journey to this realisation illustrates the potential for students to be guided toward discovering their own creative capacities, and to valuing this as an aspect of landscape design process. This student's initial scepticism about the value of the intervention process was considerable, and he clashed with staff before agreeing to go through with it only for the sake of his grades. He later explained how he had:

> '… missed the link between the activity and the site being a place of creative thinking and performance. It wasn't until I had completed the installation processes and started to explore options for a big idea did I realise that I could think back and draw upon this abstracted form of thinking to help my design process' (Student c. 2016).

Figure 10 A driftwood installation leads visitors through a garden (Satherley 2015).

Figure 11 At the last moment a hidden space is revealed (Satherley 2015).

Figure 12 Student b. design concept, detail (Mill-O'Kane 2015).

Figure 13 Student b. site plan, detail (Mill-O'Kane 2015).

Creative landscape inhabitance: the ReGenerate Studio | 51

Figure 14 **Student c. telling his story as a guided walk (Satherley 2015).**

Figure 15 **Student c. guided walk installation, detail (Satherley 2015).**

Figure 16 **Student c. design concept, detail (Niven 2015).**

Initially, he wrote down his process of exploring the Powerhouse landscape: the story of a frustrated man repeatedly visiting a landscape and walking around it hoping to have an idea. While walking, the man began to understand the existing circulation patterns of the landscape, where movements flowed and where they became blocked. As his intervention, the student told this story while guiding the audience around five footprint installations which represented both the stages of his journey and the circulatory conditions of the landscape (Figs. 14 and 15). Coupling this experience with the Powerhouse's electricity generating history, he created a design concept (Fig. 16) and site plan (Fig. 17) drawing the concentrated 'creative energy' out from the main theatre building and circulating it around the entire landscape, resolving creative energy 'blockages' and enhancing areas where it already 'flows' freely (Student c. 2015).

Despite his initial scepticism, this student had unconsciously inhabited the landscape in a manner which was 'the genesis of his creative incorporation of new meanings within it. His process was itself the primary authentic learning; the end products of this learning ... captured and communicated only some of its richness' (Satherley 2017: 10). Delightfully, the student responded to this experience by offering to address future students about what he had learnt, and to urge them to trust themselves to the creative landscape inhabitance process.

Figure 17 **Student c. site plan, detail (Niven 2015).**

In conclusion

At the end of semester, the students' final site plans are presented at Brisbane Powerhouse (Fig. 18), and ten selected to participate in Masterclasses with senior landscape architects, followed by a public exhibition in the Powerhouse art gallery (Figs. 19 and 20). These exhibited works have influenced the current development of a 'real' Masterplan for the Powerhouse landscape: a testament to the creative and pragmatic strength of the ideas generated (Maxwell 2017).

Combining the security of familiar site planning methods with the often-unfamiliar methods of creative arts practice, the ReGenerate Studio teaching strategy of creative landscape inhabitance has been a successful experiment in encouraging student creativity. It guides students to experience a landscape from within, not only as a set of practical problems needing solutions applied upon it, presented as assessable outcomes. In this way it addresses the identified tension between the prioritising of learning 'outcomes' over learning process, and the potential of this to diminish student engagement with the imaginative dimension of landscape design, and thus their own creativity. It reaffirms the importance of the 'art' in landscape architecture as an 'art of instrumentality' (Weller 2006).

Creative landscape inhabitance: the ReGenerate Studio | 53

Figure 18 A student presents his site plan to Brisbane Powerhouse management and design practitioners (Job 2014).

Figure 19 One wall of the ReGenerate Studio #1 exhibition (Satherley 2015).

Figure 20 Students discuss their work in the ReGenerate Studio#1 exhibition (Satherley 2015).

REFERENCES

Brisbane Powerhouse, 'Our Story' [website], https://brisbanepowerhouse.org/the-building/history-heritage/our-story/, accessed 12 June 2017.

Buchanan, R. (2007), 'Wonder and Astonishment: The Communion of Art and Design', *Design Issues* 23/4: 39-45. www.jstor.org/stable/25224131

Doughty, H. A. (2006), 'Blooming Idiots: Educational objectives, learning taxonomies and the pedagogy of Benjamin Bloom', *The College Quarterly* 9/4. http://collegequarterly.ca/2006-vol09-num04-fall/doughty.html

Ellsworth, E. A. (2005), *Places of Learning: Media Architecture Pedagogy* (New York: Routledge).

Ingold, T. (1993), 'The Temporality of Landscape', *World Archaeology* 25/2: 152-174.

Latz, A. and Latz, P. (2001), 'Imaginative Landscapes out of Industrial Dereliction', in M. Echenique and A. Saint (eds.), *Cities for the New Millennium* (London: Spon Press), 73-78.

Latz, P. (2001), 'Landscape Park Duisburg Nord: The Metamorphosis of an Industrial Site', in N. Kirkwood (ed.), *Manufactured Sites: Rethinking the Post-Industrial Landscape* (London: Spon Press), 150-161.

Lyon, P. (2011), *Design Education: Learning, Teaching and Researching Through Design* (Farnham: Gower Publishing Ltd).

Maxwell, F. [CEO, Brisbane Powerhouse], Interview with Shannon Satherley 31 May 2017.

Nussbaum, B. (2013), *Creative Intelligence: Harnessing the Power to Create, Connect, and Inspire* (New York: Harper-Collins).

OED Online (3rd ed.), (2010), Creative, adj. (Oxford University Press). http://www.oed.com.ezp01.library.qut.edu.au/viewdictionaryentry/Entry/44072

Red Earth [website], http://www.redearth.co.uk/about.html, accessed 22 July 2017.

Satherley, S. (2014-2016), *The ReGenerate Studio Design Brief*, (Unpublished. Brisbane: Queensland University of Technology).

Satherley, S. (2017), 'The Creative Landscape: Experimenting with a Hybridised Teaching Strategy', Proceedings of the Australian Council of University Art and Design Schools Annual Conference, 29-30 September 2016, Brisbane, Qld Australia. http://acuads.com.au/conference/article/the-creative-landscape-experimenting-with-a-hybridised-teaching-strategy/ Student a. (2015), 'Intervention' [Design concept and site plan].

Student a. [Email to author], 1 August 2016.

Student b. [Email to author], 3 August 2016.

Student c. [Email to author], 29 July 2016.

Student c., (2015), 'Transmission' [Design concept and site plan].

V2_Institute for Unstable Media, 'V2_Knowledgebase' [website], http://knowledgebase.projects.v2.nl/component/knowledgebase/?view=list&type=ecology-&Itemid=108>, accessed 22 July 2017.

Weilacher, U. (1996), *Between Landscape Architecture and Land Art* (Basel: Birkhäuser).

Weller, R. (2006), 'An Art of Instrumentality', in C. Waldheim (ed.), *The Landscape Urbanism Reader* (New York: Princeton Architectural Press), 69-85.

Wilson, S. E. and Zamberlan, L. (2017), 'Design Pedagogy for an Unknown Future: A View from the Expanding Field of Design Scholarship and Professional Practice', *International Journal of Art and Design Education* 36/1: 106-117.

Urban Intervention Studio
being site specific: temporary design installations in transforming urban areas

Bettina Lamm, Anne Margrethe Wagner

At the Urban Intervention Studio, we explore methods of creating spatial design solutions by making and building temporary, small-scale, 1:1 interventions in urban settings. We set up studio courses away from the university and within sites that are undergoing transformation. This provides us with interesting and relevant contexts in which we can explore and to which we can respond. We focus on urban areas in transition, such as former industrial sites, challenged public areas, and landscapes with the potential to hold new content. Each year, a new location provides us with a site-specific context in which to work in terms of spatial qualities, planning conditions, and communal-social character.

The course takes its point of departure in the contemporary urban approaches of tactical urbanism and temporary architecture, in which urban transformations are based on smaller strategic interventions rather than large-scale redesigns. The term *urban acupuncture* was coined by Finnish architect Marco Casagrande as the notion of tackling urban challenges through strategic "incisions" that can create a ripple effect on its surroundings and kickstart wider transformation. Spatial interventions are seen as potential agents of change by inserting new meanings, experiences, and translations into existing conditions (Casagrande, 2014).

The Urban Intervention Studio is also grounded in some of the main research themes present in the *Landscape Architecture and Urbanism* research group at the *University of Copenhagen*, namely transformation studies (Braae, 2015), temporary use (Wagner, 2016), public space, social interactions, and co-design (Wagner, Lamm, Winge, 2018). Other landscape and urban design educational institutions have utilized similar approaches as a pedagogic tool. One of the most radical setups of a tactical design-build studio environment was *University of the Neighbourhood* from Hafeniuniversität where an abandoned building in the Wilhemsburg's neighborhood of Hamburg was inhabited and transformed through both spatial changes and social activations between 2011 and 2014 (Lamm, Wagner, 2016 : 27-28). Here students lived, worked, demolished, and built extreme installations such as *The Human Hotel*, while engaging in local social activities through weekly dinners, music clubs, and children's workshops. Although the *Urban Intervention Studio* is less extreme in its setup, the *University of the Neighbourhood* has served as an inspiration through the *in situ* manner in which site, life, architectural creations, and social practices merge as both an architectural and a didactic methodology.

Studio gap

In the more traditional setting of design studios, landscape architecture students mostly act upon the hypothetical and work through various representations. These are important for any design work but can also cause a gap in the ways that students analyse site, understand scale, and create appropriate designs that ultimately will be lived, seen, sensed, and experienced. At the Urban Intervention Studio, we attempt to bridge this gap through a studio setup where students explore and disseminate a specific site in situ throughout the course and in which students' design responses become full-scale local actions. Our experience is that the embeddedness of the studio course creates valuable lessons on how to merge and translate multifaceted site analysis into site designs. In praxis, this means that we relocate our studio to the site where we are working. The drafting table is replaced by a strong on-site presence, developing projects in an almost hand-crafted process (Lamm, Reynolds, 2015).

Structure

The course has run for seven years and is now entering its eighth season. For nine weeks during the spring semester, we set up a studio workspace within the actual environment that we will use as testing ground for approximately 25 students. With teaching activities two days a week, the course content is a mix of day-to-day assignments, lectures, discussions, workshops, presentations, and group production of actual build designs. Over the years, we have developed a set of formats for creating a learning environment. Rather than simply instructors, we see ourselves as facilitators of a process in which the learning takes place through on-site doings and makings. The structure creates a framework and a set of methods that embeds students in the situation and practical philosophies of the course.

Collaborative context

The course is grounded in a close-knit collaboration with external partners and local stakeholders, who play a significant role in the didactics of the studio. This requires substantial resources during the preparatory process to scope out interesting sites and create the collaborator agreements that make the studio possible. Usually agencies, land owners, cultural institutions, and municipalities are very open towards university collaborations. They see the studio as a refreshing contribution to their daily agendas, helping them reflect on how a site can be developed. As building activities have picked up in and around Copenhagen, following a stall between 2008 and 2015, it has, however, become more challenging to scope out suitable areas. Spaces are today simply more contested, making it more complex to provide room for student experimentation.

Studio space

We borrow space on site that becomes our studio and workspace for the duration of the course. Sometimes this entails spending the first day cleaning and furnishing our temporary studio. Other times, we need to negotiate our presence, sharing the space with others. The spaces can be anything from a former military station to an office setting to a run-down warehouse. At the *Theatre Island*, we shared a building with a rehearsing opera troupe, and at *Køge Harbor* we had model boat builders as roommates. Other spaces doubled as event spaces, in which we could never be quite sure what setup we would enter into in the morning. Sometimes challenging but never boring, these quite specific encounters add another layer of site engagement. The studio becomes part of the site, allowing us to apply structured site studies while also (ephemerally) soaking up the site's atmospheres and conditions simply through our presence. Students also learn to interact, negotiate, and make the most of available local skills and resources.

Phenomenological and strategic approach

We simultaneously explore site from two directions and from two scales. First, we work in a practice-based and hands-on manner to prototype urban interventions into existing place conditions. The course is philosophically rooted in a phenomenological tradition in which sensuous embodied experience takes precedence, and we seek to train students directly and indirectly in becoming aware of these qualities. This is matched by a more strategic approach through engaging local stakeholders and integrating historic conditions, policy documents, and potential visions for the place. A wide strategic planning scope is thus addressed through small, specific interventions.

Site specificity

The course takes its point of departure in two notions of site specificity. We apply Miwon Kwoon's definitions of site specificity developed around contemporary public art, in which the multiple layers of context consist of 1) the phenomenological, spatial, and experiential; and 2) the social, cultural, and historical. Both categories of which can be understood and untangled through site analysis and applied as departure points for design interventions (Kwoon, 2004). We also deploy the understandings of sites as featuring an "area of control" and an "area of affect", as discussed by Andrea Kahn to elaborate upon the scaled and relational dynamics of design and context (Kahn, 2005).

Understanding site

We begin site exploration exercises on one of the first days of class, and we do so without providing any information concerning the site, the brief, or the local policies and agendas. We believe that this more immediate, embodied experience heightens students' awareness of local atmospheres and spatial characteristics when they can explore and experience the site first hand in a primarily perceptual mode. Students wander the site individually, perceiving and discovering, curating this exploration through a set of photo and drawing exercises that keep them focused on the perceptible spatial qualities through what they can see, hear, smell, and sense. Inspired by Keri Smith's *How to be an Explorer of the World* (Smith, 2008), this exploration is set up as a kind of wandering with no map and no specific tour to follow—just with a boundary and a time by which to be back. Part of the objective is to get lost or to lose oneself, dwell, wander, and discover. The aim is to create a strong imprint of the immediate site atmospheres and characteristics, creating a vocabulary around these qualities before venturing into the cultural and political spatial layers that often tend to overshadow more imminent spatial qualities. The drawing and photo exercises allow students to look for certain spatial characteristics through themes such as edge, surface, horizon, trace, texture, etc. The outcome is a series of individual interpretations that shape a collective reading. A poster is produced for each theme, connecting all visual inputs from students. These images become part of a common pool from which all students can draw.

Following the spatial explorations and mappings, we begin investigating the cultural, historical, legal, and political planning situations around the site. We set up a seminar in which students encounter local stakeholders, their perspectives on the sites, and what kind of collaborative frames each of them can offer the students. Speaking with local planners, landowners, administrators, and often also cultural institutions provides students and instructors with a first-hand introduction to the current cultures and conditions surrounding a site, its policies, its uses and users. Students remain in dialogue with the stakeholders throughout the course as their primary "client". As teachers, we facilitate the foundations for the local collaborators, but in the process itself, students must negotiate directly with local stakeholders, understanding their positions as well as creating support for their ideas.

Figure 1 **Mapmaking by hand follows exploration of atmospheres and spatial qualities of former military site in the process of transforming. Urban Intervention Studio, Theatre Island, 2016.**

The brief

The students are given a brief that provides a design challenge addressing particular on-site issues and potentials framing what the intervention should do and respond to. We use the theme of urban interventions as an open-ended method of conceiving and affecting our spatial surroundings, addressing the relationships between body, space, and cultural context. Students explore a place's physical, social, and processual conditions and create interventions that respond to and reinterpret this context. The brief is usually quite open, having students both pick a spot on site or a situation within the site from which to work as well as develop a concept for their design intervention. They work in interdisciplinary groups of up to four members. Each year, we have a particular theme, such as *Follies*, *Landscape Scenographies*, *Spatial Dialogues*, and *Spaces & Interfaces*. One year, the aim was to transform a warehouse loading dock into a playful public landscape. Another year, the metaphor of the folly challenged students to create visible destinations within the complex former industrial landscape of Refshaleøen. In 2018, the challenge was to rethink a heritage and harbor site, a location with numerous agendas but also with spatial challenges in terms of local connections and inviting spaces. Interventions must relate to the body and human scale, providing an invitation for people to sit, lie, walk, hold, etc. Installations must simultaneously be in conscious spatial and cultural relation to the space and site conditions.

PHOTO SAFARI

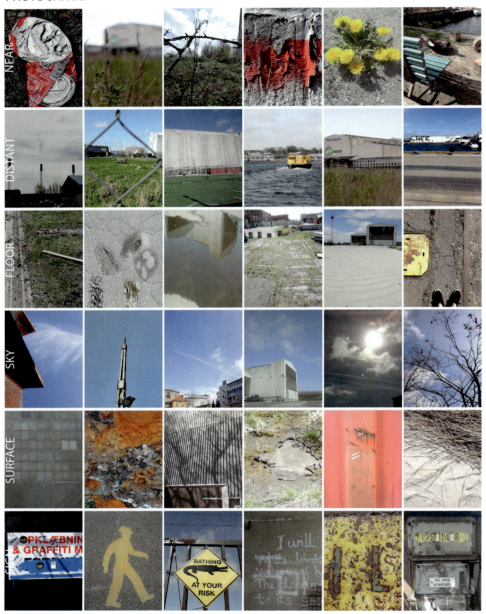

Figure 2 Collage of images from site exploration of Refshaleøen, 2015. Each student takes images of the site based on a set of themes and vocabularies. Images are grouped and displayed as a collective analysis of morphological and textual characters. Photo collage from student photos. Urban Intervention Studio (Lamm, Reynolds, 2015: 8).

Interventions as transformative agents

The studio thus asks how the ongoing site transformations and potentials of the cultural layers can be experienced and communicated through urban interventions, promoting new dynamic relations and interactions between visitor and site. In each project, the installation as interactive artistic work aims to reframe the selected setting, taking "the situation as its 'object'" (Massumi, 2008: 13). In this framework, installations are conceived and reflected upon in relation to what they do and how they create interactions and affect. An interface can connect phenomena and experiences and provide embodied access to new exchanges with and within the environment. Interfaces are thus not merely things but are processual directions and effects that carry transformative power (Galloway, 2012: vii). Urban interfaces can here be regarded as seismographs of the existing ambience of a locale, simultaneously setting the stage for new readings and interpretations of what a site is and how it can be addressed. New body-scaled objects in the *terrain vague* landscape can open up the site, inviting in human interaction, bridging specific relationships to both phenomenological and narrative qualities. As a result, zones are created in which different realities can interact (Galloway, 2012: vii). Interfacing can here be understood on the one hand as the manner in which physical objects "afford" (Gibson, 1979: 127), attract, and position a person at a particular spot at the site, creating a scaled relation to the environment, and on the other hand as the manner in which the installation narrates the cultural layers of the context.

1:1 design action

Although students construct small projects in full scale, this is not a technical tool course *per se*. The aim and ambition is instead to teach students to test and explore how an intervention can both respond to the narrative of a place and provide an installation that allows human bodies to engage on and with site. By constructing spaces and spatial interventions, they learn about space in relation to the human body—including their own. They can experience first hand how their space is used and received. The tools and the making process prompt students to become precise in their projects when designing and building in 1:1. Concepts must be translatable into actual physical and spatial designs, measurements must be defined, and details must be solved in a way that goes beyond what usually is done in a drawing. Here they experience first hand how design decisions translate into design solutions and what iterative steps they must go through to reach an outcome.

Halfway through the course, students make a 1:1 mockup of their idea, allowing fellow students and local stakeholders to give feedback and providing an opportunity for local authorities to grant approval. The mockup is a turning point for students in understanding their own concepts and gaining support on how to execute their ideas and transform them into reality. The crafting of the physical intervention itself seems to embed spatial knowledge into the students on a much deeper level than would be the case if the students worked in a more traditional representational mode. It requires them to be specific about their project ideas, and it allows them to immediately experience how their interventions are integrated in the local setting. Throughout the course, students are in contact with citizens, municipalities, sponsors, etc. and are thereby trained in the skill of communicating and interacting with local stakeholders.

Breakfast salon

One didactic action in the course is the hosting of a weekly breakfast salon. We set up a table somewhere on site, each time in a different location, and have a shared meal. We find that combining the intake of food in a social event with sensing of the site from

Figure 3 Model and 1:1 mockup of the installation The Red Carpet that creates a visual and physical marking of the quay. Installation by Linnea Carlov Jacobsen, Vivica Gardarsson, Morten Gosta Svennson and Alexander, Urban Intervention Studio, Refshaleøen, 2015.

Figure 4 Material preparations and building activities of students' 1:1 interventions that take place on the site of Urban Intervention Studio at Refshaleøen, 2015.

Figure 5 Urban Breakfast Salon, sharing a meal and conversations about design iterations, planning issues and site experience at the Urban Intervention Studio, Theatre Island, 2016.

new positions deepens the understanding of place and the shared experience of the course themes. The urban breakfast salon also frames collective reflections concerning the group projects as well as conversations with invited guests around themes that relate to the brief. Guests include architects, planners, artists, local stakeholders, and researchers, who meet students at eye level, without the usual use of PowerPoint. Particularly towards the end of the course, when the groups are busy completing their interventions, the salon functions as a structured yet informal way of maintaining common ground. It adds a theatrical and performative aspect to the process, also present in the project briefs, asking students to create their designs based on how their installations stage interactions, experiences, narrations, and behaviors.

Figure 6 Water Within Reach gives access to the water surface through a set of stairs and a deck that seems to float on the rocks. Installation: by Cæcilie Andrea Bue, Helene Bruun Sørensen, Kasper Foldager, Marlene Kjeldsen, Urban Intervention Studio, Landscape Scenographies, Theatre Island 2016.

Figure 7 In Theatre Quay a crane was renovated and appropriated into a swing that moves between deck and water redefining the space as a recreational locale. Installation: Gudni Brynjolfur Asgeirsson, Martha Gottlieb, Thomas Nichini, Nanna Kontni Prahm, Urban Intervention Studio, Landscape Scenographies, Theatre Island, 2016.

Figure 8 Waves of wind define and transform a landing dock into a destination in the harbor. The sail gives the wind a form and creates a dialogue between horizontal layers of water surface, dock and sky. Installation by Laura Vangsgaard, Frans Elinder, Natasja Lund, Simon Madsen and Katrine Dalsgaard at Urban Intervention Studio, Cultureyard, Helsingør, 2018.

Figure 9 JOY the Rocking Boat brings a playful element to the meadows of the Theatre Island with a clear reference to the harbor boats. Here visitors can swing or rest, together or in solitude. Installation by Joan Campos, Kristine Wallin Jensen, Marta Derska & Theresa Burre, Urban Intervention Studio, Theatre Island, 2016.

Figure 10 The Performance stairs connects the loading dock and the paved grounds with a big staircase that can be used as a connector, as a place for rest in the sun and as a performance space. Installation by students at warehouse turned into temporary cultural venue, LOD67, Urban Intervention Studio, 2013.

Contextual challenges

The setup of the Urban Intervention Studio seeks to develop methods of site understanding that link and activate across scales, relating to experiential aspects as well as wider urban development agendas. These poles meet *on site* and *in dialogue with the site*. This also means that students will encounter challenges related to the execution of their 1:1 installations, challenges that reveal themselves in the specific situation of the intervention but relate to larger issues such as politics, stakeholder agendas, or regulatory constraints. We see these experiences as important learning points since students learn in a very hands-on way to navigate around issues with which they may be confronted in their professional lives. The process of Urban Intervention Studio is not easy for students and often presents many frustrating moments when they are met by obstacles.

Over the years, the Urban Intervention Studio has resulted in a wide range of site-specific design interventions, and the students' production skills and design precision continue to amaze us. While the process can be challenging, with many unforeseen obstacles, the result is almost always a good experience. Making something real and seeing it come to life brings about both profound satisfaction and an understanding of how design thinking translates into actual produced interventions.

Vernissage

The Urban Intervention Studio culminates in a vernissage and a public event at which students get to present their build design interventions to local stakeholders, the public, and one another. Working towards a deadline and then sharing and celebrating a job well done is important. Here students also experience how other people experience their project. The final outcomes gives students a sense of pride and accomplishment when they can present their produced landscape settings at the vernissage.

Sometimes installations stay for just a brief moment—a few days or a week—either because they are fragile or due to conflicts with permissions. At other times, the installations last for a long period and are adopted into the daily uses of the site, becoming what they were intended: small additions or interventions that slightly alter the discourse of a place by offering new experiences, uses, and behaviors.

Conclusion

By taking our point of departure in an embodied site analysis, various scalar approaches, and manifesting thoughts in physical installations, we seek to explore the field of design pedagogy in terms of the methodological spectrum and the topics addressed, supplementing more established representational modes and engagement methods. The method has some interesting implications for the design process, for the interpretation of the site context, and particularly for learning about space through the act of making it by hand. Students develop both strategic and technical skills as well as a sensitivity to the environments with which they engage.

Not everything about landscape architecture and urban design can be taught in this type of *in situ* course, but experimenting with local site interactions and constructing real spaces in full scale give students knowledge about the complexity of localities and a deep understanding of the relationship between place, body, and scale that will support them throughout their studies and professional practice.

REFERENCES

Braae, E. (2015) *Beauty Redeemed—Recycling post-industrial landscapes* (Risskov/Basel: Ikaros Press & Birkhäuser)

Casagrande, M. (2014) Paracity: Urban Acupuncture. Conference: Public Spaces Bratislava (Bratislava, Slovakia)

Diedrich, L. (2013) 'Translating Harbourscapes. Site-specific Design Approaches in Contemporary European Harbour Transformation' Ph.D. diss. (Copenhagen University)

Galloway, A. (2012) *The Interface Effect* (Cambridge: Polity Press)

Gibson, J. (1979) *The Ecological Approach to Visual Perception* (HMH)

Ignasi de Solà-Morales Rubió (1995), 'Terrain Vague' in Davidson, C (ed.), *Anyplace* (Cambridge: MIT Press) pp 118-123

Ingold, T. (2013) *Making: Anthropology, Archaeology, Art and Architecture* (Routledge)

Kahn, A. (2005) 'Defining Urban Sites' in Burns, C. & Kahn, A. (eds.), *Site Matters* (Routledge) pp 281-296.

Kwoon, M. (2004) *One Place after Another—Site-Specific Art and Locational Identity, A critical history of site-specific art since the late 1960s* (MIT Press)

Lamm, B. & Wagner, A.M. (2016) *Book of Pilots— Transforming Cities and Landscapes through Temporary Use:* [SEEDS Workpackage 5]. University of Copenhagen.

Lamm, B. & Reynolds, R. (2015) *Follies Staging Refshaleøen, Urban Intervention Studio,* (Landscape Architecture and Planning, University of Copenhagen)

Lamm, B., Kural, R. & Wagner, A. (2015) *Playable, Bevægelsesinstallationer i by – og landskabsrum,* (Humlebæk: Rhodos)

Massumi, B. (2008) 'The Thinking-Feeling of What Happens' in Thain, A., Brunner, C. & Prevost, N. (eds.), *INFLeXions* No. 1– How is Research-Creation?

Smith, K. (2008) *How to be an Explorer of the World: The portable life museum* (Penguin)

Wagner, A.M. (2016) *Permitted Exceptions: Authorised Temporary Urban Spaces between Vision and Everyday.* Department of Geosciences and Natural Resource Management, Faculty of Science, University of Copenhagen, Frederiksberg.

Wagner, A.M., Lamm, B. & Winge, L. (2018) 'Move the Neighbourhood with children: Learning by co-designing urban environments' *Charette – Journal of the association of architectural educators* (aae), vol. 5, no. 2.

All photos by Bettina Lamm

Digital design:
opportunities and challenges for design studios

Jillian Walliss, Heike Rahmann

In the two years since the publication of our book *Landscape Architecture and Digital Technologies: re-conceptualising design and making*, the application of digital tools has moved from their predominant use for representational techniques to a more comprehensive engagement with computational design. Introducing digital techniques into design studios is challenging, for example often requiring the teaching of software during valuable studio time. Even more difficult is developing the necessary design thinking required to effectively engage with the power of parametric modelling, simulation and real-time data. Through a discussion of digital studio approaches from the University of Melbourne and RMIT University, this paper introduces the characteristics of a digital design logic and highlights strategies for developing student capacity to engage with this thinking at beginning and more advanced levels.

A parametric pedagogy
Understanding the conceptual and operational features of a parametric design process is central to conceiving digital studio pedagogy. At its simplest, a parametric model is constructed through a series of rules known as parameters. This model has an internal logic, which facilitates the modification of parameters and relationships in a related and coordinated way (Woodbury, 2010; 11). In contrast a 3-D model is created by the direct manipulation of space using tool-like operations. In this process, the model must be rebuilt if changes are made. However, a parametric model responds directly to input changes without the need to reconstruct the model.

It is therefore the establishment and maintenance of relationships which distinguishes a parametric model from a 3-D digital model or analogue representations such as a plan. This characteristic presents a major change in the manner that designers engage with information and form in a design process. As Daniel Davis (2013; 210) comments 'the presence of explicit relationships linking parameters to outcomes' not only disrupts this separation between 'maker' and 'user,' but also acts to 'distinguish parametric models from traditional manual tools and from other forms of design representation.' Parametric models, states, Davis (2013; 212), 'merge making and using to the point of indistinguishability.'

A growing body of architectural discourse (Woodbury, 2010; Burry & Burry, 2010; Oxman, 2008) interrogates the shift in design thinking which accompanies the adoption of parametric modelling. In particular, Oxman highlights a new interactivity between the designer, process and information, which departs from the visual reasoning associated with paper-based design processes. She argues that the concept of 'designerly thinking' made popular by Donald Schön's influential cognitive research into 'paper-based' design processes is premised on a process of 'talk back' or a 'dialogue with the materials of the problem,' informed primarily by visual representation (Oxman, 2008; 101). However, within a parametric model, cognitive processes of design are reconceptualised as 'our ability to formulate, represent, implement and interact with explicit, well-formulated representations of knowledge,' as design processes move from implied to explicit knowledge (Oxman, 2006; 243).

Applied within landscape architecture, the parametric model forms a powerful proxy for the site, collapsing analytical information and design explorations within the same digital model. This process departs from more accustomed linear and segmented design and planning processes, which frequently position the generation of a design concept after the synthesis of extensive site analysis. Rarely does the parametric model translate literally into form, instead presenting a medium for interrogating site behaviours and exploring the implications of design decisions. Consequently, Girot et al. (2010; 376) describe this design process as directive rather than prescriptive:

> 'Rather than relying on a design process of random variations as often associated with parametric processes of design, controlled decision-making can lead to clear performance orientated results. The resulting design operations are a hybrid between intuitive physical interventions and "variable" manipulation, and are therefore conceived as "directive" rather than "prescriptive" in design outcome.'

Folding these computational approaches into design studios is challenging. As Brian Osborn (2014) comments 'many of the contemporary design tools, like parametric modeling, …tend to require a great deal of exposure and practice before students begin to feel comfortable with them.' The adoption of non-linear workflows adds further complexity while the extensive possibilities afforded by real-time data and simulation require a high level of critical thinking as well as familiarity with scientific and mathematical principles. Consequently, it is important to expose students to digital techniques as early as possible in their studies to allow adequate time for them to explore their potential in subsequent years with increasing confidence.

We begin our discussion of digital design pedagogy with a focus on strategies for embedding digital skills and related thinking into early design studios. The first studio example Design Techniques forms an entry point for a three-year (non-cognate pathway) Master of Landscape Architecture at the University of Melbourne. With no separate representational curriculum, the studio crosses representational techniques and design generation and is a core studio offering. Our second example is a vertically integrated undergraduate studio which forms part of RMIT University's Bachelor of Landscape Architectural Design programme. With a dedicated communication stream, students enter with basic digital knowledge, with this studio offering the chance to apply these skills in a design project.

Foundational workflows

Design Techniques introduces digital software (the Adobe suite, Rhinoceros and Grasshopper) alongside design processes and theory in eight hours a week over a 12-week semester. Students come from diverse backgrounds with the majority having no previous design experience. Activities are structured around the design of a small topographically driven park, with a focus on learning design processes, which encompass physical, digital and parametric modelling. Assignments are carefully planned to move across these techniques to encourage an understanding of their potentials, limitations and workflow sequences.

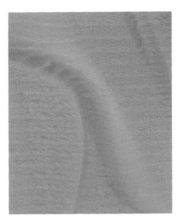

Figure 1 **Design explorations moving from physical (clay) to digital (Rhino) to physical (routed).**

With such a diverse student group, it is important to acknowledge different learning paces, reinforce achievements throughout the studio and define deliverables to maximise learning outcomes. The studio is also supported by a lecture series that introduces late twentieth century design thinking including the influences of a digital design practice.

The first half focuses on form generation beginning with an introduction to the Adobe suite, which is used to present research into design precedents. Armed with this knowledge, students complete a half-day design workshop. Working with modelling clay and a nominated topographic operation such as tilting, carving or stepping, the site's topography is manipulated to produce a first design iteration. This clay model forms the basis for introducing Rhinoceros (Rhino). The operations used for the physical model are now replaced by selected Rhino tools, which construct landform in a digital space. Students work to transform the attributes of their physical model in a digital model (Figs. 1 and 2), allowing it to develop as they gain more control over form and scale with their emerging digital skills. Two additional explorations are developed—a further landform iteration and the integration of a ramp into one of their schemes using Grasshopper.

The addition of the Grasshopper script parametrises the model, and offers a clear demonstration of how the model repairs and changes with the altering of the ramp slope, size and location. This phase concludes with their preferred Rhino scheme transformed into a CNC routed model, along with the development of one rendered panoramic view. This work is displayed in a quick pop-up exhibition: an important moment to acknowledge what has been achieved over a short time.

Phase two shifts to ideas of performance, introducing techniques for refining their topographic form through the consideration of materiality, planting, circulation and scale. For instance, working parametrically with the Grasshopper plugins (Lady Bug and Honey Bee) and meteorological data, the siting of proposed planting and the orientation of key elements is tested in relation to climatic factors. In these final three weeks, students develop a series of images generated from the digital model, including an exploded isometric, a long section elevation and two rendered panoramic views (Fig. 3). In just 12 weeks, students develop confidence and competency in working with digital tools, and most importantly gain a clear conceptual and technical understanding of the parametric model.

Turning to the RMIT studio, it is important to acknowledge that RMIT run vertically integrated studios which allow students across multiple year levels to study design together. Within this structure, students bring knowledge accessed from the communication subjects at their respective levels. While students have had more exposure to design than those

Figure 2
Testing the human experience of form in the digital model.

Figure 3
Final images from a student with a background in philosophy.

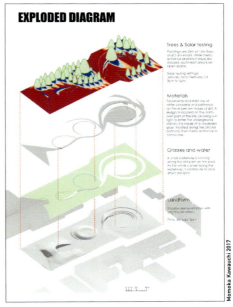

Digital design: opportunities and challenges for design studios | 71

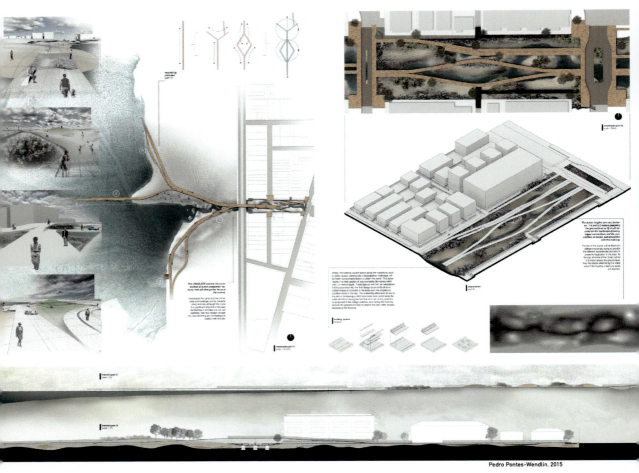

Figure 4 **A systems driven response to dredging.**

undertaking the University of Melbourne studio, the diversity of skill levels still requires the studio leader to navigate design techniques and processes depending on individual students' abilities and design experience.

Working across analogue and digital techniques, the studio explored design interventions responsive to the fluctuating water levels found in a small suburban stream in Melbourne. Intuitive explorations of form are mixed with a rule-based approach, along with the introduction of testing for performance through consideration of parameters such as slope gradients, flow dynamics and material movement (erosion and deposition).

Students began with the reconstruction of flow processes based on drawing exercises from site observations and research into flow dynamics. These exercises were then translated into physical form studies using clay and kinetic sand. In a similar process to the previous studio example, the physical model is then transformed into a digital model constructed in Rhino. This digital model forms the basis for interrogating the relationship between water processes and landform. At this point the testing took different turns. Students who had studied the parametric communication subject could embed parametric techniques (Grasshopper) into their design, while beginning students adopted visual judgement to understand the implications of their design decisions.

Those engaging with parametric processes established faster and more powerful generative explorations—aided by real-time feedback—than those adopting visual decision-making. For example, one project (Fig. 4) challenged the current dredging process based on the mechanical excavation of sedimentation, to instead offer a system-driven response, which recasts processes of sediment deposition as a productive land forming operation. Working with the vertical parameters of slope combined with the horizontal forces of water, various relationships were explored to produce a new landform that influences the location of sediment deposition, and accordingly the flow path of the stream. The result is an adaptive landscape, which responds to two water forces—stormwater flows (from the urban context) and wave action (from the bay).

Student diversity significantly influences the structure and the manner in which digital tools are introduced in both studios. In the University of Melbourne model, students from diverse non-design backgrounds are introduced to digital as their first design language. Emphasis is placed on developing an understanding of design processes. Within the RMIT example, peer-to-peer learning through the vertical studio structure offers beginning students exposure to the potential of advanced digital applications, which they are yet to experience in their own studies. Importantly both studios encourage a fluid workflow crossing digital and analogue techniques.

In the following section, we shift to more advanced studios, which harness computational techniques to engage with issues of climate change relevant to Australian and Asian cities; namely heat and pollution. While designers can do very little to minimise the frequency of heat waves or general levels of air pollution, they can influence the human experience of these phenomena, understood through real-time data and simulation. We highlight the value of these computational approaches through a discussion of an intensive Master studio from the University of Melbourne which interrogates heat wave conditions on a small urban site in suburban Melbourne and an undergraduate landscape studio from RMIT University which explores opportunities for design interventions to alleviate exposure to harmful pollutants in Ho Chi Minh City (HCMC), Vietnam.

Defining Design Problems through Data and Simulation

Increasingly accessible real-time data and simulation offer valuable techniques for engaging with the dynamic and invisible behaviour of atmospheric phenomena. Working with data demands a high level of critical thinking to identify unusual or influential events that can be filtered into 'high value' problems. While many students develop proficiency with digital tools, this criticality is far more elusive. This becomes even more important when working with large-scale and complex environmental problems where spatial design has a limited impact on solving the underlying issues responsible for the problems. Consequently, challenging tendencies towards literal problem solving and instead encouraging more lateral and tactical approaches forms an important role for the studio. In this context, the studio requires a clear articulation of the value of data to design and careful navigation between evaluative and generative design techniques. Critically, the studios are not aiming to achieve the level of specialised data analytics evident in science; rather, to develop a design process which interrogates the behaviours of systems 'informed by a combination of simulation, design theory and existing scientific research' (Walliss & Rahmann, 2018; 135).

One of the limiting factors in working with environmental conditions is access to valid and comprehensive datasets specific enough for their respective design context. In the case of the HCMC studio, existing pollution data was limited to a single site reading focusing on a single pollutant type. It was therefore necessary for students to record their own data through intensive fieldwork using Arduino devices (microcontroller) and handheld sensors (Fig. 5). Similarly, the Melbourne heat studio used small i-buttons to record five weeks of continuous temperature data drawn from different site microclimates. Recorded at the scale of human inhabitation, this data provided an important counterpoint to the broader scale meterological data available in Melbourne; most typically recorded at airports and other major landmarks.

These self-gathered localised datasets encouraged a more rigorous exploration of the explicit interrelation between build form and environmental conditions, and most importantly, aided the identification of stress points (locations with high impact and high consequences), which evolved into site of intervention. Working in HCMC, students uncovered variations in pollution types and different conditions across the city. One team revealed a link between urban morphology and the accumulation of pollutants (SO_X, NO_X, O_3) despite the neighbourhood's distance from major traffic roads.

Another identified higher concentration levels of particulate matter ($PM_{2.5}$ and PM_{10}) related to construction activities in sections of the city. This analysis highlighted the need for highly site-specific design responses, demonstrating the danger of using generalised datasets to define the pollution problem. For example, the first team's discovery demonstrated the need to 'wash' the pollution out of the urban form by increasing air flow, while conversely the second team's observations revealed the reverse recommendation, the importance of introducing wind breaks to settle pollution associated with construction sites.

Returning to Melbourne, careful analysis of the temporal pattern of site data by one group highlighted an intriguing anomaly: at a particular hour each day, the site temperature would drop below the ambient air temperature for over an hour before building back up again. This unexplained data glitch revealed the possibility of interrupting a cycle of heat build-up and inspired the concept of 'reset pods'—places of rest designed to limit the accumulation of heat in site materials.

Moving from the interrogation of site data, both studios introduced physical prototyping into the design process to validate data driven site observations. The HCMC studio had a team based in Melbourne verify conditions and effects identified on site through physical wind tunnel simulations (Fig. 6). Isolated from other site conditions, this process offered the in-situ studio a clearer understanding of the relationship of observed thermo-dynamic principles in physical space. Similarly, students in the Melbourne studio interrogated material responses (timber and concrete) to heat, working in a combination of digital simulations and physical prototypes to isolate performance according to fluctuating thermal conditions, as shown in Figure 7.

This isolation of site behaviours offered a further refinement of the 'high value' problems during subsequent design generation processes. For example the HCMC group who identified the need to 'wash' their site proposed the insertion of a series of small awnings into alleyways to increase wind turbulence and encourage the flushing of pollution from confined urban spaces. Working closely with vernacular awning structures the students developed various design solutions informed by the exploration of set parameters to achieve the desired wind flow behaviour (Fig. 8). In contrast the group working with the particulate matter from construction, proposed an urban scale strategy for phasing construction processes to encourage pollution deposition. This strategy considered the effect of both land formation processes and housing configurations in the future masterplan, as depicted in Figure 9.

Developing their 'reset pods' further, the Melbourne group tested the siting and forms against the dynamic site conditions using simulation and real-time datasets (Figs. 10 & 11). These findings, combined with the material research, led to a series of sitting pods which vary according to their detailed environmental context, thereby creating their own specific climatic conditions for inhabitation.

Figure 5 Mobile sensors provide the opportunity to record site and context specific datasets.

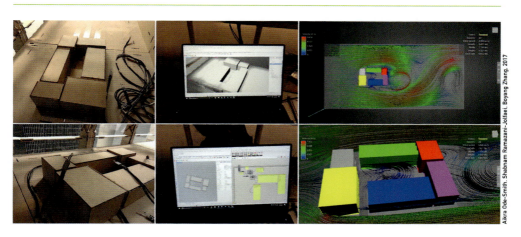

Figure 6 Wind tunnel simulations provide an interface between physical and digital prototyping.

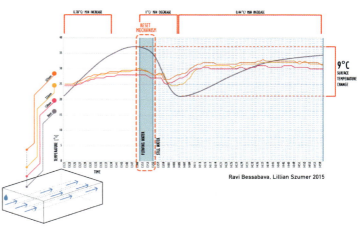

Figure 7 Testing the material behaviour of concrete.

Digital design: opportunities and challenges for design studios | 75

Figure 8 **Design studies informed by controlled exploration of set parameters.** (Source: Will Mulheisen, 2017)

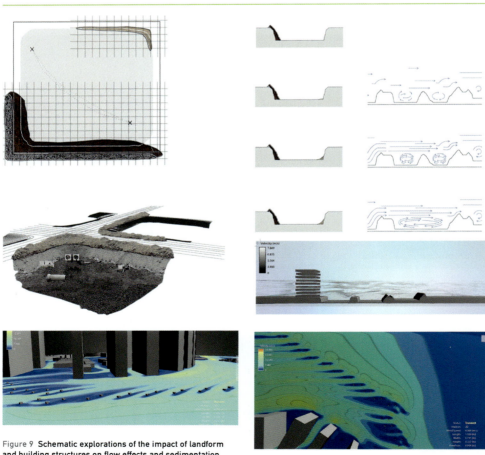

Figure 9 **Schematic explorations of the impact of landform and building structures on flow effects and sedimentation.** (Source: Louella Exton, Robbie Broadstock, George Willmott, 2017)

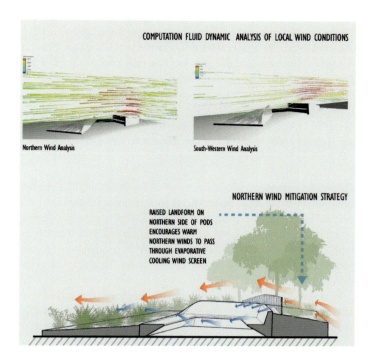

Figure 10 Testing the reset pods in-situ using simulation.

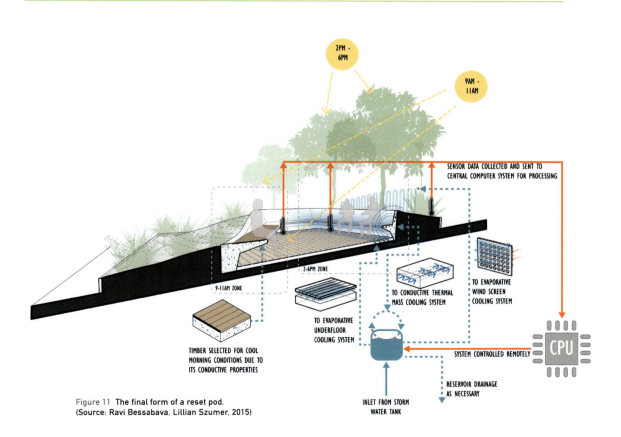

Figure 11 The final form of a reset pod.
(Source: Ravi Bessabava, Lillian Szumer, 2015)

These design approaches demonstrate how simulation and physical prototyping, along with real-time data, facilitate an iterative process of problem redefinition, where the designer gains greater insight into how the behaviour of phenomena might be altered. Rather than 'solve' a problem, students are directed to identifying a specific designed effect, which in turn leads to novel design outcomes. While these design approaches foreground performance, this does not mean that other design qualities such as aesthetics, materiality and human experience are ignored. These qualities are explored as part of the design process, once performance attributes are understood.

Conclusion

To design parametrically entails a shift from implicit to explicit knowledge, requiring the breakdown of design explorations into influential parameters and rules. This design process differs from more familiar design and planning processes which develop the design concept after the synthesis of extensive site analysis. Further parametric processes challenge the dominance of visual reasoning in guiding design decisions, with real-time data and simulation offering powerful new ways for engaging with site conditions and testing design interventions.

However, these new design potentials require the careful conceptualisation of studio structure and intent. For the beginning student it is important to emphasis non-linear workflows encompassing analogue and digital techniques and to introduce a design thinking underpinned by rules and behaviours. For more advanced studios, the extensive possibilities afforded by real-time data and simulation needs to be controlled within a design process shaped by a high degree of criticality. Far from offering the solution, digital tools such as parametric modelling and simulation allow landscape architects the ability to understand relationships between physical form and dynamic systems in an unprecedented manner. Mastering the software is a matter of time and application; knowing how to use these tools in an effective manner is far more challenging. However, a steady stream of new books such as *Codify: Parametric and Computational Design in Landscape Architecture* (Cantrell & Mekies, 2018) are making it increasingly easier for students to understand the exciting potentials and value of computational techniques to landscape architecture.

REFERENCES

Burry, J. & Burry, M. (2010), *The New Mathematics of Architecture*, (London: Thames & Hudson).

Cantrell, B. & Mekies, A. (2018), *Codify: Parametric and Computational Design in Landscape Architecture*, (Oxon: Routledge).

Davis, D. (2013), 'Modelled on Software Engineering: Flexible Parametric Models in the Practice of Architecture', Ph.D. diss. (RMIT University Melbourne).

Girot, C., Bernhard, M., Ebnöther, Y., Fricker, P., Kapellos, A. & Melsom, J. (2010), 'Towards a Meaningful Usage of Digital CNC Tools: Within the field of large-scale landscape architecture', in *Future Cities: Proceedings of the 28th Conference on Education in Computer Aided Architectural Design in Europe*, September 15-18, 2010, Zurich, Switzerland, (ETH Zurich) 371–378.

Osborn, B. (2014), Email communication.

Oxman, R. (2006), 'Theory and Design in the First Digital Age', *Design Studies*, 27: 229–265

Oxman, R. (2008), 'Digital Architecture as a Challenge for Design Pedagogy: Theory, Knowledge, Models and Medium', *Design Studies* 29: 99–120.

Walliss, J. & Rahman, H. (2016), *Landscape Architecture and Digital Technologies: re-conceptualising design and making*, (Oxon: Routledge).

Walliss, J. & Rahman, H. (2018), 'Computational Design Methodologies: an enquiry into atmosphere', in *Codify* (eds) B. Cantrell & A. Mekies, *Codify: Parametric and Computational Design in Landscape Architecture*, Routledge, (Oxon: Routledge). 132–143.

Woodbury, R. (2010), *Elements of Parametric Design*, (Oxon: Routledge).

79

A phenomenological method for the landscape studio

Susan Herrington

Girot's four trace concepts

In 1999 Christophe Girot's chapter, 'Four Trace Concepts in Landscape Architecture,' appeared in the anthology, *Recovering Landscape: Essays in Contemporary Landscape Architecture*, edited by James Corner. According to Girot, 'In the course of my own work I have unravelled four operating concepts that serve as tools for landscape investigation and design, especially with regard to recovering sites. I call these trace concepts because they cluster around issues of memory: marking, impressing, and founding' (1999: 60). Girot's four trace concepts are landing, grounding, finding, and founding. Landing involves a phenomenological approach during the first site visit of a project. Phenomenological methods privilege knowledge gleaned during direct experience. For Edmund Husserl (1859–1938) 'Natural objects, for example, must be experienced before any theorizing about them can occur. Experiencing is consciousness that intuits something and values it to be actual; experiencing is intrinsically characterized as consciousness of the natural object in question and of it as the original' (*Husserl* 2002: 125). Resonating with Husserl's conception of phenomenology, Girot's landing comprises unbiased descriptions of phenomena that appear in an experience of the site, and are not limited to physical objects, as phenomena can also include imagination and memory as well. 'Landing thus requires a particular state of mind, one where intuitions and impressions prevail…' (*Girot* 1999: 61).

The second concept involves grounding, which entails repeatedly visiting, interpreting, and studying the site. Girot contends, 'Grounding is a process implying successive layers, both the visible and the invisible' (1999: 63). Thus, this phase involves the layering of what has been discovered during direct experiences with the site and information gleaned through research. Girot's third concept, finding, 'discloses the evidence to support one's initial intuitions about a place' (1999: 64). Finding reveals the evidence to support a design proposition; however, the methods of finding are diverse. It 'can result from either a surprise discovery or some painstaking, methodological quest…Such discoveries may be tangible, like a relic or a significant tree or stone, or they may be more evanescent, like the death of a significant person' (1999: 63). Lastly, founding lays the ground for future events. For Girot, 'Founding is probably the most durable and significant of the four trace acts. It comes at the moment when the prior three acts are synthesized into a new and transformed construction of the site' (1999: 64).

> *'The recovery of landscape will begin only when we are ready to reconcile our senses with our science'* Girot 1999: 66

Girot's aim in developing 'Four Trace Concepts in Landscape Architecture,' is two-fold. First, he supports the goals of *Recovering Landscape*, which seeks to reinstate the imaginative and cultural dimensions of landscape architecture that had been overshadowed by environmentalism and a sentimental, static image of landscape. Girot argues that French landscape architects chiefly concerned themselves with environmental conservation and restoration. 'The work is seen as a significant ameliorator of ecological damage and urbanization.

It is, therefore, not surprising to find the notion of landscape recovery central to this field of action because it implies a focus on people's concern with the quality of and image of their immediate environs. It is possible, however, to broaden this sense of recovering landscape, invoking cultural and imaginative horizons' (Girot 1999: 59). The second aim for Girot 'underlines the fact that a designer seldom belongs to the place in which he or she is asked to intervene. How can an outsider designer acquire the understanding of a place that will enable them to act wisely and knowledgeably' (1999: 60). Girot notes 'the introduction to a site project has all too often been reduced to systematic and quantitative formulas for analyzing the site from a distance. By contrast, trace concepts enable the designer to come to grips with their intuitions and experiences of place, allowing these impressions to direct the unfolding of the project' (199: 65). Thus, 'Four Trace Concepts in Landscape Architecture,' aims to tap the designer's creativity and inventiveness as part of the design process and also overcome the designer's own personal detachment from unfamiliar projects sites.

But is this chapter on design process, written in 1999, relevant today? It is germane now more than ever. Since 1999, landscape urbanism has dominated theory and design in landscape architecture schools in North America. Landscape urbanism was coined in 1997 by Charles Waldheim, who suggests, 'landscape urbanism can be read as a disciplinary realignment in which landscape supplants architecture's historical role as the basic building block of urban design' (2006: 37). Since its coinage, the movement has been championed for its privileging of systems, particularly non-human systems, over form giving and human concerns. Moreover, its rise has been advanced by the alacrity of digital media and social networks developments.

Some have argued that landscape urbanism and the rise of digital means to analyse and visualize landscapes have further distanced designers from the sites they design. In 2016, Lisa Diedrich, Gunilla Lindholm, and Vera Vicenzotti organized an international conference, *Beyond ism: the landscape of landscape urbanism*, in Alnarp, Sweden to garner the insights of critics and promoters of landscape urbanism (Beyond ism: the landscape of landscape urbanism 19-21 October 2016). Participants such as Thorbjörn Andersson, Elizabeth Meyer and Noël van Dooren noted that the movement was hampered by a lack of concern with human (or even urban) issues. Likewise, its fixation with the aesthetics of digital representations of landscapes, rather than the aesthetic qualities of built works, ignored contributions made by physical landscapes. The following example from a studio experience in Vancouver illustrates how the four trace approach augments the opposite attitude.

ECOLOGICAL SURVEY OF THE ARBUTUS CORRIDOR

A section every 500m along the corridor was drawn, flora and fauna was documented. Though the survey is not all inclusive, it gives a broad understanding of the ecology throughout the corridor while providing in depth detail at 500m intervals. See "Arbutus Corridor Field Guide" for section details.

Figure 1 **The Arbutus Corridor by landscape architecture students at the University of British Columbia.**

Figure 2 **Landing on the corridor.**

Four Trace Concepts and the Arbutus Corridor

'Four Trace Concepts in Landscape Architecture' guided the design process of a master of landscape architecture studio at the University of British Columbia, Canada. The students' site was the Arbutus Corridor, an abandoned urban railway line in Vancouver (Fig. 1). Stretching across six Vancouver neighbourhoods, the corridor connects numerous terrains, geographies, land use types, and most poignantly the hidden with the visible. Seemingly 'abandoned' yet teaming with life, the Arbutus Corridor has been the landscape of conflict since the last freight train travelled the line in 2001. For 16 years, the Canadian Pacific Railway could not agree on a price to sell the land to the City of Vancouver. In the meantime, a liminal landscape emerged with an informal ecosystem of human settlements, roving wildlife, and guerrilla gardens.

The corridor site was apt for translating Girot's trace concepts into a design process for a studio. Our programme attracts students from all over the world, so most of the students were outsiders to the Arbutus Corridor. Moreover, the nature of the site required an approach that that was not based only on distanced analyses and interpretations.

The corridor's unusual dimensions—10 to 20 metres in width by 11 kilometres in length–demanded an approach that exploited its experiential qualities. Once developed as a public space by the city, this veritable thread in the urban landscape would be encountered first-hand by the dense population that surrounded it. In the adaptation of Girot's theory to the studio, students were asked to read 'Four Trace Concepts in Landscape Architecture' in sequence with four major assignments called landing, grounding, finding, and founding, which culminated in a design proposal at the conclusion of the studio.

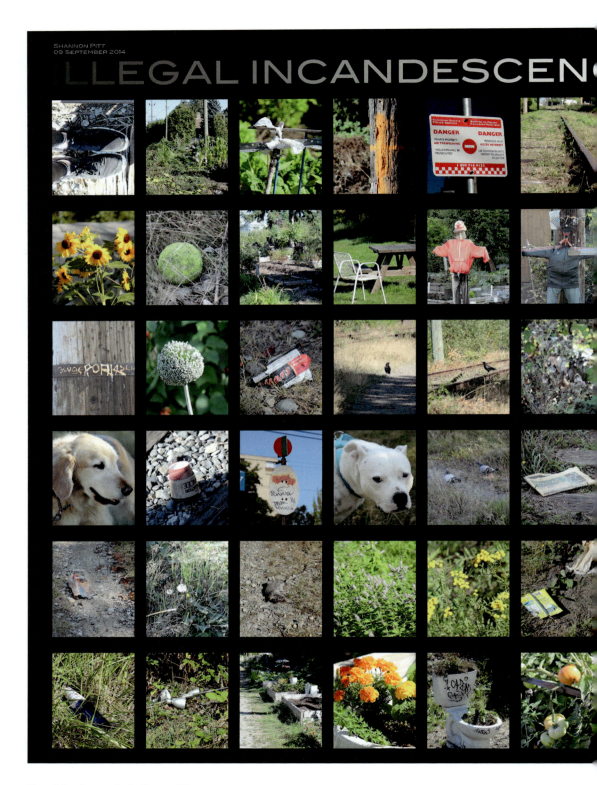

Figure 3 Landing exercise by Shannon Pitt.

Landing

Girot's first trace concept, landing, echoes Husserl's method of phenomenology. According to Girot, 'During landing, nothing is allowed to remain obvious or neutral to the designer, rather everything is apprehended with wonderment and curiosity' (1999:61). To reinforce this phenomenological introduction to the site, GIS files and other digital data describing the site were withheld from the students. None of the students had ever attempted to walk the Arbutus Corridor in its entirety, so they were asked to land on the corridor by walking its full length—by themselves or in groups. They could start at the north end or south end, and they could go anytime during the first two weeks of the course. It was suggested that evening was a good time to go, if they could bring a friend. They were also encouraged to take along a pet, the more exotic the better. Students were asked to directly describe their experiences and to juxtapose what they thought they knew about the corridor with their direct experiences. Once students had landed, each student was required to produce either a visual assembly of site photos; a tactile collage of found objects collected sequentially; an auditory collage of sounds taken at consistent intervals of space (metres) or time (minutes); or a brief IPhone film of their landing. They were also asked to include textual information about their experience, which was to be documented immediately during their landing (Fig. 2).

Shannon Pitt's landing occurred during the daylight hours and she was impressed with the numerous infractions that she encountered along the corridor. From dogs, to guerrilla gardens, to large billboards, to clothes collection bins, to litter—this contested site spoke volumes to her regarding the multiple ways people were using and experiencing the site on a daily basis. For Pitt, people seemed unconcerned that they were using a private space owned and regulated by a corporate railway company—despite the ample signage warning against the corridor's use for dog walking or gardening. She created a systematic documentation of these illegal uses, entitled Illegal Incandescence (Fig. 3). Derived from the Latin word, incandescens, meaning to glow, Pitt selected this title as she was illuminated by these illegal uses through her landing.

Tamara Bonnemaison attempted a psycho-geographical account of her landing, much like Husserl's direct, unbiased descriptions of experiences. Every time she encountered unusual phenomena while landing, she named it with an invented name that occurred to her. The names reflected the immediate impressions that the phenomena made on her. She then created a linear collage of these new names, which included titles such as mechanical ivy, romantic hops overlook, and big bee meadow. Reviewing these names later on during the grounding process, Bonnemaison was struck by the colonizing plants of the corridor and their wild growth as a central theme to her experience.

Grounding

Grounding is the second phase in Girot's four traces. For Girot, 'The difference between landing and grounding is essentially linked to time and moment. Landing only happens once, at the beginning, immediate and distinct, whereas grounding recurs indefinitely. Grounding is more about reading and understanding a site through repeated visits and studies.' (1999:62-63). Two weeks later, and throughout the remainder of the studio, student groups engaged in a grounding exercise that we called Necessary Digressions. This grounding exercise involved speaking and obtaining information from stakeholders involved with the corridor, the First Nations (communities whose land the corridor occupies), the railway corporation (who owns the property), and City of Vancouver representatives (potential owners of the site). These digressions brought layers of knowledge about the site that were not visible. As Girot notes, 'it is not necessarily what remains visible to the eye that matters most but forces and events that undergird the evolution of a place' (1999:63).

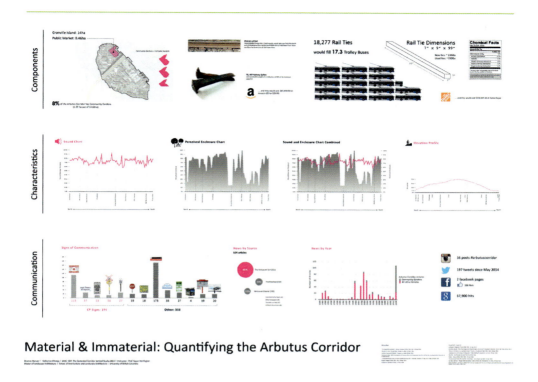

Figure 4 **Grounding by Deanne Manzer and Katherine Pihooja.**

Using ideas and information gleaned from the grounding, students began to reveal linkages among the layers of visible and invisible phenomena of the site. Working in small groups, this phase involved examination of the corridor's material and immaterial features, natural features and infrastructure, its competing histories (public) and memories (private), its local and regional logistics, its informal and formal uses and events, and its spatial and temporal dimensions.

Considering the corridor's material and immaterial features, Deanne Manzer and Katherine Pihooja quantified the major communicative elements they discovered about the corridor (Fig. 4). For example, they counted the physical and textual features of the site, such as 194 official Canadian Pacific Railway signs and 318 other signs. As a corollary, they also counted the corridor's immaterial features, such as two Facebook pages for the Arbutus Corridor, 197 tweets that year about the corridor, and 67,900 Google hits. To link these worlds, they created their own Facebook Page called All Aboard the Arbutus Corridor and posted their grounding work on this page. Manzer and Pihooja also discovered that the corridor contained 72,907 railway spikes, which shopping online on Amazon would cost $87,459CD. They also counted 18,277 railway ties, and when consulting The Home Depot, these would cost $236,947USD online. By linking information that was materially present on the Arbutus Corridor with this material's immaterial presence (monetarily online), Manzer and Pihooja connected visible site conditions with information not visible on the site.

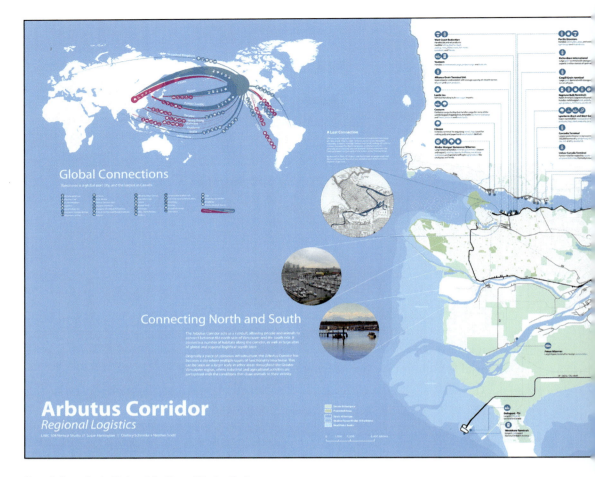

Figure 5 **Grounding by Chelsea Schmitke and Heather Scott.**

Chelsea Schmitke and Heather Scott examined the local and regional logistics of the Arbutus Corridor (Fig. 5). Logistics entailed the procurement, maintenance, and transportation of resources and goods. Regarding the immediate local north to south logistics, they found that the Arbutus Corridor served as a conduit, enabling the flow of people and animals between False Creek to the north and the Fraser River to the south. Bird and bat habitats along the corridor served as some of the most important primary ecological functions of the site. On a larger scale beyond the Greater Vancouver region, industrial and agricultural transportation routes were linked to various trading sites the corridor once served by linking resources and products from land to water. Connecting ports in Asia to regional Vancouver sites, such as the Alliance Grain Terminal Limited and Kinder Morgan Vancouver Wharves, Schmitke and Scott discovered the numerous logistical linkages that the corridor supported during its life as a railway corridor. They also discovered the habitat logistics that the space now provided for as an abandoned railway site.

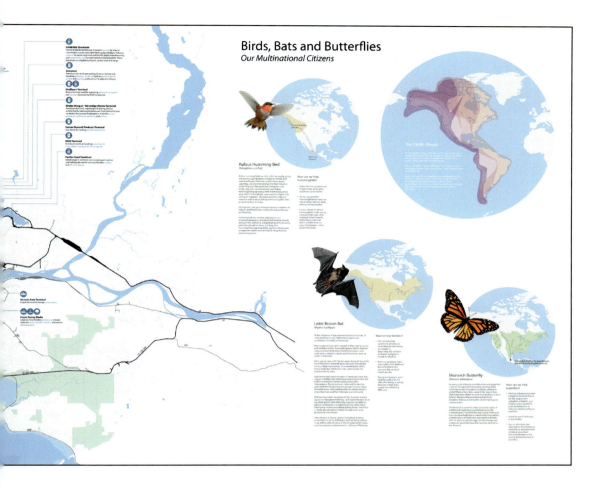

Finding

Finding commenced halfway through the term and this was the most challenging of the three concepts to adapt to an assignment. For Girot, it could be 'a surprise discovery or some painstaking, methodological quest' (1999: 63). Students were asked to create a visual matrix, using photos, sketches, plans, montages, and textual material. The matrix columns compared transformation, succession, and operation with the rows of scales ranging from the region, neighbourhood, and body. Each student selected a scale to work across (Fig. 6).

Beginning with the regional, transformation addresses the future multiple uses of the corridor, and in this example, flight, particularly by birds and bats, created a constant modification of the site. Succession demonstrates how this transformation might evolve over time and some students considered the corridor as a linear space for human flight. Operation concerns the economic logistics of this transformation and succession, and Katherine Pihooja proposed that the corridor be used as a beta-testing laboratory where

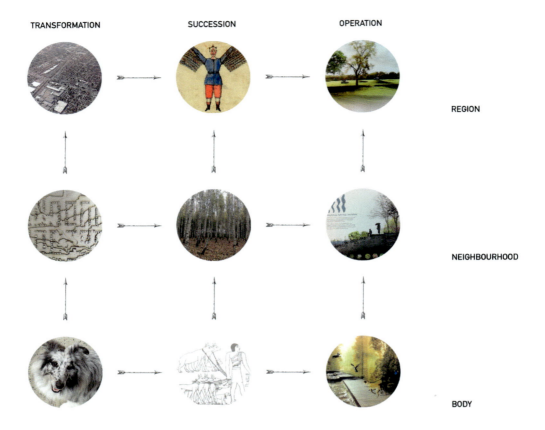

Figure 6 Finding matrix.

Figure 7 Grounding by Chelsea Schmitke and Heather Scott.

ecological and sustainable systems could be monitored and documented through hover-crafts and other flying vehicles (Fig. 7). Starting with the neighbourhood scale that crosses paths with the corridor and which directly transforms the site, Heather Scott speculated a new hydrological condition to evolve over time. Operationally, as it was envisioned by Scott, the corridor would become a linear wetland network. At the scale of the body (human and/or animal), dogs were frequently identified as actors in the corridor. Although they were not allowed to occupy the site, people frequently walked their dogs along the corridor, transforming the site with their markings. Dogs have a long history of cohabitation with humans and have evolved in succession with human activities and customs. Chelsea Schmitke's operational cell envisions a linear area for the cities' canine populations. Her landing was conducted with a go-pro camera strapped to her dog's head.

Founding

In the founding phase, students synthesized design futures for the corridor across multiple scales, temporal stages, and velocities. Students were asked to consider the corridor for experiential potential. This included, but was not limited to, the corridor as a transportation infrastructure for humans and wildlife, an experimental ground for new types of technology, a site for informal and formal economic networks, and a logistical landscape where the desires and wills of multiple participants must be negotiated. Given the highly polemic nature of this linear landscape (extensive media coverage on the internet, TV, radio, and grey literature presenting all types of opinions), it was important that students understood the potentials that the corridor offered as an urban experience. This required students to present a conceptual plan for the entire 11km site, detailed designs that communicated materials and the human scale experiences afforded by their design (perspectives, photo-shopped interventions, etc.), programming, and connections to the immediate and regional context, as well as virtual connections.

Steph Aitken proposed bat habitats. In North America, the white-nose syndrome (WNS) has devastated insect-loving bats of many species. The syndrome is called white-nose because of the white fungus that grows on the hibernating bat's face, ears, and wings, which eventual contributes to the bat's death. The USGS National Wildlife Center estimates 'bat population declines in the north-eastern US since the emergence of WNS are approximately 80%,' (US Geographical Survey 2017) and the syndrome has spread to the west coast of North America. WNS inflicts several species of bats, including the little brown bat (Myotis lucifugus), which students identified on the Arbutus Corridor site during grounding.

Aitken's proposal not only involved creating bat habitats, since they return to the same areas for mating and nursing. To attract insects, wetlands were proposed with shallow water and emergent plants for larvae anchorage. Aitken also planned rocky crevices and bat habitat structures. Lighting was to be removed from the corridor so as to not disrupt the bats' nocturnal activities. Aitken also envisioned community involvement in the monitoring of the bats along the Arbutus Corridor. She proposed the Arbutus Bat Group and the installation of Live Bat Cameras that could be viewed by local residents, university researchers, and schoolchildren. She repurposed the billboard signs to advertise the bats and their needs (Fig. 8). Entitled Dark Fascinations, the billboards promoted the web cams and Arbutus Bat Group as well as the reduction of light pollution.

Tamara Bonnemaison returned to the section of the Arbutus Corridor that she named Romantic Hops Overlook during her landing exercise. She designed lookout platforms that she oriented based on the location of the setting sun during different times of year. The platforms themselves, as well as gateway markers leading to the platforms, also provided

Figure 8 **Founding by Steph Aitken**.

nooks and crannies for the abundant wildlife living in the corridor. The sun setting platforms were designed to shelter a range of small mammals, and pathways in this area were raised to allow for the safe crossing of mice, raccoons, and other small animals (Fig. 9). For the gateway markers, the upper level provided shelter for screech owls, northern flickers, downy woodpeckers, chickadees, purple martins, Carolina wrens, nuthatch, crested flycatchers, or Benwick's wrens. In the lower stratum (below one metre), tree swallows, mourning cloaks, praying mantis, hummingbird clearwings, and Isabella tiger moths could find refuge (Fig. 10).

Conclusion

By incorporating phenomenological methods of Girot's landing exercise, students explored the nature of experience in the role of the standard site visit that is conducted in many design studios in landscape architecture programmes. Since they acquired knowledge about the corridor through their experience, this brought insights into the site visit that they may have overlooked. Students were shocked that they were not provided with a base map or digital plan of the site at the start of the studio. However, this gap in knowledge enabled them to more fully concentrate on the experience of the site during landing.

Grounding enabled students to study the site distinctly from the landing experience, and many of the students conducted detailed analyses in this phase. The finding charrette enabled students to leap quickly between different ideas and scales. Founding also produced unusual approaches in planning the corridor's future. Moreover, Girot's cumulative theories helped students maintain an awareness of the role that intuition plays in the relationship to the factual information, which is often gathered during the site analysis phase. The four trace theories strengthened the relationship between the site and the students' imagination in the design synthesis process. Lastly, the four traces build upon one another. This is not always recognized when simply reading Girot's chapter. Enacting the four trace concepts in the design studio reveals how students' discoveries are iterative and also how these discoveries retain the power to inspire other students' design proposals.

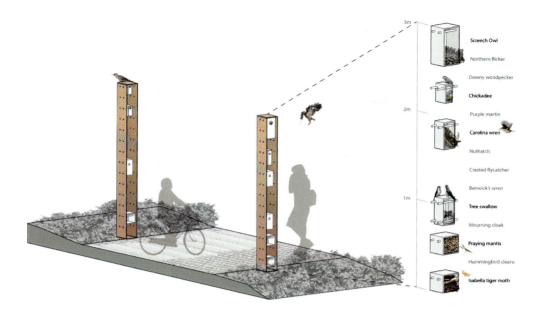

Figure 9 **Founding** by Tamara Bonnemaison

Figure 10 **Founding** by Tamara Bonnemaison

REFERENCES

Husserl, E. (2002), 'Pure phenomenology, its method, and its field of investigation,' in Dermont Moran (ed.), *The Phenomenology Reader* (London: Routledge), 124-133.

Girot, C. (1999), 'Four trace concepts in landscape architecture,' in James Corner (ed.), *Recovering Landscape: Essays in Contemporary Landscape Architecture* (New York: Princeton Architectural Press), 59-68.

US Geological Survey (White-Nose Syndrome (WNS)), https://www.nwhc.usgs.gov/disease_information/white-nose_syndrome/ Accessed 14 April 2017.

94

LANDSCAPE CONSTRUCTION CLASSES

Technical subjects, such as those involved in teaching landscape construction are often seen as lacking the glamour of traditional studio teaching which tends to focus more explicitly on the creative aspects of landscape architecture. Creativity, however, should no less be a characteristic of construction than it should of design, something which the two chapters in this section underline, both of them stressing the need to take an holistic approach to problem solving in which technology is the means and not the end.

An holistic approach to dealing with rainwater within design projects is the focus for Peter Petschek's chapter which treats it as an integral part of the site engineering process. Rainwater is viewed here as a valuable resource to be treasured rather than as a problem to be dealt with. In addition to outlining the technical aspects related to the materials and techniques involved in the management of site runoff, this contribution goes on to describe how this can best be taught within the context of digital landscape construction workflow for infrastructure BIM (Building Information Modelling).

Design strategies for green infrastructure within an urban context is the theme of the second chapter in this section. Here Maria-Beatrice Andreucci describes a landscape architecture studio taught within the University of 'La Sapienza' in Rome, centred around project based learning. This student centred approach involves teaching in small multi-disciplinary groups, focussed around a specific site and based on a project brief developed by the students themselves.

Rainwater management as part of the HSR site engineering education

Peter Petschek

Abstract

It is imperative that rainwater be protected! Rainwater is essential for our drinking water supplies. In Switzerland, like in many other European countries, there is a common understanding that clean water has to return to the natural hydrological cycle, and this belief is clearly supported by Federal Law, construction standards and city regulations (VSA 2004). HSR University of Applied Sciences Rapperswil Switzerland emphasizes Rainwater Management in its Landscape Architecture site engineering education. Terrain grading is one of the most fundamental and effective ways in returning the water to its natural cycle. The HSR Rainwater Management approach uses digital grading as a part of landscaping-SMART (BIM process) to achieve this goal.

Introduction to rainwater management

Clean water is an essential and very precious asset. Precipitation replenishes the ground-water needed for domestic, agricultural and industrial use. In order to keep groundwater free of the toxins and other contaminants, stormwater management is necessary. The author prefers the less dramatic term rainwater instead of stormwater, which the US publications use, because rainwater is a valuable asset one has to take care of; it is not a hazard like stormwater.

The strategy for rainwater protection by The Swiss Federal Law for the Protection of Water requires that unpolluted water is percolated or filtered into the ground as it would have before the natural ground was built on by various impermeable constructions. If this is not possible, the water must flow with reduced speed into rivers and lakes.

Swiss guidelines for the percolation, retention and guidance of rainwater in urban areas (VSA 2004) explain the rainwater management process and they are a standard to which Architects, Civil Engineers and Landscape Architects must adhere.

Today different products to retain, filter and percolate water help to manage rainwater. Green roofs are a good way to reduce the water runoff from buildings, and many green roof products are available. Permeable paving stones also provide another rainwater management solution. Some of the concrete products are porous, while others have openings or wider joints where the water can penetrate. On sites where ponds, basins and swales are not possible for retention and percolation, underground modular retention systems can be used. The products are made of polyethylene (PE), and they work like sponges with a retention rate of 90% and are able to withstand soil pressures at a depth of up to 4 metres. Before the water can be retained in these structures and then slowly percolate, it has to go through a natural filtering process in the topsoil. If this is not possible, special filter systems (rainwater adsorption filter) which can be part of a manhole or gutter systems, will simulate the filtering ability of the natural soil. Because of these types of engineering solutions, rainwater management is now possible in places where before a simple excuse like, 'We have no space for retention ponds or swales' was used. All standards and materials are ineffective if the water does not flow towards the intended location or structure designated for infiltration. The act of designing the surface and guiding the water is called terrain grading. In the further text the term grading will be used.

Grading and rainwater management

'Simply put, grading is design' (Storm 2009: 1). Although the professional spectrum is very broad, and intense grading is not necessarily part of each project, every intervention designed by a Landscape Architect involves some modification of the earth's surface. Grading therefore plays a key role in Landscape Architecture. 'The shaping of the earth's surface is one of the primary functions of site planners and landscape architects' (Storm 2009: VII). Grading with contour lines, spot elevations and profiles is the first step to control the rainwater and guide it to areas where it can percolate. Standards with minimum and maximum slopes make sure the water runs off different surfaces in an efficient manner. Grading does not stop on top of the surface.

'It is difficult to separate the act of grading from the act of accommodating and controlling storm water runoff, since one directly affects the other' (Storm 2009: 24). Subsurface drainage design consists of manholes, gutters and pipes. If there is no space for percolation on a site, water has to flow to manholes and gutters, where pipes then lead it to retention areas. Subsurface drainage design, which includes the calculation of the amount of water in order to size all elements, belongs to the overall grading process. It is important not to forget that subgrades must also have slopes. They are normally graded to the same slope as the top surface.

Grading is also needed for the design of retention and percolation ponds, bio swales and rainwater gardens. It helps to integrate the elements in an overall design concept. Profiles created via grading provide volume information (profile volume method), which is necessary together with the specific infiltration rate of the soil on a site for the sizing of infiltration systems like retention and percolation ponds.

BIM, landscapingSMART and rainwater management

Building Information Modelling (BIM) was originally developed for complex architectural projects. It is also important to keep in mind, BIM is a method and a process not just a software. The three levels of tasks within the BIM process are BIM construction, BIM coordination and BIM management. The main idea of BIM for Infrastructure, similar to that of BIM for Architecture, is the use of one complete data model by the different project partners. Partners may include civil, structural and environmental engineers, planners, landscape architects, building contractors and government or city agencies. All planners and engineers use only one model and therefore can detect conflicts during the planning phase instead of on site during construction. BIM for infrastructure is not yet as clearly defined as BIM for Architecture, with infrastructure projects tending to be more diverse and spread over larger geographical areas. On the other hand, the infrastructure industry has been using Little BIM for quite a while. The term little is used when only one discipline is using the data, as is the case with GNSS earthworks.

Today most mid and large size civil construction companies in Switzerland are using the Global Navigation Satellite Systems (GNSS) technology together with digital terrain models for earthwork projects in order to reduce costs and to allow for higher precision. This

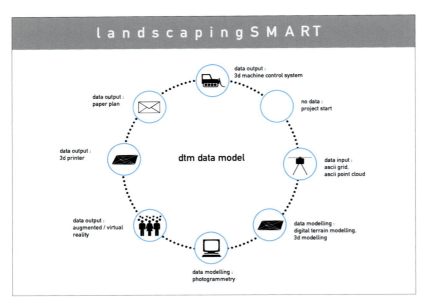

Figure 1 The landscapingSMART process with the DTM data model in the centre is part of rainwater management.

combination is an important aspect of a BIM. landscapingSMART (Petschek 2014: 179 - 211) describes the workflow starting with data generation, via modelling to preparation of data for a Landscape Architecture GNSS machine controlled earthwork construction site. It does not cover BIM topics like data structure and work organization. landscapingSMART emphasizes the following:

- In order to build a Digital Terrain Model (DTM) for GNSS controlled machines precise data of the existing conditions are necessary. It is better to hire a surveyor to acquire the data, as it is not the job of Landscape Architects.
- The DTM is the central element in landscapingSMART. The DTM for the proposed site enables a correct, efficient and precise surface and subsurface design. The knowledge to model a detailed DTM is one of the main competences of Landscape Architects.
- Only the combination of civil engineering and architectural software will result in a BIM for Landscape Architecture model.
- Analogue terrain models are also very important tools in Landscape Architecture. While hand built models will always play an important role in grading design studies, eventually they must be transferred to digital terrain models. Photogrammetric software facilitates this transfer. Landscape Architects must be familiar with the concept of photogrammetry and able to apply the software.
- Excavators and dozers with Global Navigation Satellite Systems (GNSS) based 3D machine control (guidance) systems need the DTM data for shaping the proposed site. The machines guarantee high precision surfaces. Contractors are responsible for this task, but Landscape Architects need a basic understanding in order to create a correct DTM.

landscapingSMART not only improves the efficiency and precision of the construction process and is part of a BIM for Infrastructure, but landscapingSMART also supports rainwater management. All DTM surfaces have to have slopes for water runoff. Slopes, curbs, gutters, catch basins, manholes, pipes, swales, percolation areas and retention ponds are all defined within a digital terrain model. By understanding digital grading and how a DTM works, Landscape Architects can precisely analyze and design the flow of water on the site. Simply speaking: the one who controls the DTM also controls the machine and in turn controls the rainwater.

HSR site engineering education and rainwater management

In comparison to other schools in Europe, e.g. in Germany, where the topic is briefly taught as part of surveying courses, grading is the most important element of the site engineering education at HSR. The curriculum on grading is very similar to US and Canadian schools where a rigorous training in the design with contour lines, spot elevations, profiles, volume calculations, subsurface drainage, etc. is required. 'I do know that probably all landscape architecture programs in the USA have included these subjects in their curricula since WWII and perhaps even much earlier' (e-mail by Prof. Bruce Sharky on the topic of history of grading education in the USA). One can assume that the very important licensing exam in the USA, with an entire chapter dealing exclusively with grading and drainage, has a big influence on the curricula. A whole array of books published in the USA on grading also shows the importance of the topic.

At HSR, the teaching of grading happens both in analogue and in digital. With a solid background in manipulating contour lines by hand, catch basin, manhole and pipe dimensioning in the first semester, and a good understanding of surveying equipment, HSR students are then exposed almost exclusively to digital grading in their second semester. 'Most computational and drafting tasks associated with site engineering have become completely automated', (Storm 2009: VIII). The digital grading course includes the following aspects:
- Import of survey and GIS data.
- Triangulation of points, contours and breaklines.
- Theory on TIN (Triangulated Irregular Network).
- Using point and feature line commands for site design.
- Volume calculations, digital pipe and manhole layout.
- Roadway alignment and corridor design.
- Close range photogrammetry using UAV technology (drone).
- Instruction of a GNSS excavator.

The developments in the construction industry are one reason for the emphasis on digital grading, the second reason being it is easier for students to use. How can you prove that students are solving grading problems better with digital tools? An experiment using a comparative approach a couple of years ago demonstrated the advantages of digital tools. HSR students had to take part in two exams in which they had to solve a typical grading problem. The first exam asked them to calculate and draft the placement of a tennis court in the traditional analogue hand-calculated and hand-drawn method. In the second exam, the students used Civil 3D, a software dedicated to digital grading tasks. The findings were clear, more students solved the task with digital than analogue grading. Today more intuitive software would likely show that the results tend even more in favour of digital grading.

The site design project in the second semester is the core of the site-engineering education in the first year and is very important for understanding rainwater management. Here the students must apply their knowledge of grading in a project. The students define the location of a building, drop off area, access road parking spaces, terraces, paths and grade all of it into an existing landscape. The scale of the project is typical for professional

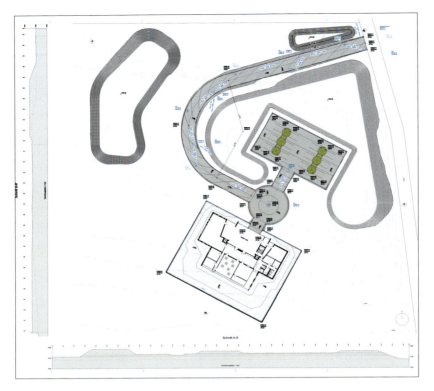

Figure 2
HSR site design project with digital grading for rainwater management.

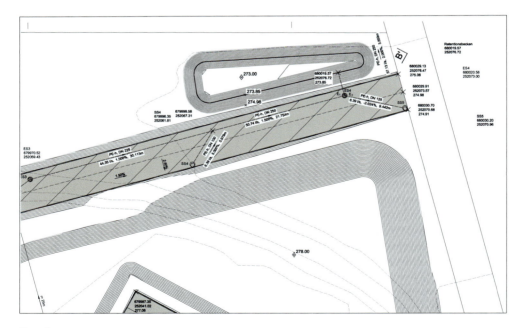

Figure 3
Retention and percolation pond detail of the HSR site design project.

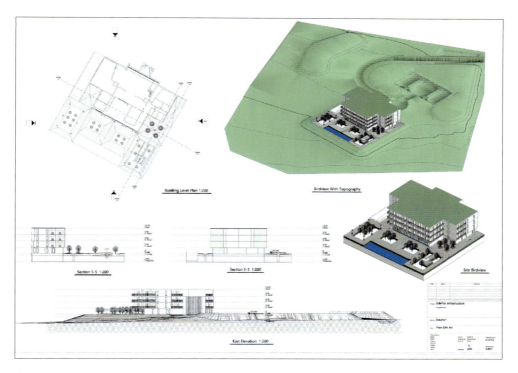

Figure 4
Combined Civil 3D (civil engineering software) and Revit (architecture software) model with a detailed grading design of the terrace over the parking garage.

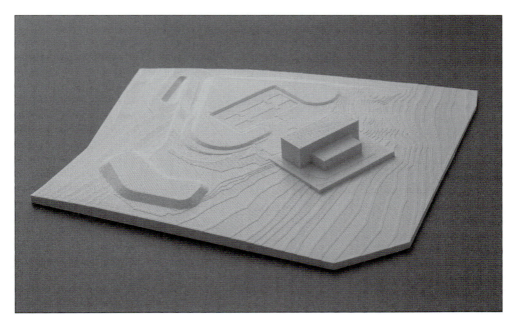

Figure 5
3D printed model of the HSR site design project.

Figure 6
HSR student using a drone for generating terrain data via Close Range Photogrammetry. HSR students also very often use smartphone data for creating terrains.

Figure 7
HSR students working with a 3D GNSS excavator.

Landscape Architecture jobs in Switzerland. The students use Civil 3D for the digital grading tasks. The site grading of the project must also include the subsurface drainage design and dimensioning of swales and ponds. All water runoff from the roofs, drop offs, access roads and parking lots has to be collected and guided by pipes to bio swales, retention and percolation ponds. The dimensioning of these elements is important. Therefore calculations for the specific infiltration rate of soils on site and the dimensioning of infiltration systems have to be taken into account. Professional software for modelling rainwater runoff like HydroCAD or STORM are too complex and time consuming for second semester beginners. Therefore the students use a simple and easy-to-use rainwater management workflow for smaller sites developed at HSR. Following this step-by-step workflow with tables, videos and preliminary calculations helps make sure the students understand the process.

Starting in the 2018 fall semester, Revit, a BIM for Architecture software, will be integrated into the first semester CAD teaching as well as in the fifth semester site design project. In the first semester course, students must model a small architecture project, for example a bus stop, rain shelter, or pavilion. In the fifth semester, the site design project from the second semester is refined. Students will be required to combine the 3D Revit architecture model and the Civil 3D civil engineering model into one BIM model. The architecture model includes a large terrace covering a parking garage, which is a typical structure in urban Switzerland. This area is constructed using combined Revit and Civil 3D and leads to a BIM construction model for checking possible conflicts (catch basin depth, crossing pipes, grade changes, location of tree bales etc.). BIM Coordination and Management topics are covered in a separate project management course. Main tasks in this project are grading and rainwater management. All the water on top of the parking garage must drain into a retention pond on site. Our YouTube channel 'HSR Landschaftsarchitektur' presents first BIM student projects.

Besides traditional engineering courses on materials, surveying, geotechnics and construction techniques, grading is the most important topic in the site engineering education at HSR. Digital grading as part of the landscapingSMART process leads to a BIM construction model and is the foundation of rainwater management.

REFERENCES

Autodesk Civil 3D, 'software' [website], https://www.autodesk.com/products/autocad-civil-3d/overview, accessed 22.7.2017

Autodesk Revit, 'software' [website], https://www.autodesk.com/products/revit/overview, accessed 16.9.2018

HydroCAD, 'software' [website], http://www.hydrocad.net/index.htm, accessed 22.7.2017

Petschek, Peter (2014), *Grading. landscapingSMART, 3D Machine Control Systems, Stormwater Management* (Basel: Birkhäuser).

Sharky, Bruce (2015), *Landscape Site Grading Principles* (Hoboken: Wiley & Sons).

STORM, 'software' [website], http://www.sieker.de/de/produkte-und-leistungen/product/storm-16.html, accessed 22.7.2017

Storm Steven, Natham Kurt, Woland Jake (2009), *Site Engineering for Landscape Architects*, 5th Edition (Hoboken: Wiley & Sons).

Untermann, Richard (1973), *Grade Easy* (Washington: Landscape Architecture Foundation).

Verband Schweizer Abwasser- und Gewässerschutzfachleute VSA (2002), *Planung und Erstellung von Anlagen für die Liegenschaftsentwässerung SN 592 000* (Zürich: VSA).

Verband Schweizer Abwasser- und Gewässerschutzfachleute VSA (2004), *Regenwasserentsorgung, Richtlinie zur Versickerung, Retention und Ableitung von Niederschlagswasser in Siedlungsgebieten* (Zürich: VSA).

Teaching environmental technological design: fostering meaningful learning integrating green infrastructure into architectural and urban design

Maria-Beatrice Andreucci

Introduction

Environmental risks such as failure of climate-change mitigation and adaptation—which is considered the most potentially impactful risk and the third most likely, with water crises, biodiversity loss and ecosystem collapse (WEF 2016: 6)—are rising up the list of world-wide concerns.

Landscape architects, and other professionals from related disciplines, are deemed to contribute with 'adaptive' architectural and urban design levering on nature-based solutions and appropriate technologies[1] (Schumacher 1974; Thormann 1979) in order to mitigate negative impacts and strengthen resilience.[2]

While researchers and scientists have discussed ecosystem services for many decades, the Ecosystem Services concept itself became popular with the Millennium Ecosystem Assessment (MA) only in the early 2000s. The specific contribution of 'Green Infrastructure' (GI) to the provision of Ecosystem Services (Alcamo et al. 2003) is still mostly unexplored in European landscape architecture and architectural and urban design professional practice. It is therefore important that students of building professions—landscape architects, architects and engineers—exchange experience and co-learn how the integration of GI into architectural and urban design can help create more sustainable urban settings.

In the environmental technological design studio taught by the author at the Faculty of Architecture of 'Sapienza' Università di Roma, students are asked to develop their project focusing on GI specialised design strategies and construction techniques in order to implement adaptive interventions aiming at resilient architecture and inclusive urban design. The key learning objectives of the courses are: the provision of cultural and methodological references and of technical and operative tools to realise—in a coherent relationship with the built environment—bio-eco-oriented environmental technological design interventions at both architectural and urban scale. The learning activities help develop experimental knowledge of the diagnostic methods for environmental and cultural heritage, and of the key strategies for its requalification, valorisation and restoration, in particular through the GI design approach. The main goal is to sensitise students to the urgent need of long-run equilibrium conditions among settlements, anthropogenic activities and Natural Capital, in a dynamic scenario of technological innovation and sustainability.

Fostering meaningful learning through environmental technological design

Fostering meaningful learning teaching environmental technological design to architects and landscape architects requires going beyond the mere transmission/reception of technical-scientific information, while committing to knowledge that is robust and transferable to real-life professional practices and contexts, and that looks at co-operative learning as a possible pedagogical approach to facilitate interdisciplinary education.

Problem (or project)-based learning (PBL)

Problem (or project)-based learning (PBL) is a way of building knowledge in which the problems act both as context and driving force for learning, in a student-centred, active approach to education (Barrows 1986: 483). Usually, the problems are based on real-life problems that have been selected and edited to meet educational objectives and criteria. The learning content is directly related to the context, thus promoting student motivation and comprehension.

Six pillars characterise the PBL process (Barrows 1996). The first characteristic is that learning needs to be student-centred. Secondly, learning has to occur in small student groups under the guidance of a tutor. The third characteristic refers to the presence of a tutor acting as a facilitator or guide. Fourth, authentic problems are primarily encountered in a learning sequence, before any preparation or study has occurred. Fifth, the problems faced are used as a tool to achieve the required knowledge and the problem-solving skills necessary to eventually solve the problem. Finally, new information needs to be acquired through self-directed learning.

PBL has been adopted in educational programmes in a variety of disciplines, including Architecture, Law, Engineering and Social Work (Boud & Feletti 1997; Maitland 1997, both cited by Bridges 2006: 755-759), and PBL techniques are widely endorsed as methods of achieving meaningful learning (Ausubel 2000: 6) and simultaneously encouraging a mature participation within the educational process (Roberts 2004: 1-3) with students engaging in scientific activities, presenting similar cognitive challenges.

Green infrastructure design approach

The topic of the GI project is part of the broad, scientific and operational debate on the development of methodologies and integrated design frameworks for sustainable urban transformation in a regenerative perspective.

Urban GI are 'the elements of biodiversity, Natural Capital, and organized systems linked to any urban area, with intrinsic qualities or degraded, including individual environmental technological devices, integrating biodiversity in the built environment, such as green roofs and bio-walls, permeable paving, rain gardens and other sustainable urban drainage systems, in order to promote, through the provision of ecosystem services, environmental protection, economic feasibility, health, well-being, equity and social inclusion' (Andreucci 2013).

Urban GI is an evolving concept, where the urban ecosystem—a place of interaction between biotic and abiotic elements—represents the complex and vital system by which to pursue the rebalancing imposed by the erosion of resilience abilities. In particular, open spaces that counteract fragmentation due to increasingly intense flows of people, materials and information, as well as other surfaces and buildings (Andreucci 2017).

Interdisciplinary co-operative learning

Interdisciplinary work, where learners integrate information from two or more disciplines to create artefacts and explain or solve problems (Boix Mansilla 2004), has been linked with promoting critical and holistic thinking skills, where the holistic thinking (Holm

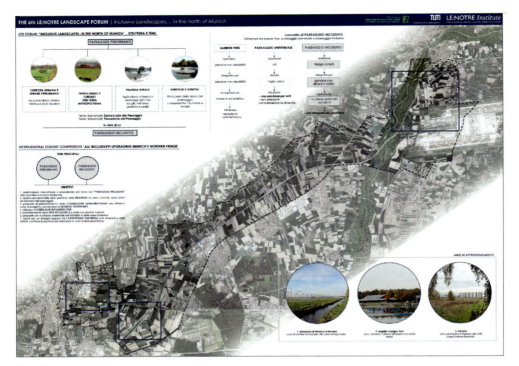

Figure 1

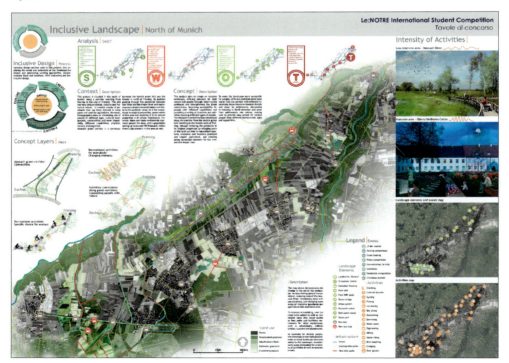

Figure 2

Figures 1-3 LE:NOTRE Landscape Forum 2017 students competition, 1st Prize Project 'Inclusive Landscapes Munich North': Giada Di Sante ('Sapienza' Università di Roma), Ziou He, Eliza Salman, Evgeniia Telnykh (IMLA).

Figure 3

2006) is the ability to understand how ideas and information from relevant disciplines, relate to each other, and to the problem. Many argue that this is a powerful and engaging strategy that leads to sustained and transferable learning (Hiebert et al. 1996; Jones, Rasmussen & Moffitt 1996).

Teaching and learning green infrastructure design in PBL
Course units description

The experience described represents different types of academic work developed by the students under the author's responsibility across different types of academic programmes offered at the Faculty of Architecture of 'Sapienza' Università di Roma in the academic year 2015/2016.

'Environmental Technological Sustainability' is a 5 credits core course of the Master degree programme in Landscape Architecture.

'Technologies for Environmental Design and Urban Requalification' is an 8 credits optional course of the Master degree in Architecture.

Within the 'Technology of Architecture' curriculum[3], the two design studios focus on elements and systems of GI design for urban regeneration, addressing the issues of sustainability in relation to the environmental technological requalification of urban open spaces (Master in Landscape Architecture), and to the sustainable design and construction of residential buildings, taking into account the micro-climatic and social factors of the surrounding urban neighbourhood (Master in Architecture).

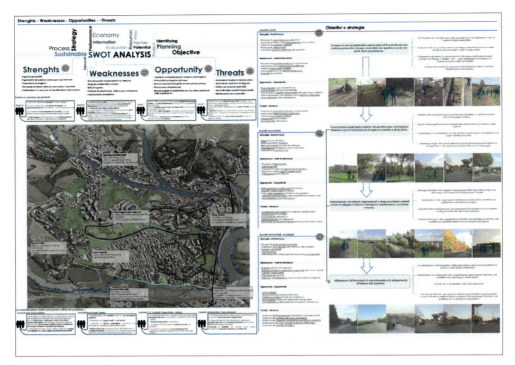

Figure 4

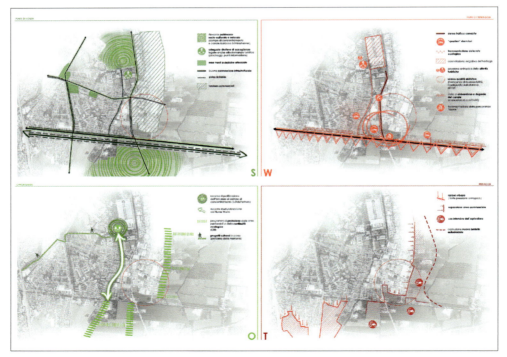

Figure 5

Figures 4 and 5 LE:NOTRE Landscape Forum 2017 students competition, 1st Prize Project 'Inclusive Landscapes Munich North': Giada Di Sante ('Sapienza' Università di Roma), Ziou He, Eliza Salman, Evgeniia Telnykh (IMLA).

The learning process

Levering on the multidisciplinary teaching and professional experience of the professor (landscape architect and economist) the two Master courses focus on environmental, social and economic issues, as they relate to sustainability in architecture, landscape architecture and urban design.

Students initially select with the help of the tutor a project site and then work in small groups questioning each other and researching additional information and relevant case studies. Students have the opportunity to determine their own problem formulation within the given subject area guidelines. Self-directed study groups discuss and analyse selected cases. The typical study group (3-5 students) meets regularly twice a week. Each individual student in the study group presents his/her work. It is then discussed and the group decides who will continue with what tasks. Often students organise their work in such a way that their individual work integrates the work of the group, enabling them to develop a broader perspective of the interrelated themes. The role of the professor who attends the meetings in class is primarily to facilitate the learning process, i.e. to expedite the group's work and knowledge transfer through internal communication. It is important for the students, at this early stage, to be able to identify specific sustainability issues that they need to learn more about, or that they do not fully appreciate.

On-field group analyses are complemented with the individual research of specific environmental, social and economic 'landscape performances'[4], through case-study selection and project critics. International teamwork and sharing of information lead to an enhanced learning experience (Figs. 1-3).

Understanding the concept of 'landscape performance' and why it is important to the development of metrics and measures of environmental, social and economic sustainability; learning about available instruments and methods to quantify landscape benefits; and recognising the essential role of most appropriate environmental technological strategies and adaptive design in creating high performance urban and peri-urban landscapes are the key objectives of this educational phase.

Students are then asked to organise in a 'SWOT matrix' the data and information they have collected, to generate scenarios, and only subsequently to identify the most effective nature-based design solutions (Figs. 4-5).

Students consistently draw a 'Masterplan', a programme of the envisaged interventions which reflects objectives and strategies pursued, taking into account the integrated— and often conflicting—environmental, social and economic problems and opportunities, detected during the previous phases. Later in the semester, these studies advance to greater specificity and students are asked to further develop their project, focusing on specialised design strategies and construction techniques to implement adaptive interventions of landscape architecture for resilient architecture and inclusive urban design. Among the key aspects to be investigated and 'translated' into design solutions are: the implementation of sustainable urban drainage systems; tree planting design and forest management in the urban environment; nature-based solutions for bio-climatic comfort and urban heat island (UHI) mitigation; energy-efficient architecture and open space design; low-impact mobility; and re-permeabilisation strategies for the built environment. 'Multifunctionality' and 'transcalarity' are fundamental characteristics of the GI, and are constantly tested and 'measured' throughout the two 'greening the grey' courses (Figs. 6-13).

This approach is based on the consideration that scholars as future practitioners need a methodological approach to the study of critical issues—that are non-linear and more complex in their interactions (Andreucci 2017: 121-126)—aiming at understanding the relationships among innovative nature-based solutions and environmental technological devices, informed adaptive design and sustainable construction.

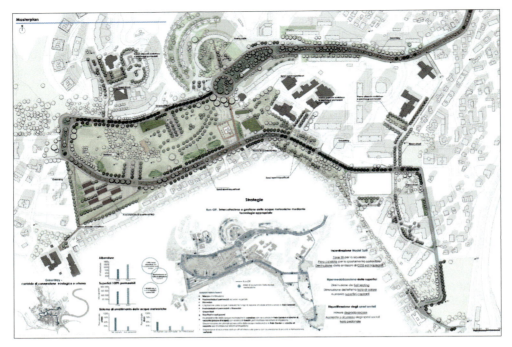

Figure 6

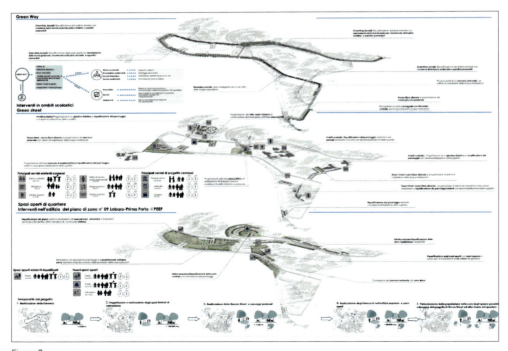

Figure 7

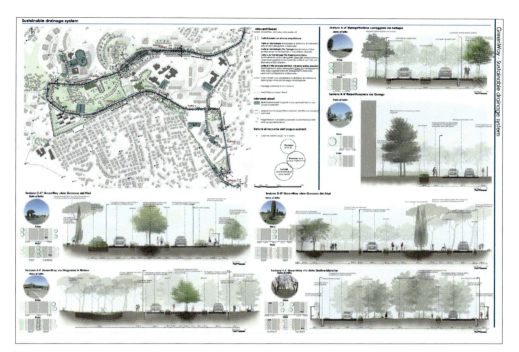

Figure 8

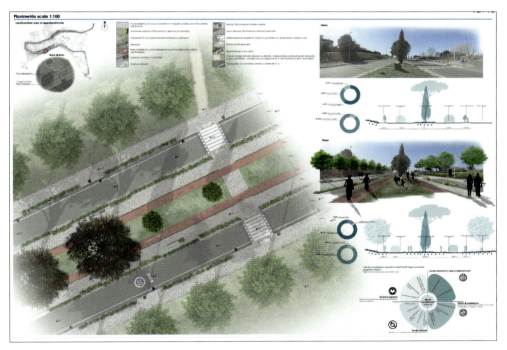

Figure 9

Figures 6-10 Masterplan, strategies and solutions for 'Labaro Prima Porta' in Rome: Jessica Pettinari, Master thesis in Landscape Architecture, professors Luciano Cupelloni, Maria-Beatrice Andreucci, 'Sapienza' Università di Roma, 2017.

Teaching environmental technological design | 111

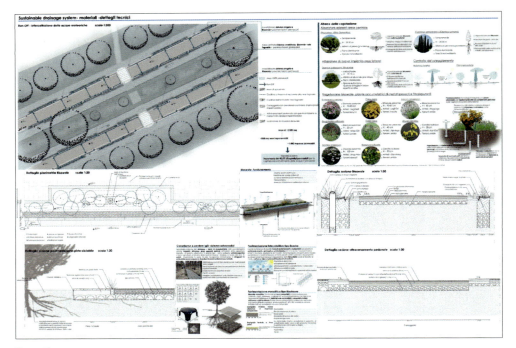

Figure 10

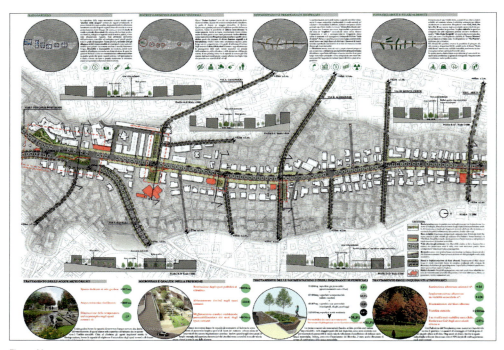

Figure 11

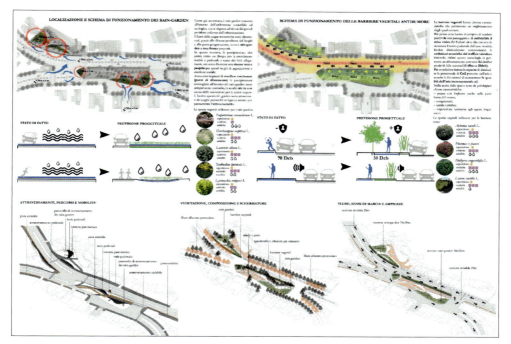

Figure 12

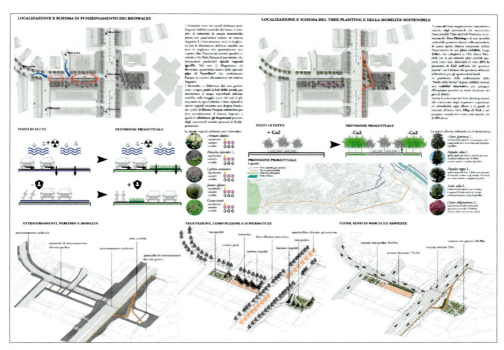

Figure 13

Figures 11-13 **Masterplan, strategies and solutions for 'Viale Colli Portuensi' in Rome**: Gugliemo Pirri, Master thesis in Landscape Architecture, professors Luciano Cupelloni, Maria-Beatrice Andreucci, 'Sapienza' Università di Roma, 2017.

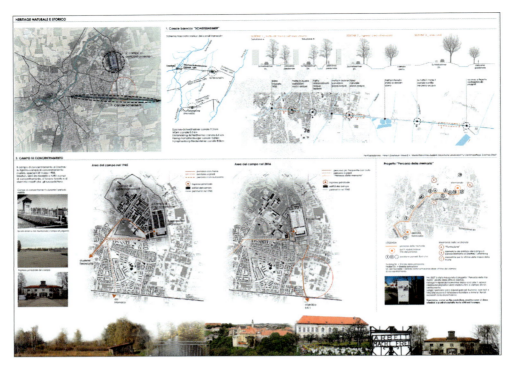

Figure 14

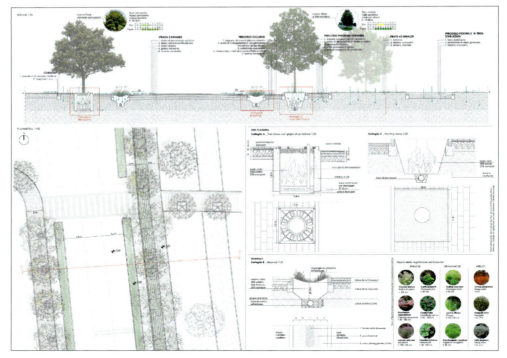

Figure 15

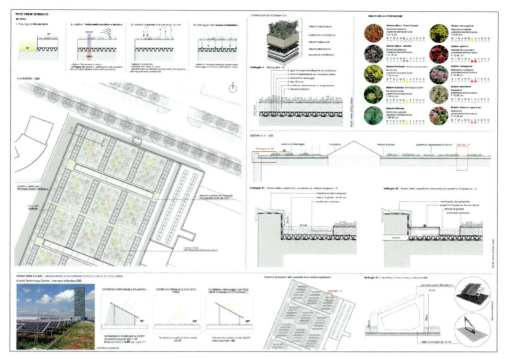

Figure 16

Figures 14-16 Project for Dachau-Scheisseimer canal (DE): Giada Di Sante, Master thesis in Landscape Architecture, professors Luciano Cupelloni, Maria-Beatrice Andreucci, 'Sapienza' Università di Roma, 2017.

Students are encouraged to learn by working in multidisciplinary teams (landscape architects and architects) as they become opportunities for collaboration and interaction that have the potential to greatly enhance knowledge exchange. In terms of curriculum structure, the design studios are used as the arena for integrating architectural, landscape architectural and environmental design knowledge.

Careful consideration of the specific knowledge acquired upon re-organisation of the data and information acquired is an integral part of the active learning approach, whereas assessment takes place on both individual and group members' contribution to the class's knowledge building and exchange. The assessment methods implemented respond to the objectives of the adopted learning process, this means progress testing to enable the students to evaluate their own individual knowledge, and final testing for acquired competence, rather than for isolated factual knowledge.

Conclusions

The present review of a problem-based approach to teaching and learning Environmental Technological Design at 'Sapienza' Università di Roma indicates that it can be considered a valuable method, which promotes situated learning through contextualised problem setting and interactive group work. In comparison to traditional architecture and landscape architecture teaching approaches, the PBL model appears to inspire a higher degree of involvement in study activities and, consequently, a more advanced level of complex comprehension.

Figure 17

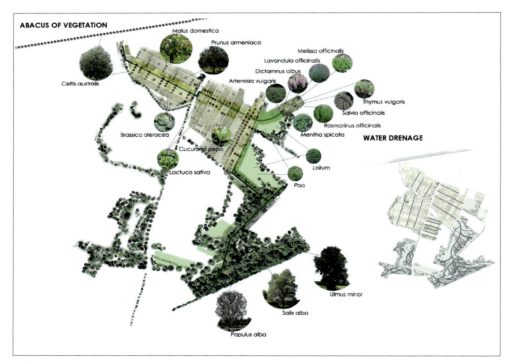

Figure 18

Figure 19

Figure 20

Figures 17-20 IFLA 'International Students Charette' 2016, 1st prize project for 'Barca Bertolla', Turin: Consuelo Cenci, Chiara Patamia, Delfina Saccone ('Technologies for Environmental Design and Urban Requalification' course, Master degree in Architecture); and Giada Di Sante, Guglielmo Pirri, ('Environmental Technological Sustainability' course, Master degree in Landscape Architecture), professor Maria-Beatrice Andreucci, 'Sapienza' Università di Roma, 2016.

Students progressively achieve upper levels of research and analytical skills, of reading comprehension and of problem-solving, in a very dynamic and inclusive learning environment. Such an active learning milieu successfully provides future landscape architects, architects and urban designers with references and guidelines, as well as effective learning methodologies that they can recall and adopt in their future careers.

The six core characteristics of PBL distinguished in the core model originally described by Howard Barrows (1996) can all be traced in the described teaching approach. In the actual experience at 'Sapienza', it has been important, however, to adapt the PBL framework to the specific subject taught by the author (scientific disciplinary sector: Environmental Technological Design). This meant providing the students with an initial series of lectures—originally banned within the PBL learning techniques—on GI design, and on the metrics and valuation methodologies of the multiple ecological, environmental, social and economic benefits, deriving from the practice of evidence-based design.

When completing higher demanding tasks, students are engaged in a productive interdisciplinary confrontation, which challenges them to make connections to concepts and to other relevant knowledge. An authentic learning environment is created: one in which the cognitive demands, i.e. the thinking required, are consistent with the key challenges characterising the urban built environment, and for which the teacher is preparing the learner (Honebein, Duffy, & Fishman 1993, cited by Herrington & Oliver 2000: 4). Students also investigate history in order to engage in urban landscape construction 'learning from the past', and not only from the application of the most advanced technologies. Similarly, students engage in a state-of-the art scientific discourse, and take a problem-solving approach (Figs. 14-16).

In the academic year 2015/2016, 60 students joined the 'Environmental Technological Sustainability' core course; and 120 students joined the 'Technologies for Environmental Design and Urban Requalification' optional course. More than 95% of the students in both courses successfully completed the exams during the semester. Both courses received very high scores in the students' opinion poll. These students were also able to apply their understandings of the GI design approach to generate recommendations for improvements of environmental technological design instructional methods.

Scholars who participate in a problem-based learning approach construct a deeper understanding of the concepts supporting environmental technological design than do the students in comparison classes, as demonstrated by the outstanding performances attained in IFLA 2016 Student Charette competition (Figs. 17-20). This evidence gives weight to the claims made that interdisciplinary learning, using a problem-based approach, can promote deeper thinking and aid the making of links between the sustainable design disciplines.

NOTES

1 Green Blue Infrastructure can be viewed as 'living technologies', key components of the urban setting that helps maintain a healthy environment for urban dwellers.

2 Resilience in this context is a measure of robustness and buffering capacity of the ecosystem to changing conditions.

3 Master degree in Landscape Architecture, 'Sapienza' Università di Roma, 'Planning, Design, Technology of Architecture' Department. The two courses belong to the 'Technology of Architecture' curriculum.

4 Landscape performance can be defined as a measure of the effectiveness with which landscape solutions fulfil their intended purpose and contribute to sustainability.

REFERENCES

Alcamo, J. et al. (eds.) and Bennett, E. M. et al. (contributing eds.) (2003), *Ecosystems and human well-being: a framework for assessment / Millennium Ecosystem Assessment* (Washington, DC: Island Press). http://pdf.wri.org/ecosystems_human_wellbeing.pdf

Andreucci, M. B. (2013), 'Towards a Landscape Economy', Introductory keynote to the Italian Association of Landscape Architects Conference, MACRO Museum of Contemporary Art, Rome, Italy, 13 December 2013.

Andreucci, M. B. (2017), *Green Infrastructure Design: Technologies, values and tools for urban resilience* (Milan: Wolters Kluwer Italia).

Ausubel, D. P. (2000), *The Acquisition and Retention of Knowledge: A cognitive view* (Dordrecht: Kluwer Academic Publishers).

Barrows, H. S. (1986), 'A taxonomy of problem-based learning methods,' *Med. Educ.* 20: 481-486.

Barrows, H. S. (1996), 'Problem-based learning in medicine and beyond: a brief overview', in L. Wilkerson, & W. H. Gijselaers (eds.), *Bringing Problem-based Learning to Higher Education: Theory and practice* (San Francisco, CA: Jossey-Bass), 3-12.

Boix Mansilla, V. (2004), Assessing Student Work at Disciplinary Crossroads. [Online], http://thegoodproject.org/pdf/33-Assessing-Student-Wo.pdf

Boud, D. and Feletti, G. (1997), *The Challenge of Problem-Based Learning* (London: Kogan Page Ltd).

Bridges, A. (2006), *Problem Based Learning in Architectural Education*, University of Strathclyde, Glasgow, UK. [interview], https://pure.strath.ac.uk/portal/files/64389413/strathprints006150.pdf

Herrington, J., and Oliver, R. (2000), 'An instructional design framework for authentic learning environments', *Educational Technology Research and Development*, 48/3: 23-48.

Hiebert, J., Carpenter, T. P., Fennema, E., Fuson, K., Human, P., Murray, H., Alwyn, O. and Wearne, D. (1996), 'Problem solving as a basis for reform in curriculum and instruction: The case of mathematics', *Educational Researcher*, 25/4: 12–21.

Holm, I. (2006), *Ideas and Beliefs in Architecture: How attitudes, orientations, and underlying assumptions shape the built environment* (Oslo: School of Architecture and Design).

Honebein, P. C., Duffy, T. M., and Fishman, B. J. (1993), 'Constructivism and the design of learning environments: Context and authentic activities for learning', in T. M. Duffy, J. Lowyck, and D. H. Jonassen (eds.), *Designing Environments for Constructive Learning* (Heidelberg: Springer-Verlag), 87-108.

Jones, B. F., Rasmussen, C. M. and Moffitt, M. C. (1996), *Real-life Problem Solving: A collaborative approach to interdisciplinary learning* (Washington, DC: American Psychological Association).

Maitland, B. (1997), 'Problem-based learning for architecture and construction management', in D. Boud and G. Feletti, *The Challenge of Problem-Based Learning* (London: Kogan Page Ltd).

Roberts, A. (2004), 'Problem based learning and the design studio', *CEBE Transactions*, 1/2: 1-3.

Schumacher, E. F. (1974), 'Economics should begin with people not goods', *The Futurist*, 8/6: 274-275.

Thormann, P. (1979), 'Proposal for a program in appropriate technology', in A. Robinson (ed.), *Appropriate Technologies for Third World Development* (New York: St. Martin's Press), 280-299.

World Economic Forum (2016), *The Global Risk Report 2016*, 11th Edition. http://wef.ch/risks2016

LANDSCAPE PLANNING STUDIOS

In the case of studios which work at a larger landscape scale, a different kind of creativity is called for. Many more variables are involved, many if not most of which are not under the direct control of the landscape architect or planner. This section presents both concrete examples of landscape planning studios as well as general reflections on principles for studio teaching. All the examples have a strong urban character and, while some of the studios presented are 'one-off' examples, others are long-standing courses which have been running in similar, if evolving, form over a significant time period.

The logistics of and the respective roles of student team and faculty members in organising and running collaborative landscape planning studios in a variety of international contexts is the subject matter of the opening chapter in this section. Carl Steinitz presents his experience in orchestrating the dynamics of many such complex projects to illustrate this approach using a range of examples of landscape planning studios involving local actors and cohorts of students working in locations from Bermuda and Mexico to Spain, Italy and Portugal.

An interdisciplinary group of landscape, architecture and planning students were the participants in a landscape planning and design studio focusing on streams within a river basin within the City of Izmir as a basis for an urban transformation process. Adnan Kaplan and Koray Velibeyoğlu's studio also included lectures, site surveys, discussions and design charrettes after which students were able to choose between different possible themes. Examples of three of the resulting projects are presented, each of which represented aspects of green and blue infrastructure as a basis for urban development.

The place of scientific, and in particular, ecological enquiry in the planning and design studio is the subject of Joan Iverson Nassauer's contribution. A plea is made for the conscious development of mutual respect and understanding of the benefits landscape science and landscape design can bring to the conception of new landscape futures. Potential problems arising from differing languages and approaches between the two fields can, it is argued, be overcome by explicitly taking landscape science approaches into the design of studio teaching.

A series of studios investigating the potentials for restoring the coastal waterfronts of transformed Mediterranean tourism landscapes are the focus of the studios described in the chapter by Maria Goula, Ioanna Spanau and Patricia Pérez Rumpler. Recreating the hydrological conditions of the coastal plains which tourism developments have altered has provided one ongoing theme, as has the interpretive cartographic representation of these transformation processes from an experiential point of view. Projects develop the idea of a reclaimed 'second coast' associated with the landscapes of the hinterland as an alternative focus for new leisure activities.

Karin Helms and Pierre Donadieu present an historical perspective on the teaching of landscape architecture in the urban context starting in 1970, when horticultural scale teaching gave way to site-based approaches which in turn began to be expanded to deal with larger urban territories from a landscape perspective. These developments, which pre-dated the invention of the term 'landscape urbanism', were initiated at the Versailles school but later they were also adopted at other French landscape programmes. French approaches to landscape urbanism continue to develop in both teaching and practice and this chapter reflects on its future applications.

Teaching about urban landscapes also forms the subject matter of Lisa Diedrich and Mads Farsø's chapter, which focuses on coming to terms with their unpredictability through the use of innovative approaches which combine science-based methods and creative artistic paradigms. Uncertainty as a feature of contemporary urban landscape is what today's students will have to learn to address, and to do this, the authors suggest that design thinking is a key competence. Studio courses focusing on these skills are presented here.

Teaching in a collaborative studio context: on educating conductors and "getting started"

Carl Steinitz

The vast majority of professional education in Landscape Architecture and other design professions is directed towards training soloists.

Relatively few students see their long-term objectives as preparing themselves for conducting—for being the leaders or managers of teams, yet a surprising number of the students whom I have taught are in professional practice as conductors.

The approach

In this chapter I want to focus on two related themes: educating "conductors" in a collaborative context, and "getting started." I consider the beginning period to be the most important stage of any project because if the beginning is unsatisfactory, then the ending must also be.

The reasons for my teaching in a manner which requires students to work in teams, and frequently in large, self-managed, multidisciplinary teams, are many but normally centre upon the scope and complexity of the problem around which the studio is focused: invariably a large and highly valued landscape region undergoing considerable pressures for change.

The studio is normally organized in a manner analogous to a large multidisciplinary office, with the students themselves being maximally responsible for the entire project. Unlike the more traditionally organized studio, in which the students are given a site, a client and a program, the students are responsible for problem identification, much of the methodological approach, product definition, production and presentation of work, and all aspects of project management including budget allocation. The faculty responsibilities are diverse but emphasize the roles of "producer," "consultant" and "presence."

Identifying projects which are important and interesting both to the faculty (me) and potential students is not so difficult. Successful projects share some characteristics; they are large in terms of geography, number of participants, conflicting objectives, landscape complexity and financial and political implications. The academic setting allows much more free and flexible thinking to be directed toward the problem and it allows the work to be publicized under the students' authorship. This means that it can be freely discussed and dismissed if necessary.

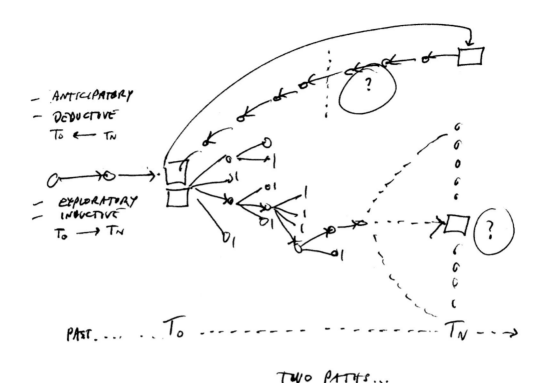

Figure 1 Two very different paths toward a design: the Anticipatory based on deductive logic, and the Exploratory based in inductive logic. Each has elements which must be identified and synthesized.

At the end of the semester prior to the studio, the students volunteer knowing that the project will be organized by themselves functioning as a large team. The initial problem statement is concise: "Be prepared to spend the first week of September in _____ and figure out what is going on there." The initial field trip is crucial to the definition of the study and to the creation of an effective working team. The organization of that field trip is the first studio task. During early summer four students volunteer for the first management team and are responsible for the assignment of research responsibilities, be they based on functions, systems and/or geographic areas.

The field trip is an intensively scheduled working session with both group and individual responsibilities. Of prime importance are the tasks associated with becoming familiar with issues, geography and people. I make a major point of telling the students that we are on the field trip to observe and ask questions.

An especially important part of the collaborative studio is "getting started," the initial set of exercises that begin on the site visit and that are aimed at developing the studio's overall structure, methods and design strategies. I teach my students that there is no such thing as "THE design method" or "THE planning method." Rather, there are many methods, and they must be adapted to issues and questions raised by the problem at hand. Every landscape design, regardless of size or scale, has three groups of influences which should be considered: the history of the place and past proposals, the "facts" of the area which are not likely to be changed, and the "constants" which should be incorporated into any proposed alternative.

There are two fundamentally different ways of getting started: these two paths are "anticipatory" and "exploratory," and they can be seen in Figure 1.

The anticipatory approach embodies the idea that the designer is expected to make an heroic leap forward in time and implicitly make correct choices among the many assumptions and contingencies inherent in the situation, and present a proposed future change: the design. This anticipatory method then requires the use of deductive logic in order to figure out how to get from the desired future state back to the present. But if the present circumstance is large and complicated, it is too often difficult or impossible to connect the future back to the present. And an early wrong decision can be fatal to the design.

The alternative exploratory method requires the explicit development of a scenario, a sequence of the assumptions which will shape the design. It requires the use of the inductive logic. Again, this approach is relatively easy if the problem is a simple one but if it is large and complex, and if each single assumption has several options, there are too many combinations to consider and too many risks of taking the wrong path.

Therefore, the essential initial steps must be to "sensitivity-test" the most important assumptions. Most frequently, one skips back and forth between these extremes. But which way should we begin? Here the issues of "size and scale" and "risk" must be considered.

In my view, the smaller project types such as a residential site plan present fewer real risks of being wrong than do the larger design projects and regional landscape plan studies which are rarely directly built. Rather, their aim is to influence the way society values and changes its landscapes, including aspects of water and land use.

At the extremes, these varied scales require different initial strategies. For the larger size and complexity of the problems, exploratory methods are the more appropriate starting strategies. They can result in one dominant design strategy or they can produce several made by smaller teams or they can produce individually differentiated designs.

Technically, the methods rely on the making of simple and clear diagrams to represent ideas, be they physical changes or policies. ALL ideas, are included without pre-judgment as to their value. A core concept is making a distinction between the generation and "ownership" of ideas, and their use: (Albert et al. 2015; Steinitz 2013, 2011, 2009, 2007, 1997, 1990; Steinitz et al. 2010, 2007).

The case studies

Bermuda, 1982

This studio concerned the future of the garbage dump of that small, then newly independent, island nation. It was surrounded by civic institutions, a large wetland, the well fields which supplied drinking water to most of Bermuda, and important playing fields. It was in the midst of the residential area of the poorest people in the country.

The studio travelled to Bermuda and visited the study area (Figure 2). There were several presentations and several open meetings for interested persons. Each evening I met with the students and had them list and categorize the issues which had been raised, and prepare simple line diagrams to a standard scale of every idea and proposal which they had been offered or which they themselves had.

Upon returning to the University, and in the first working session of the studio, the students agreed on a final list of about 20 issues which had to be resolved in any design. These were of two kinds: the constants which had to be incorporated into every design, and the variables, for which there might be alternative diagrammatic solutions. Pairs of students were asked to produce between two and five alternative strategies regarding each issue. There were approximately 80 diagrams each drawn with permanent black marker on thin clear plastic so that they could easily be selected, overlain, and looked at together as a set. The next exercise was to rank the issues and alternatives, using a modified Delphi

Figure 2 The Bermuda dump and its context. The wind blows to the north, where the black population lives. The then-Prime Minister (and the first black person to be Prime Minister) lived immediately north of the dump, and so did the British Governor General in the estate to the upper-right. It was important to conserve the existing wetland and playing fields.

technique (Figures 3, 4). Figure 5 represents what was actually the laying out of the small diagrams on a very large table. The constants all are in the left-most column. The variables are listed along the top row, from the left in order of their perceived importance.

One can interpret the positions of the diagrams on the table in the following way: every constant diagram must be included, and in addition the most likely successful design strategy would be to select the top row of issue alternatives starting from the left. This process was completed at the end of the third studio class.

In the next phase of the studio, each individual student was required to prepare an initial design by selecting an appropriate set of the diagrams. A total of 14 substantially different initial diagrammatic designs were then available after the fourth studio class.

Each student then prepared a physical model of his or her initial design in a standard form and these were presented at the end of the sixth week and reviewed by a Bermudan committee, which decided that three of the designs should be moved forward to the next stage. Those students whose designs were not chosen to go forward then had to join the team of one of the three designs which would be presented at the end of the semester.

The Bermudan authorities decided to place the choice of one of the three park concepts before the electorate in a special election with the aim of identifying the preferences of the general public for the strategies which were embedded in the design options. The winning design was, interestingly, the one which most closely conformed to the upper and left hand section of the diagram layout with which the studio got started (Figure 4).

The following are applications of the diagramming method to problems at different scales and with different products, but using digital adaptations of the basic approach.

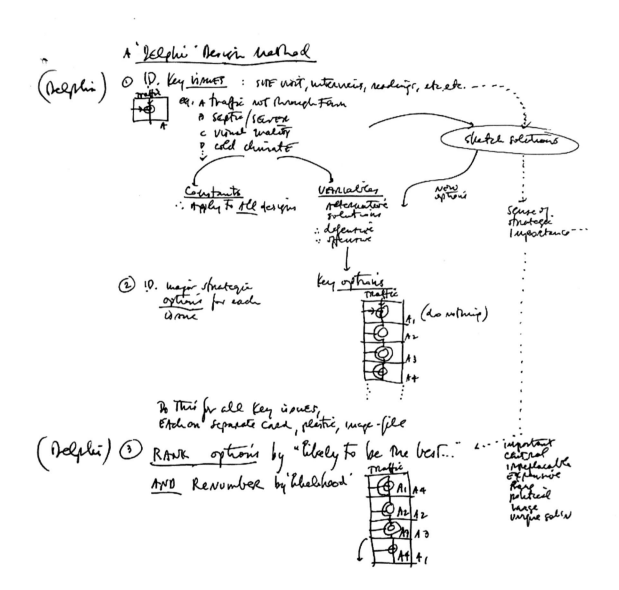

Figure 3 A diagrams-based design method inspired by Delphi methods

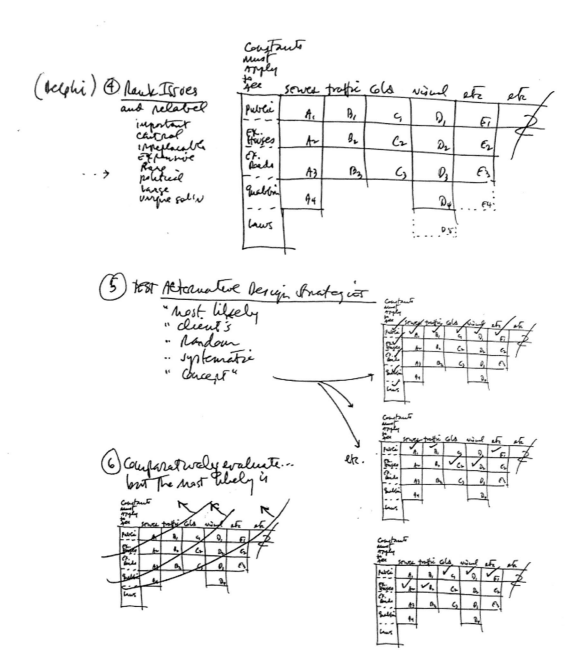

Figure 4 A diagrams-based design method inspired by Delphi methods

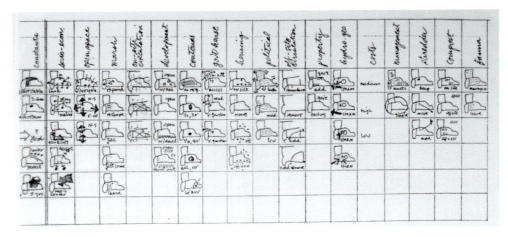

Figure 5 The interviews-generated diagrams arranged as constants and variables, with the variable-columns ranked in importance from local interviews, and the diagrams in each column ranked in likely success by the students.

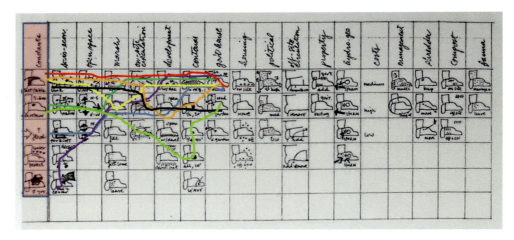

Figure 6 Each student's individual design must provide for all the constants, and must be based on a different set of diagrams from all other designs. Priority for diagrams selection was based on a numbers-lottery, and symbolically shown by colored lines.

Figure 7 a, b, c
These are the final three designs, each developed by its initial designer and a team of other students whose designs were not premiated by the Bermuda Dump Committee in week 6. These were publicly presented in Bermuda. The Prime Minister then ordered a public referendum, which chose 7c as the most favored design. It was then developed as an implementable design by two of the students after they graduated.

Tepotzotlan, Mexico, 2004-5

With Anibal Figueroa Castrejon, Juan Carlos Vargas-Moreno

We worked in collaboration with a faculty/student team from the Universidad Autonoma Metropolitana (UAM) led by Professor Figueroa, and with the full cooperation of the municipal government.

Tepotzotlan is a municipality at the northern edge of the Mexico City metropolitan area. It is facing enormous development pressures as it is on the main highway to the north of Mexico. It has, and is surrounded by, considerable amounts of social housing and distribution warehouses. There are increasing amounts of "informal housing". The untreated sewage of the entire Mexico City area flows via Tepotzotlan, some in canals and some in a broken pipe system. Yet the municipality retains the character of a group of relatively small settlements, with some agriculture and large adjacent National Forest lands. The main attraction of the town of Tepotzotlan is the church and monastery of St. Francis Xavier, founded in 1584.

During the five-day visit to Tepotzotlan, Mexico, the students created a list of projects and policies as reactions to the daily meetings, discussion, visits and information gathered. Each project was proposed by one or more students and presented in brainstorming sessions that were held at the end of each day. By the end of the eight-day field visit, the students had identified around 200 projects. These were first entered in a "project list" in an Excel spreadsheet and then diagrammed by hand on a large regional map of 3 by 6 meters comprising high-resolution orthophotography and several layers of transparent plastic sheet. In the spreadsheet, each project was characterized and classified into one or more of eight color-coded categories: national or municipal government related, neighborhood related, transportation, industrial, ecological (including hydrology), heritage, utilities or wildlife restoration.

During the last day of the site visit, students were divided in groups corresponding to each category, and asked to select up to 20 of the most significant projects in each category. A new short-list of around 80 projects was selected for further development and digitized as diagrams in a GIS, each as a separate layer in the color code of its assigned category and the attributes entered in the Excel spreadsheet. With this electronic database of individual projects the students created different clusters of projects as overlays in a 3-D visualization. Different clusters such as tourism or ecological-related projects were created as initial explorations. This allowed the students to visualize the cumulative effect of different projects and categories. Later, through class discussion, three alternative scenarios were developed by combining different projects: tourism, ecological and economically driven. Each scenario was presented in a 3-D visualization, coded as a group of project numbers and discussed for future refinement. This had been accomplished within the site visit. Later, several further scenarios of more complex objectives were prepared and compared before the studio team decided to focus on one. This was developed into an alternative municipal plan, and several projects elaborated at more detailed scales (Steinitz and Figueroa et al. (eds) 2005).

Zona Industriale Padove (ZIP) Italy, 2005-6.

With Tess Canfield, Juan Carlos Vargas-Moreno

ZIP (la Zona Industriale di Padova) is the largest "industrial park" in Italy. The ZIP consortium owns a large adjacent area, the Parco del Roncajette, which will become a major new park for the city. The site has flood control channels containing polluted water from the city, industry and the upstream areas, which eventually flow into the nearby Venice Lagoon. It also has the city's sewage treatment plant, the famous analog model of the Venice Lagoon, and residential and agricultural holdings.

ZIP and the city are committed to building a new city park on this land, but there are many unknowns and related issues; Padua's "green spaces strategy" which includes connecting many small "green areas"; the reconsideration of the future of an existing local airfield and ZIP expansion.

The studio was organized as a collaborative effort with substantial student self-management. Its aim was to produce and compare three or four alternatives for the park and its ZIP and urban context, based on different sets of assumptions (Steinitz, C. et al. 2006).

Castilla La Mancha, Spain, 2006-7

With Christian Werthmann, Juan Carlos Vargas-Moreno

The studio was intended to lead to design proposals for the protection and development of the landscapes of Don Quixote, between Madrid, Toledo and Cuidad Real in the Province of Castilla-La Mancha, and to support the Province's interest in promoting landscape protection, tourism and economic development associated with the 400th anniversary of the publication of Don Quixote. It was sponsored by the Fundacion Civitas Nova and had the full cooperation of both the provincial and local authorities in Castilla-La Mancha. The specific studies and projects undertaken were identified during initial investigations and discussions with provincial and local authorities. The studio proposed landscape plans, policies and designs directed at the long-term sustainability of the attractiveness of the region.

Projects included an assessment of the implications of Madrid's growth on the province, implications of climate change on the region's agriculture, a regional landscape management plan with a visual management component, a landscape plan for the road between Madrid and Toledo, a development strategy and designs to protect the historic image of Toledo, and a growth strategy for Cuidad Real, all coordinated into a single overall landscape plan for the chosen portions of the Province.

The studio was an organized collaborative effort with substantial self-management by the students. They spent the first five days of the studio in the region, following a similar digital diagramming strategy as in the Tepotzotlan example; however, here the diagramming of projects and policies was at three scales: national, regional and local, and the students were asked to select up to 20 layers to assess the "worst" and the "best" alternatives for various important themes (Steinitz and Werthmann et al. (eds) 2007).

Workshop—Technical University of Lisbon, 2008

This was a four-hour exercise as part of a wider workshop. Participants were faculty and pre-doctoral students from universities in Lisbon, Porto and Coimbra, The tradeoff between rapidly working through an entire process versus carefully considering design strategies and their consequences favored working through a method very rapidly.

The case study considered the future of the waterfront and the viewshed of the Tejo river estuary of Lisbon. After a discussion which identified key interest groups and their main objectives, "students" were assigned the tasks related to rapidly drawing the many alternative color-coded diagrams by hand. These were presented and organized on a long table, following the basic methods of the Bermuda example, while a simple spreadsheet model was used to estimate the capital cost of each proposal. Teams of two were then assigned to make a proposal which best suited the needs of a stakeholder group by selecting the best 5 to 10 strategy diagrams in order of importance. These were then replaced on a large table identical to that described in figures 3, 4 and 5, for use by the next presenters. It became obvious that there was a significant similarity in the diagrams which had been selected and incorporated into these designs. Furthermore the most often chosen component diagrams were those in the uppermost and left hand positions on the table, where all the diagrams had been placed according to the Delphi method, and similar to that in Figure 4.

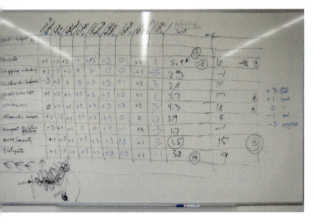

Figures 8-13

The diagrams of the elements for the design strategy, all uniquely named and numbered by its system, and drawn in the system color. They are being discussed prior to selection into the team's design synthesis.

Presentation of the design "sandwich" of the design's diagrams, clipped together and shown additively

Impacts assessments of all designs by teams which had previously assessed site systems for attractiveness and vulnerability

Each system-based evaluation team assesses the designs of all the design teams, for comparison and improvement.

Redesigning after impacts assessment, by changing or adding diagrams as needed

An important question was whether there might be a consensus among the stakeholders groups if they could collectively evaluate all the alternatives. This is not so different from asking whether the techniques of rapid assessment using diagrams could be used to develop a single dominant design strategy.

The students were reorganized with each pair being assigned to evaluate all designs for an impact-category and to compare all designs while representing a stakeholder group. Each row of the large chart in Figure 5 represents a stakeholders/design and each column represents a category of impact, e.g. hydrological, ecological, visual, social, cost, etc. The students used a simple five-level numerical assessment scale, and each pair evaluated each stakeholder design alternative with inputs from real stakeholder representatives and faculty experts. This was followed by a final discussion in which it appeared that coalitions could be formed around a small number of alternative strategic plans (Steinitz 2014 a, b, 2017, 2012 a, b, 2011).

Organizing the team and managing the project

I have illustrated several variations of an approach to a studio's beginning phase, all of which rely on a mix of diagramming and Delphi methods and of judgment.

The first phase of work after the site visit and the diagramming exercises is that of developing the detailed work plan for the study. This is the only other part of the semester which I organize. It consists of two phases, individual and group. The first one-day task is for each individual participant to diagram, write or describe on one large piece of paper, how he/she sees the project developing. What are its objectives? Its principal proposed methodologies? Its expected products? Its schedule? (Some of the students have previously taken my lecture course on theories and methods of landscape planning.) In a silent and anonymous review, each student ranks each presentation for similarity to his or her own ideas. Then, on the basis of similarity of approach, teams are formed for a one-week exercise in proposal preparation.

At the end of that week, each of the teams must present a fully professional written proposal for the entire study, again describing objectives, methodology, product, budget, etc. The written proposals are publicly reviewed by a panel including myself, a representative from the study area, and outside faculty and professionals. They are ranked and those rankings and comments are publicly communicated with the students. Then the students negotiate the critical path of the project under the leadership of the first management group. This occurs about two weeks into the semester and has as its end product an agreed study plan in which all of the issues have been publicly decided and to which all participants can willingly commit themselves. My role in this is one of "expeditor." It is certainly not that of "decider."

Having decided what to do, the student managerial roles come into ascendancy again. As part of the study plan, management responsibilities are assigned for the entire semester-long project period. Normally, there are four management teams, each responsible for a major phase lasting about four weeks. Everyone takes a responsibility in the management committee, and everybody has a turn to be a conductor. Responsibilities include overseeing project direction, task identification and work assignment, product review, budget decisions and communications. However, being a conductor does not mean that you are "the boss."

In making assignments, people should recognize that there are normally two reasons for undertaking a task (other than project needs). The first is that you can do something, enjoy it and want to do more. The second reason is that you can't do something and want to learn how to do it. Even though project efficiency may favor the former reason, the latter is a better rationale for an educational institution.

The project belongs to the students as a group. Credit is shared by the team in alphabetical order. The space which the studio occupies is organized for group activity, with one very large central table for meetings, and smaller individual work spaces. All classes start at the table, and all important discussions and presentations, including reviews of individual work, take place there.

Because managerial responsibilities are frequently transferred, considerable importance is given to organized documentation. It is obvious that each student cannot and does not do all tasks. Because of this, students are encouraged to make presentations to the class meetings of things which they are doing and which may be of interest to others. ALL students play a role in each presentation and intermediate reviews involving study area representatives, faculty and outside professionals.

The final, highly polished, public presentations usually take place in at least two loca-tions, the School, and the study region. They have included a half-hour television program, newspaper supplements, regional magazine issues, demonstrations and published reports. The faculty roles are varied and challenging. Clearly there is the role of producer, there is a considerable consultant-in-chief role in which advice is sought both by management teams and individual students. Without doubt, there is a substantial "hidden hand" role, in which constant observation is necessary. Students are often overly ambitious.

There are also important mediation roles, frequently around social questions and issues of organization. There is the real responsibility of ensuring that the educational needs of individual students are met within the scope of the team organization. There is the faculty role as "critic." Finally there is the legal responsibility of oversight, to ensure the project is completed within the constraints of time and money available. Yet the most difficult faculty role is that of purposefully abstaining from controlling the many difficult managerial and design decisions, and letting the group learn by experience.

For many years I told the students in the very beginning that they will all get the same grade, and that I and they should expect it to be a high one. This is not the policy of my school, but it is how any collective enterprise really is judged … collectively.

I believe that our educational institutions should recognize and support the difference in education, style and skill required of conductors versus those demanded of soloists.

REFERENCES

Albert, C., C. von Haaren, J. C. Vargas-Moreno and C. Steinitz (2015) "Teaching Scenario-based Planning for Sustainable Landscape Development: An Evaluation of Learning Effects in the Cagliari Studio Workshop", *Sustainability* (open access), www.mdpi.com/journal/sustainability, 7(6), 6872-6892; doi:10.3390/su7066872

Ballal, H. and C. Steinitz, (2015) "A Workshop in Geodesign Synthesis", in Buhmann, E., Ervin, S., and Pietsch, P., (Eds) *Digital Landscape Architecture 2015*, Herbert Wichmann Press, Germany, pp. 400-407

In Hoversten, M. E., and S. R. Swaffield, (2019) "Discursive Moments: Reframing Deliberation and Decision-making in Alternative Futures Landscape Ecological Planning", in *Landscape and Urban Planning*, Volume 182, February 2019, pp. 22-33

Steinitz, C. (2017) "Beginnings of Geodesign", in *Geo-Design: Advances in Bridging Geo-information Technology, Urban Planning and Landscape Architecture*, Nijhuis, S., Zlatanova, S., Dias, E., van der Hoeven, F. and van der Spek, S. (Eds), Delft University of Technology, 2017, pp. 9-24

Steinitz, C. (2014a) "Which Way of Designing?", in Lee, Danbi, Eduardo Dias and Henk Scholten (Eds) *Geodesign by Integrating Design and Geospatial Sciences*, Springer, pp. 11-43

Steinitz, C. (2014b) "Geodesign with Little Time and Small Data", in Wissen Hayek, U., P. Fricker and E. Buhmann (Eds) *Digital Landscape Architecture 2014*, Herbert Wichmann Press, Germany, pp. 2-15

Steinitz, C. (2013) "Getting Started: Teaching in a Collaborative Multidisciplinary Framework", in *Landscape Architecture/China*, Special Issue on Digital Technology and Landscape Architecture, pp. 16 – 24, (in English and Chinese)

Steinitz, C. (2012a) *A Framework for Geodesign, Redlands California*, Esri Press (in English) In Japanese, Italian, Spanish, Portuguese, Chinese forthcoming 2019

Steinitz, C. (2012b) "Public Participation in Geodesign: A Prognosis for the Future", in Buhmann, E., S. Ervin, D. Tomlin and M. Pietsch (Eds), *Teaching Landscape Architecture, Proceedings, Digital Landscape Architecture, Anhalt University*. Herbert Wichmann Press, Germany, pp. 240-249

Steinitz, C. (2011) "Getting Started: Teaching in a Collaborative Multidisciplinary Framework", in Buhmann, E., S. Ervin, D. Tomlin, and M. Pietch, *Teaching Landscape Architecture, Proceedings, Digital Landscape Architecture, Anhalt University*. Herbert Wichmann Press, Germany

Steinitz C., E. Abis, C. v. Haaren, C. Albert et al. (2010) FutureMAC09 Scenari Alternativi per l'area metropolitana di Cagliari: Workshop di sperimentazione didattica interdisciplinare / FutureMAC09: Alternative Futures for the Metropolitan Area of Cagliari: The Cagliari Workshop: An Experiment in Interdisciplinary Education, Gangemi, Roma, 2010

Steinitz, C. (2009) "A Framework for Collaborative Design Workshops", in *Landscape and Ruins*, Proceedings ECLAS, September 2009

Steinitz, C. (2007) "Some Notes on Landscape Planning: Towards the Objectives of the European Landscape Convention", in *Landscape and Society*, Fourth Meeting of the Council of Europe Workshops on the Implementation of the European Landscape Convention, Ljubljana, Slovenia, May 2006, pp. 143-145

Steinitz, C. and C. Werthmann, et al. (eds) (2007) Un Futuro Alternativo para el Paisage de Castilla La Mancha – An Alternative Future for the Landscape of Castilla La Mancha, Foro Civitas Nova and Communidad de Castilla La Mancha, Spain (in Spanish and English)

Steinitz, C. et al. (eds) (2006) Padova e il Paesaggio-Scenarui Futuri peri l Parco Roncajette e la Zona Industriale / Padova and the Landscape – Alternative Futures for the Roncajette Park and the Industrial Zone, Commune de Padova and Zona Industriale Padova (in Italian and English)

Steinitz, C. and A. Figueroa et al. (eds) (2005) "Futuros Alternativos para Tepotzotlan/Alternative Futures for Tepotzotlan", Universidad Autonoma Metropolitana-Azcapotzalco, Mexico, (in Spanish and English),

Steinitz, C. (1997) Keynote Lecture: "Landscape Design Processes: Six Questions in Need of Answers… and Three Case Studies." Proceedings, 33rd World Congress, International Federation of Landscape Architects (IFLA) Congress

Steinitz, C. (1990) "A Framework for Theory Applicable to the Education of Landscape Architects (and other Environmental Design Professionals)," *Landscape Journal*, Fall 1990, pp. 136-143. (In *Process Architecture*, no. 127 (English and Japanese). In *Planning*, March 2000, (Chinese) In U.S. Environmental Protection Agency, Office of Research and Development, Environmental Planning for Communities, Cincinatti, OH, 2002. In Chinese, Planners, March 2000)

Teaching a regional landscape project studio in the interdisciplinary setting

Adnan Kaplan, Koray Velibeyoğlu

Introduction

Regional and urban landscapes in the age of the Anthropocene need to support recognition of complex and dynamic ecosystems. As one of these ecosystems, river/stream systems are inherently capable of acting as major landscape infrastructure in a multi-scalar context. Thus both regional context and landscape infrastructure provide physical, ecological and social advocacy while addressing multiple challenges associated with rapid urbanization and its resultant effects such as dense and uncontrolled urban development (Kaplan 2016: 201).

Water-based regional context and its transformative power at regional and urban scales have been themed on (interdisciplinary) landscape studios of some scholarly works such as Kondolf et al. (2013) and Nijhuis and Jauslin (2013). The interdisciplinary landscape project studio that aims to elaborate on the above-mentioned context lies at the epicentre of this study. The studio emerged with a basic agenda of 'who should be the motivator of regional context and urban transformation in question?', and hereby suggested two contradictory approaches of 'market-driven development' and 'regional landscape context'. In educational studies, market context—alongside global, local and regulatory—inform all areas of urban and regional design projects. In general, studio projects start with given market and regulatory settings. However, well-conceived landscape infrastructure formed the basis of this studio to steer stream-based regional and urban transformation. Thus regional landscape context harnesses urban resilience and landscape infrastructure to reclaim the urban realm deteriorating by market-driven development.

The regional landscape project studio approach and examples

The interdisciplinary 'regional landscape project studio' follows a didactic approach that combines regional (in this case water-based) planning and specific mode of regional and urban transformation thinking. The assumption is that this kind of transformation thinking can help to effectively deal with the myriad of challenges that planners/designers need to address at regional landscape scales, including ecological, spatial, social and engineering issues. The studio is for graduate students who are majoring in landscape architecture, urban planning and architecture.

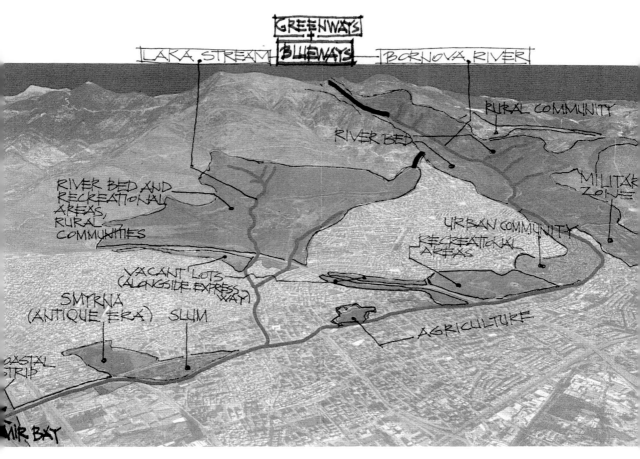

Figure 1 **Bornova stream pattern within the regional landscape context**

The examples used in this chapter draw from a research-based joint project studio called 'Re-naturing, Healing the Cities' that combines the graduate courses (Landscape Planning and Design Studio, LPD548 of Ege University Landscape Architecture Program and Urban Design Studio, UD502 of İYTE Department of City and Regional Planning Urban Design Program). The area employed for this project studio is the Bornova stream micro-basin (47 km²) (Fig. 1) that is located around İzmir Bay. The graduate studio considers the wide regional context (i.e. Bornova stream micro-basin, Homeros Valley (Bornova) down to İzmir Bay) as the medium of the transformation (Figs. 1, 2 and 3).

The studio took a multi-scalar approach (Fig. 2) and is particularly concerned with the stream pattern and its engagement with the regional landscape context involving İzmir Bay and associated urban and rural communities (Fig. 3). Bornova stream (9.6 km in length) acts as a key figure guiding future urban transformation within the Bornova and Bayraklı Metropolitan Districts (Kaplan and Velibeyoğlu 2016). The multi-scalar nature of the Bornova stream micro-basin has relevance regarding the 'region-urban-local' hierarchical order that is important for the project studio. This order ranges from the outskirts of the city through urban fabric to İzmir Bay.

It is important for applying the Regional Landscape Project Studio Approach and its application in the river basin context and at scales given below:
- Region/basin (L): Bornova stream and its tributaries within 'Homeros Valley-Bornova Plain (urban)-İzmir Bay' continuum
- Urban (M): Bornova Plain
- Local (S): urban settlement, CBD, squatter, brownfield, historical settlement, rural community, coastal strip (İzmir Bay) (Fig. 2).

Another point is that the studio devises an urban-nature continuum within the regional landscape context, rather than urban-nature conflict promoted by market-driven development. On this basis, the studio primarily aims to help familiarize students with regional landscape context. It also aims at designing for a cohesive system of blue and green infrastructure that would act as a catalyst for urban transformation. A comprehensive ecological network would be installed, instead of a series of rather isolated and individual channelled water courses that are exposed to the current exponential urban growth and to serious water contamination. The new context would then be capable of supporting and sustaining a consistent linkage from urban fringe through urban central business district (CBD) to İzmir Bay.

Basic concepts and terms of the studio

The project studio justifies regional landscape context and design thinking through:
- highlighting nature types (zero nature through fourth nature) and 'nature-urban' transect in the healing/restoration of pre-selected parts of the region (Center for Applied Transect Studies 2016),
- regional landscape system across scales; regional landscape infrastructure will replace conventional planning process.

The project studio, therefore, defined water-based urban transformation by using landscape infrastructure based on regional design thinking (The Infrastructure Research Initiative at SWA 2013; Bélanger 2016) on Bornova stream micro-basin (Fig. 4). In order to focus into studio themes/concepts each student/group created their own 'mind map' before the design (Fig. 5).

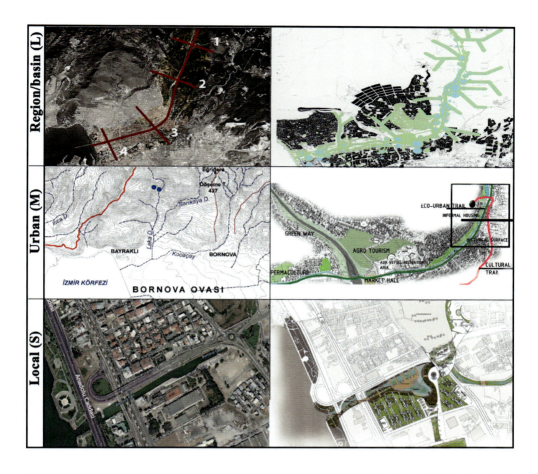

Figure 2 Multi-scalar context of the project theme

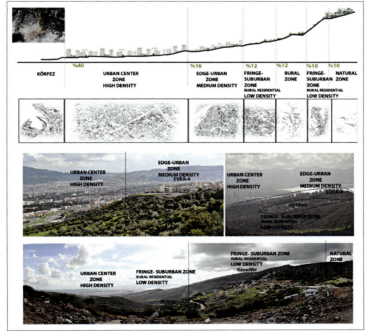

Figure 3 Urban-nature continuum through Bornova stream micro-basin (from the project sheet of Berna Saba)

An interdisciplinary landscape studio | 139

'Nature' types

The most common delusion is to think about natural ecosystems as one single entity. The question here is which ability we should add in our design thinking about multiple natures. Within the plurality of nature, we can define a cyclical process. The 'first nature' can be seen as unchanged nature, it is untouched by human activity. These sites are generally in-situ nature protection areas. For the project, this resembles the watershed protection area of the regional stream system of Bornova District. Second nature is the land changed by human intervention. It is man-made and characterized by the use of nature for utilitarian purposes such as agriculture, urban. Third nature is the designed landscape such as gardens, parks, recreational fields etc. (Hunt 2000). Today, a shift within the cycle of the 'nature-culture' sequence is observed towards a fourth nature, which can best be described as an act of restoration/(re)creating or re-naturing. It refers to redressing the balance with ecosystem (Carver 2016). The essence of the fourth nature could be treated as planetary understanding of nature as a whole that requires massive regeneration and restoration via re-naturing activity of the human (Jencks 2004).

The whole idea of the graduate studio is, therefore, to apply landscape infrastructure and the fourth nature into 'the regional landscape-urban transformation' equilibrium, as a novel way to healing our living environments. In the students' projects, fourth nature or re-naturing is to be interpreted by means of hybridization (overlapping multiple natures), restoration (healing of the ecosystem) and natural process-oriented approach for self-transformation.

Regional design thinking and landscape infrastructure

'Forming a theoretical description of the regional design process is recognition of the breadth of the spectrum of ways that land can be used: urban core, central business district, suburbia, productive farmland, forest, wilderness fringe, wilderness, and all the variations among these uses' (Lewis 1996: 31). Regional design phenomenon takes on Bornova stream micro-basin as a basis to formulate design brief at multi-scalar framework. And as its primary tool, landscape infrastructure—a suite of blue and greenways—merged hydrological/stream pattern with natural and cultural tissues.

Landscape infrastructure is being explored in urban studies as a concept/reality that expands the traditional set of spatial planning and design strategies towards the multi-functional system. 'It engages the full capacity of post-Euclidean planning and global contextualism of capital flow while exploiting the techno-spatial capacity of 21st century civil engineering in order to deploy ecology as the agent of urban transformation, and is developing new ways to conceive and shape the organization of the human/natural environment for the future transformation of urban regions' (Bélanger 2016: 215).

In a new anthropogenic age where exact dichotomy between nature and city destroys (Crutzen 2002), the project studio exploits landscape infrastructure for re-naturing regional context and particularly built environment.

Applyingthe regional landscape project studio approach

The course work involves lectures, site surveys, discussions and project evaluations with design charrettes. Following the introduction of the course schedule (Table 1), some academics/experts—specializing in landscape architecture, urban planning, architecture, geography, engineering and agriculture—were invited to the studio and field research to disseminate different aspects of the regional landscape and its diversified challenges. Students in the interdisciplinary setting were, otherwise, unable to conceptualize regional landscape context and its engagement with İzmir coastal city, and thus deliver any substantial planning and design proposal for regional/urban transformation. The studio environment particularly engendered some discussions with each other, and with invited scholars

Table 1. **Course schedule for 2015-2016 spring semester**

Week 1	23 Feb	Introduction to the Course **Introduction to Studio Theme, Precedents**
	26 Feb	Literature Review
Week 2	1 March	Literature Review
	4 March	**ZERO NATURE:** Lecture 1: Asaf Koçman (EU)—Introduction to İzmir Basin and Bornova Stream Sub/Micro Basin
Week 3	8 March	Desk Critics
	11 March	Field Learning -Technical trip to the sub/micro-basin with Bornova Municipality staff and Prof. Asaf Koçman along with the studio instructors
Week 4	15 March	Desk Critics
	18 March	**FIRST NATURE (Water):** Lecture 2: Alper Baba (İYTE)—Water Resources **SECOND NATURE (Infrastructure):** Lecture 3: Orhan Gündüz (DEU) – Environmental Engineering (water resilience)
Week 5	22 March	Desk Critics
	25 March	**SECOND NATURE (Cultural Landscape, Agriculture):** Lecture 4: Yusuf Kurucu (EU), Adnan Kaplan, Koray Velibeyoğlu
Week 6	29 March	Desk Critics
	1 April	**THIRD NATURE (Understanding Site):** Lecture 5: Ebru Bingöl, (İYTE), Erdem Erten (İYTE)
Week 7	5 April	Desk Critics
	8 April	**Project Review 1: Site Analysis + Design Idea + Design Strategy (schemes, diagrams, drawings)** Erhan Küçükerbaş (EU), Nuran Altun (Consultant), A. Kaplan, K. Velibeyoğlu
Week 8	12 April	Desk Critics
	15 April	Panel Critics
Week 9	19 April	Desk Critics
	22 April	Panel Critics
Week 10	26 April	**Project Review 2 (Jury - Academics): Master Plan**
	29 April	Panel Critics
Week 11	3 May	Desk Critics
	6 May	Panel Critics
Week 12	10 May	Desk Critics
	13 May	**Project Review 3 (Jury - Practitioners): Site Plan + Details**
Week 13	17 May	Panel Critics
	20 May	Panel Critics
Week 14	24 May	Desk Critics
	27 May	Desk Critics
Week 15	31 May	Optional Review Final Review (Till 15 June 2016)
	16 June	Final Jury
	30 June	Project submission due

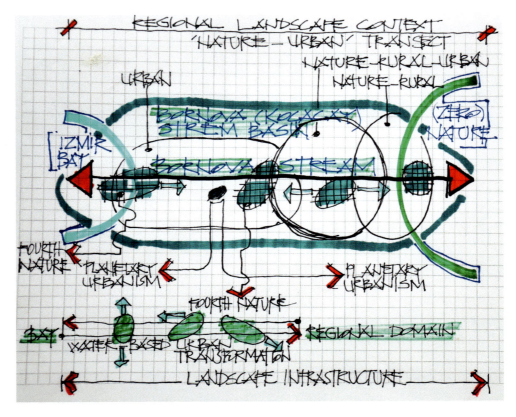

Figure 4 Regional landscape context accounts for landscape infrastructure concept and regional design thinking.

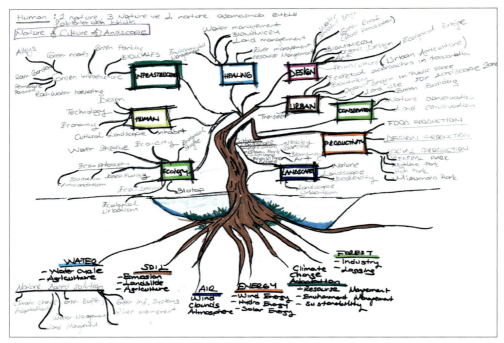

Figure 5 An example of 'mind map' (produced by Hande Gündel)

and practitioners. Students' work either individually or in project teams involved in-class presentations and research-based evaluations to deal with various project themes. The projects were evaluated consecutively in three project review meetings by interested experts from public and private sectors and academics.

Following conceptualization of the micro-basin and stream system in tune with regional and urban planning processes, students either in groups or individually are expected to apply the regional landscape approach at micro-basin level that cares for ecological/social/engineering-based concerns and delve into a site-specific project among below-mentioned possible themes:
• Nature as Green/Blueways: Homeros Valley down to Izmir Bay alongside Bornova stream and its tributaries
• Nature as Urban Development and Housing: slums located alongside Bornova and Laka streams
• Nature as Agriculture: the urban-rural continuum, rural settlements and urban farming
• Nature as Recreation: Aşık Veysel Urban Park, Homeros Valley (3rd to 4th nature)
• Nature as History: Manda stream, Smyrna (İzmir in antiquity), Yeşilova.

The students prepared their project submission as follows:
• Analysis and Planning (1/25000 − 1/5000)
• Macro Design Scenarios (schemes, diagrams, drawings and reports)
• Site Planning and Design (1/1000 − 1/500)
• Cross-sections, perspectives and other accompanied documents
• Service Design of Selected Supporting Details (in necessary scale).

Outputs from the output studios

Results of the project studio are presented below. Three studio groups are presented that each focuses on different aspects of urban transformation in regional landscape context. They deliver examples of regional design thinking from the whole basin down to site-specific district.

Project 1: Urban patches (Berna Saba)

This project concentrated upon interfaces and patches across the 'nature-urban' transect analysis. Henceforth, it provides the continuity alongside the stream and laterally into rural/urban tissue. In order to secure nature-urban equilibrium across the basin, patches and thresholds are particularly utilized in the form of interfaces to tie different or fragmented landscape types (Fig. 6).

It is envisaged that urban patches would incrementally account for balancing and healing in restoration/re-naturing phases of urban transformation for the regional continuity. Thus, patches attribute farmland, eco-boulevard and promenade while thresholds act as a balancing effect on recreational amenities, trails and stream bed (Figs. 7, 8 and 9). Patches emphasize the stream as the skeleton of the basin so that it could relate in rapprochement the urban realm with the basin. Smyrna (historical settlement) square has as well been designated to juxtapose the history with stream ecology and social life anyway (Fig. 8).

Project 2: Re-considering the Bornova (Kocaçay) Basin over the water cycle (Hüseyin Öztürk, Ahenk Karcı, Alev Orhun, Serhat Tümer)

Bornova stream micro-basin acts as an overarching phenomenon between culture and nature, and re-interprets the water cycle so as to shape urban dynamics in a cohesive way. The association of hydrological pattern with natural and urban landscapes calls for site-specific design interventions in some critical cross-sections of the stream. These inter-

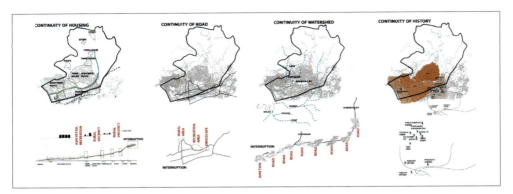

Figure 6 **Patches and thresholds secure the linkages between different parts of the micro-basin.**

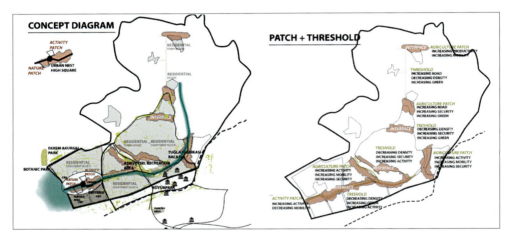

Figure 7 **The project concept originates from a suite of patches and thresholds.**

ventions would in a regenerative way help heal the complete region by water cycle/storage/purification/use while increasing the efficiency of water-related design. For instance, water pools in rural communities have been exploited for ecological and agricultural pursuits, in urban communities for ecological, social, recreational and aesthetic purposes. And the design framework also involves re-configuration of stream bed and its associated landscapes in particular sections to repurpose storage and use of the water. For instance, from the outset of the stream on, some existing levees along the course have been re-aligned to maintain stream natural course and flow of stream (Figs. 10, 11 and 12).

Project 3: Riparian city (Hande Gündel)
Linkage of Bornova stream with (un)built environments has been posed to recognize some challenges with their spatial boundaries. Urban squatters, disconnection of the stream with the urban (dwellers), degradation and loss of agricultural land, disruption of historical traces, flooding are some remarkable challenges against which some measures have been poised to under 'riparian city' concept that is contingent on three fundamentals: edges, trail system and riparian corridor (Fig. 13).

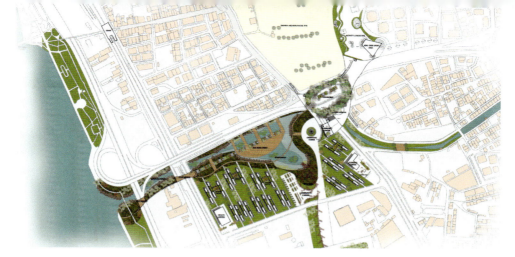

Figure 8 Urban design work associates İzmir Bay with Bayraklı District and the antique city (Smyrna) across the stream bed.

Figure 9 Bayraklı District hosts diverse and state-of-art urban and social programmes for urban infrastructure.

'Edges' is related to describe the characteristics of problems and potentials while trail system enables to experience urban landscapes and the region. Riparian corridor is the mainstream of the riparian city that places some linkage between edges and trail system around/alongside the stream to ensure 'nature-urban' continuity. Trail system—cultural and industrial—is made up of the traces of history and the stream itself. The system operates as a bridge between constraints and potentials in spatial context. Riparian corridor renders some special emphasis on infrastructure, nature restoration, retrofitting of urban squatters, improving the health of urban ecosystem, reclaiming the historical sites. Based on these, the project introduced some strategies upon conservation, water, history and ownership to appreciate riparian city concept (Figs. 14, 15 and 16).

Discussion

The studio was developed as a critical response to prosaic urban planning and design practices, market-driven and multi-layered challenges of urban development at the 'urban-nature' transect. Henceforth, a consistent regional landscape system along the stream pattern was introduced as the main agent of the urban transformation.

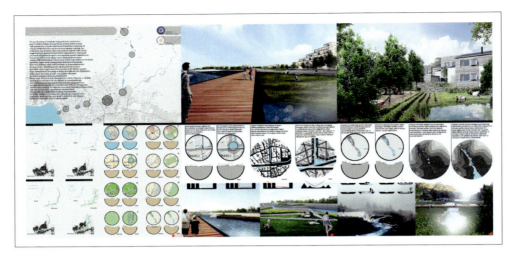

Figure 10 Re-considering the micro-basin has yielded regional landscape infrastructure as well as a set of design/engineering interventions.

Figure 11 The stream bed and its engagement with urban fabric result in well-established ecological community and social milieu.

To investigate the aforementioned framework effectively within the realm of interdisciplinary landscape project, the studio delivered:
- the water-based regional/urban transformation,
- the layout of a suite of blue and greenways into planning and design medium,
- ecologically well-defined urban fabric to sophistically reclaim the complex water system at multiple landscape scales from region to site.

The studio as espoused by Neuman (2016) acted as an effective teaching practice engaging students, faculty, practitioners and local governments into real-world problem solving activities. Therefore, more emphasis in jury deliberations attributed to how this creative studio process would progress, and accordingly which kind of revisions in political,

Figure 12 **The stream bed and its engagement with urban fabric result in well-established ecological community and social milieu.**

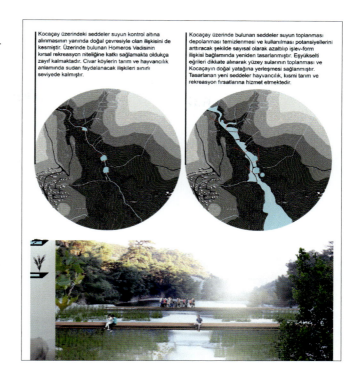

Figure 13 **Edges, trail system and riparian corridors are the necessary tools to generate a comprehensive regional landscape infrastructure.**

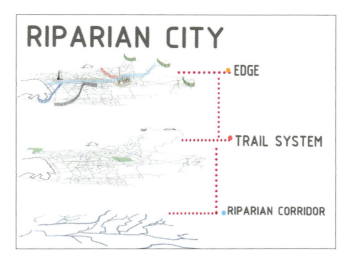

Figure 14 **Ensuring nature-urban continuum leads regional landscape thinking.**

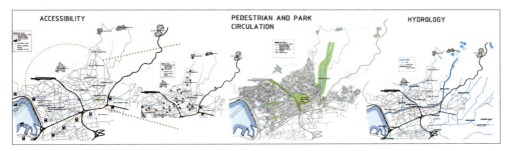

An interdisciplinary landscape studio | 147

Figure 15 The transition zone between natural and urban realms challenges highly critical design and engineering approach.

Figure 16 Stream bed and its environs are appropriate means to deliver corporate design thinking that confronts with ecological, socio-cultural and engineering challenges.

judicial and administrative landscapes has to be applied. Yocom et al. (2012) stated that the studio encouraged pushing beyond individual's disciplinary comfort zone for successful collaboration and generation of collective understanding.

Lectures and field works emphasizing planning, design and engineering matters of the micro-basin have supported students in identifying and analysing regional landscape context. They devised some cross-pollinated ideas upon the context. So they synthesized planning/design insights with engineering field to set forth interdisciplinary design approaches that have addressed multidimensional challenges and opportunities of the micro-basin in a multi-scalar framework. Kondolf et al. (2013) confirmed that this integrative pedagogy accompanied by cross-scale learning proved to be particularly effective in responding to the above-mentioned challenges.

Conclusion

The basic idea of the studio takes blue and greenways as the main component of landscape infrastructure that interacts with regional and urban landscapes. The project studio communicated the regional and urban design experience while highlighting operational and tactical interventions to urban landscapes. This accommodates regional landscape context as an alternative to current market-driven urbanization process. To this end, visionary and multi-functional aspects of regional landscape thinking should be exhibited and supported by research-based, interdisciplinary project studios.

Regional/nature-based response to spatial challenges is the coming agenda of regional/urban design in face of sustainable and resilient urbanism. The interdisciplinary landscape studios should further develop innovative and state-of-the-art methodology/tools/applications as a transformative effect on regional landscape context.

Acknowledgements

This paper has benefited substantially from the Joint Project Studio. We therefore would like to extend our appreciation to the graduate students (Hande Gündel, Berna Saba, Hüseyin Öztürk, Ahenk Karcı, Alev Orhun and Serhat Tümer) for their project works. Particular thanks are also due to guest lecturers, especially Prof. Emeritus Asaf Koçman, and jury members/evaluators.

REFERENCES

Bélanger, P. (2016), 'Is Landscape Infrastructure', in G. Doherty and C. Waldheim (eds.), *Is Landscape…?: Essays on the Identity of Landscape*, (Routledge), 190-227.

Carver, S. (2016), 'Rewilding… Conservation and Conflict', ECOS 37/2: 3-9.

Center for Applied Transect Studies [website], http://transect.org, accessed 5 March 2016.

Crutzen P.J. (2002), 'Geology of Mankind', *Nature* 415/3: 23.

Hunt, J.D. (2000), *Greater Perfection: the Practice of Garden Theory*, (London, Thames & Hudson).

Jencks, C. (2004), 'Nature Talking with Nature', *Architectural Review* 215: 66-71.

Kaplan, A. (2016), 'Experimenting Regional Stream Pattern as Landscape Corridors in Urban Transformation', in S. Jombach, İ. Valánszki, K. Filep-Kovács, J.Gy. Fabos, R.L. Ryan, M.S. Lindhult, L. Kollányi (eds.), Proceedings of 5th Fábos Conference on Landscape and Greenway Planning: Landscapes and Greenways of Resilience, Szent István University, Budapest, 201-206.

Kaplan, A., Velibeyoğlu, K. (2016), 'Syllabus of Joint Project Studio (UD502 and LPD548)', İzmir.

Kondolf, G.M., Mozingo, L.A., Kullmann, K., McBride, J.R., Anderson, S. (2013), 'Teaching Stream Restoration: Experiences from Interdisciplinary Studio Instruction', *Landscape Journal* 32(1): 95-112.

Lewis, P.H. (1996), *Tomorrow by Design: A Regional Design Process for Sustainability* (John Wiley and Sons).

Neuman, M. (2016), 'Teaching Collaborative and Interdisciplinary Service-based Urban Design and Planning Studios', *Journal of Urban Design* 21(5): 596-615.

Nijhuis, S., Jauslin, D. (2013), 'Flowscapes: Design Studio for Landscape Infrastructures', *Atlantis* 23(3): 60-62.

The Infrastructure Research Initiative at SWA (2013), Landscape Infrastructure: Case Studies by SWA (Basel, Birkhäuser).

Yocom, K., Proksch, G., Born, B., Tyman, S.K. (2012), 'The Built Environments Laboratory: An Interdisciplinary Framework for Studio Education in the Planning and Design Disciplines', *Journal for Education in the Built Environment* 7(2): 8-25.

Landscape science in studio

Joan Iverson Nassauer

Introduction: Landscape science and the ecological turn

Landscape architecture theory and practice have taken a promising new ecological turn in the past decade, and this is complemented by many practitioners' recognition that research is needed to inform practice. These trends might be understood to mean that landscape architecture increasingly draws on science. The science that could propel them is rich. Collected under the umbrella of landscape science, environmental and social sciences that are relevant to design, planning, and landscape change across scales have deep knowledge bases (Gobster & Xiang, 2012). For landscape architects, a question about how to use this knowledge remains.

In the world of science, using ecological knowledge requires experience doing or, at least, critically using research. Scientists learn to conduct their own inquiries partly to learn the substance and methods of their fields, but also to learn to test what is true: to practice skepticism. Within science, skepticism instigates research and practice that changes, advances, and corrects ecological knowledge over time. Consequently, using ecological knowledge requires attention not only to current knowledge but also to the research that generates it. In contrast, in the world of landscape architecture, theory and practice that gesture to ecological knowledge may not do or even directly use science. Different from critically querying ecological knowledge, portraying environmental phenomena may be understood as a form of urban ecology (e.g., Mostafavi & Doherty, 2010; Orff, 2016; Pickett, Cadenasso, & McGrath, 2013). Given landscape architecture's long tradition of employing environmental knowledge of sites and regions to inform design, and its rich late 20th century literature using science to develop ecological design approaches (e.g., Hough, 1984; Lyle, 1985a; Spirn, 1984; Zube, 1986), the pursuit of design as urban ecology absent scientific inquiry is surprising.

Several scholars have explored possible reasons for this discontinuity. For example, some believe that the unfamiliarity and extent of social and environmental knowledge may prevent landscape architecture from grasping relevant knowledge. Or, some may see conceptual and pedagogical conflicts between the use of science and the development of design expertise (e.g., Grose, 2014; Johnson & Hill, 2002; Nassauer, 1985; Poole et al., 2002). These perceptions imply that a sophisticated understanding of science and sophisticated practice of design compete with each other—in pedagogy, in practice, and even in scholarship. Margaret Grose (2014, 2017) has argued that design and ecology are fundamentally different in the ways in which they query landscapes and understand what is true. Like others who have considered the relationship between science and design, she notes that landscape architecture and ecology use different languages, and sometimes, use the same word to mean different things (Johnson & Hill, 2002; Nassauer, 1985; Spirn, 2002). Further, she observes that science fails to understand the value of the holistic generalists' perspective of landscape architecture. These observations may lead some to conclude that teaching students to be sophisticated in their use of science limits their creativity. Students learning to use pattern books or design heuristics may be viewed as adequate substitutes for learning functional concepts. I see these challenges as incidental to landscape architecture curricula —and in particular, studio pedagogy—rather than inherent to science or design.

The landscape science imperative for learning and practice

Discontinuity between design and science is unnecessary and avoidable. Further, at a time of existential need for ecological design that grows out of scientific understanding, a time when the truth of science is popularly dismissed or replaced by myth or rumor, activating the longtime link between landscape architecture and science is imperative. This requires that landscape architects achieve functional understanding of the social and environmental processes that affect and are affected by landscapes, and that they learn to critically observe and instigate scientific advances by identifying and reading scientific literature.

Suggestions for constructing landscape architecture curricula to incorporate environmental science were thoroughly and ably proposed by a large group of designers, scientists, and practitioners in 1998, and collected by Bart Johnson and Kristina Hill in *Ecology and Design: Frameworks for Learning* (Johnson & Hill, 2002). This work includes useful and detailed suggestions that remain highly relevant for teaching ecology in studio (Poole, et al., 2002) and incorporating ecology in landscape architecture curricula more broadly (Ahern et al., 2002). In addition, since that time, substantial bodies of interdisciplinary knowledge in urban ecology and landscape ecology have grown as a result of science conducted in Europe, the United States, Australia, China, and elsewhere. This knowledge should be at the foundation of landscape architecture students' learning.

Landscape ecology and urban ecology, two different interdisciplinary forms of landscape science to which designers and landscape scholars have contributed for decades (Ahern et al., 2002, Felson & Pickett, 2005; McDonnell & Niemalä, 2011; Wu, 2014, 2017), are abundant with knowledge that landscape architects can use. Both incorporate knowledge drawn not only from ecology but from landscape architecture, engineering, planning, environmental justice, psychology, public health, forestry, geology, and geography. Scientists engaged in both approaches advocate for moving science from the interdisciplinary to the transdisciplinary, and for conducting investigations at local to global scales. The material landscape, as both a biophysical entity and dynamic cultural artifact, is a focal object in both approaches, which link landscape structure to social and environmental functions. Important to advances in science and practice, the structure/function link requires functional causes and consequences to be integral to landscape spatial characteristics that might be displayed in visualizations or maps.

The landscape design implications of these sciences are apparent in peer-reviewed scholarly literature (e.g., *Landscape and Urban Planning, Landscape Ecology, Landscape Journal*), and in richly detailed, carefully sourced comprehensive textbooks that draw from this peer-reviewed literature (e.g., Forman & Godron, 1986; Forman, 2014). If students directly use these sources, they not only gain deeper functional understanding of landscapes, they become familiar with how to find and critically consider peer-reviewed research. This is important since double-blind peer review produces knowledge that is qualitatively distinct from other information sources—including many books, magazines, and the various products of web searches. When students are introduced to double-blind peer review as a scholarly process that screens and enhances the quality of published scientific literature, they often are surprised to learn that it is quite different from curation of other print or digital media. Because it blinds the identities of creators of new knowledge, and also blinds the identities of reviewers of proposed publications, it can allow the work to speak for itself. Combined with an inclusive and extensive reviewer network, this emphasis on ideas with evidence rather than on identities of knowledge creators can achieve community curation of trustworthy new knowledge. When students understand the trustworthiness and relative openness and fairness of the double-blind peer review process, and how this process promotes diversity among contributors, they become more inquisitive about what they can discover in the peer-reviewed literature.

Bringing landscape science into studio

Understanding scientific literature can and should be integral to studio as a means of building functional understanding, creativity, and credibility for landscape architects as designers. The time-consuming, project-based pedagogy of studio does not need to compete with learning science; rather the studio can be structured to explicitly make time and space to "go to the literature" to learn.

Seeking knowledge of social and environmental processes as understood by science does not mean abandoning the creative, holistic insights of design, or the power of visualizing its effects. In my experience, differences between designers' and scientists' traditional ways of knowing and describing landscapes actually can accelerate creativity—if practitioners of design and science expect that each has valuable knowledge to share. When people with different understandings of the same landscape strive to comprehend one another, their differences can be catalysts for invention. Drawing on that experience, I have argued that because landscapes are inherently visible and integrate environmental processes, they can be used as boundary objects among disciplines and stakeholders, allowing people with different perspectives to "tack back and forth" to build consensus around something new (Star, 2010). In this way, landscape can be an essential medium and method for bringing science into the design of landscapes and bringing design into scientific inquiry (Nassauer, 2012).

Interdisciplinary collaboration benefits from tacking back and forth between scientific knowledge and creative insight, but landscape architects also can benefit from tacking back and forth inside their own studio design processes. At key moments in that process, they can learn to turn to peer-reviewed scientific literature. In studio, I teach students to query this literature to inspire design invention and development.

To open students' creativity and imagination to scientific knowledge, I draw on John Lyle's (1985b) powerful essay, "The alternating current of design process" to teach a way of thinking about iterative design process (Nassauer, 2002). Lyle described an "alternating current" of uncritically and intuitively proposing creative possibilities and critically examining their basis, disposing of what may not work. The "dispose" phase of critical examination explicitly makes space for using landscape science to consider the social and environmental functions embodied in a landscape proposal. It makes space for aesthetic critique as well, and invites synthesis of the implications of scientific and aesthetic critiques. Further, the dispose phase prepares the student's intuitive mind for the next propose phase; it provides substance to feed the imagination for creative work. In "propose" phases of design, students work freely and uncritically, but they see things differently because of what they have learned in disposing.

Either "propose" or "dispose" is a productive way to start a project. Most important is not to linger in the beginning phase, propose or dispose, but rather, to quickly move on to consider the project from the opposite pole of the alternating current. As students learn to use this process, there is no formula for time spent in one phase or another. Since students know they have recourse to an alternative way to see their work, they are less likely to be "stuck" as they flesh out a project, because the process enables them to continue to have fresh insights. That might mean explicitly setting the science or the aesthetic critique aside to just "make" work; it might equally mean setting aside production of forms and images to consider the functions of the emergent landscape in light of relevant scholarship.

In "dispose", critical observation of their work, students are compelled to consider whether and how the landscape they propose performs as they wish. At these moments, students who have learned to use scientific literature should know what they want to know more about and go to the literature to search for that knowledge. This helps them review their initial conception, to refine it or develop a wholly new idea—based on their interpretation of scholarly evidence. These are influential moments for guiding students to learn science in studio. However, learning to use science in design requires a way in. In studio, I find it useful to draw on what I have learned from my own transdisciplinary research. This includes telling stories about working among different science and design disciplines. These stories are lessons in landscape as boundary object that demonstrate how science can help to anticipate how a future landscape should or will function.

Then, by critically reading a few influential landscape science papers that I have selected to illuminate a short, simplified design exercise, students can learn functional concepts and disciplinary vocabulary of the relevant science. This critical reading also deepens students' sense of the transdisciplinary exchange necessary to ecological design. Based on what the students read, we discuss what they would ask their collaborators in ecology and engineering, and what these collaborators need to be able learn from them, the designers. This enables students to use science concepts creatively, while effectively using the vocabulary to consider and communicate their own work (figure 1). In contrast, learning to use words from science or engineering as metaphors without having a deeper understanding of the processes they denote drains them of their potential to inspire meaningful wholistic insights, creative advances, and credible communication. In a worst case, it promotes design that may give an impression of social and environmental functions that are not delivered (Hill, 2018; Pickett, Cadenasso, et al. 2013; Spirn, 2002).

For example, critical reading and discussion of selections from Richard T. T. Forman's *Urban Ecology.* (2014), Mary Cadenasso and Steward Pickett's "Urban principles for ecological landscape design and maintenance: scientific fundamentals" (2008), Kristina Hill's *Urban Design and Urban Water Ecosystems* (2009), Christopher Walsh and colleagues' "The urban stream syndrome: Current knowledge and the search for a cure" (2005), and my papers, "Care and stewardship" (Nassauer, 2011) and "Urban vacancy and land use legacies: A frontier for urban ecological research, design, and planning" (Nassauer & Raskin, 2014) were related to short design exercises in the Metropolitan Design Dynamics studio in the Landscape Architecture program at the University of Michigan. My ongoing research, in which I work with colleagues in ecology, engineering, law, sociology, public health and toxicology, and urban along with city residents, further informed the student designers' own approaches to their work—giving them access to the literature we are finding relevant to our research, observations of our research test sites, and engagement with our collaborators. This prepared student designers Jiayang Li and Andrew Sell to develop their own designs by individually investigating literature that related to questions and ideas stemming from their own work (figures 1-6).

Detailed discussion of selected papers can launch individual students' further exploration of this literature. Most students are astounded by the abundance of peer-reviewed literature about social and environmental functions of landscape. Driven by their desire to effectively address social and environmental issues, students learn to use and cite this literature as part of thinking critically about their own design work.

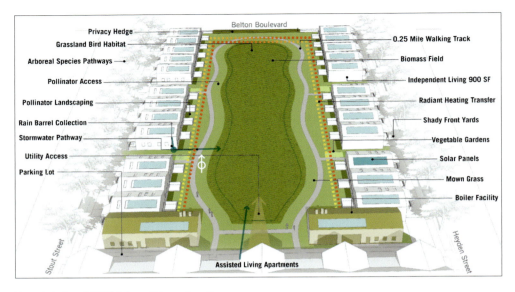

Figure 1 Andrew Sell (2016), framed his own inventive approach to an urban stormwater system. Starting with the scholarly literature we studied in class, he then drew on research in my lab with the Argonne National Laboratory and Illinois farmers, in which we investigated biofuels production (Graham, 2016).

Implications for teaching landscape architecture

However, learning science in studio cannot be only situational, driven by a project-motivated design process. Learning science in studio also should be a form of professional preparation, and the extent of landscape science requires deliberate goals for learning particular areas of science throughout a curriculum, including studio. If studio pedagogy does not change to incorporate critical understanding of new scientific knowledge, landscape architecture limits its professional capacity for ecological design. Linking introduction of scientific literature to studio content helps to narrow the overwhelming extent of landscape science to a degree that makes it possible for students to become comfortably familiar with relevant aspects of the science. When students know the content-learning objectives for a studio, they are motivated to learn that content.

Design process taught and practiced in studio can advance the new ecological turn in landscape architecture if studio engages students with scientific evidence about landscape function. In my experience, teaching an iterative design process that alternates between intuitive, wholistic spatial proposals and evidence-based critique can open time and space in studio for students to develop curiosity and competence in using peer-reviewed scientific literature. Within that propose/dispose framework, some rubrics for studio pedagogy are:

- Choose studio projects because of what they can teach students about learning from scientific knowledge rather than solely because of other curricular objectives (e.g., scale or technologies employed) or opportunities for relationship with practice, community engagement, or service.

- Give students a substantial foundation in scientific knowledge to empower their own creativity and imagination. If they know more about social and environmental functions

Figure 2 Sell adapted this research in my lab to a wholly new application—regional zone heating with locally produced biomass to make affordable living for an aging community in a highly vacant neighborhood of Detroit, MI, USA.

embodied in landscapes, students are able to use that knowledge inventively to conceive of novel formal possibilities.

- Demonstrate how the language of scientific literature empowers designers' authority in collaborating with others to invent new landscapes. If students first learn what the words of science mean to denote about social and environmental processes, they can be inquisitive and practice discernment when they use the scientific literature.

- Make it necessary for students to directly access scientific literature in order to critically evaluate it for their own design thinking. Use pattern books or heuristics sparingly and critically, only to supplement interpretation of the literature. By practicing how to critically examine the literature, students learn to evaluate the science for its legitimacy and relevance to their own design proposals. This may help them as practitioners to contribute to the development of relevant science.

- For legitimate design critique, require that students can point to evidence for their assertions about the social and environmental functions of their landscape designs.

How does an iterative evidence-based approach to studio employ other traditional aspects of studio pedagogy? It does not exclude the search for design precedents, but it is more likely to lead students to look and think beyond the obvious or superficial aspects of precedent work and to more critically examine claims for predecents' performance. It does not exclude the use of digital graphic tools or digital analytical tools, but does require that more time be spent on quick spatial ideation and critical thinking and less time spent on

GREEN LANDSCAPE, GREEN ENERGY
MULTIFUNCTIONAL STORMWATER MANAGEMENT THROUGH BIOMASS FARMING

BELTON GREENWAY

EXISTING CURB & GUTTER
48"X48" INLET STRUCTURE
5' SIDEWALK
48" DIA. ACCESS MANHOLE
12" INLET PIPE 1.5%

EXISTING ROAD

TYPICAL BIOMASS BLOCK

PASTORAL PROFILE
SECTION NOT TO SCALE

FROM FIELD TO HOME
HOW BIOMASS TRANSFORMS FLOODED STREETS TO LOW COST HEAT

Cup Plant provides a late summer food supply for pollinators and migrating birds.

Fields capture stormwater runoff from adjacent roads and buildings, creating ephemeral wetlands in early spring.

Dense root systems infiltrate stormwater and sequester CO2.

MARCH APRIL MAY JUNE JULY AUGUST SEPTEMBER

PRAIRIE INSPIRATION
As seasons progress, the biomass fields provide an ever changing landscape which benefits urban wildlife and nearby residents. Edge maintenance including mown turf and fences or shrub borders where necessary is key to provide cues that the landscape is purposeful and beautiful.

PLANT PALETTE
By utilizing native plant species adapted to both wet and dry conditions with a high biomass and competitive phenology, these stormwater biomass fields are both ecologically diverse and commercially productive.

ROOTS
A dense rhizosphere further enhances the field's ability to infiltrate stormwater and can absorb, transform, or stabilize a variety of contaminants, including soft and heavy metals and volatile organics through hydraulic control, absorption, and mycorrhizal activity.

156

Figure 3 His design fuels district heating systems with biofuels grown in the neighborhood—a technology developed by the Illinois farmers who had participated in research in my lab. This approach brings biofuel production down to an urban block scale. Importantly, Sell uses biofuel crop production to manage urban stormwater and to enhance biodiversity in a highly multi-functional landscape.

BIOMASS AS A PLANT COMMUNITY

Switchgrass *Panicum virgatum*
As the primary matrix species, switchgrass is becoming a leader in perennial biomass production. A Michigan native plant, the species is host to a variety of insects, is long-lived, regenerating and phenotypically plastic.

Hopniss *Apios Americana*
Commonly found in meadows and tall-grass prairies, hopniss is a native legume vine noted for it's ability to create dense networks of tubers and fix nitrogen. This plant provides extra nutrients to help support vigorous *Panicum* growth.

Cup Plant *Silphium perfoliatum*
As a vigorous native sunflower species, this plant can successfully compete with switchgrass. Including this flowering forb increases biodiversity and provides an early spring flush of growth, especially in wet conditions.

BIOMASS PRODUCTION:
Biomass farming is the production of perennial, herbaceous or woody plant material that is harvested seasonally, dried, and processed for combustion in boiler heating systems.

BIOMASS FARMING BY THE NUMBERS
1 Typical Block = 30 Parcels
30 Parcels = Approx. 8 acres
Typical Parcels = 40x130'
1 Acre = 8 tons of dried biomass fuel (*Average for *Panicum* spp.)
1 Ton = Heat for 8 months* (Average Warrendale 1,000 SF Home)
1 Ton Biomass = 200 lb of natural gas

Sources: Interview with Illinois biomass farmer

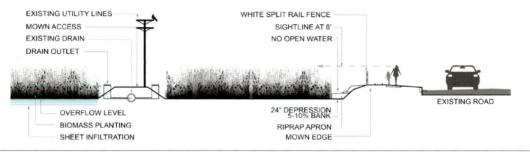

Figure 4 Sell initiated his own inquiry with some of our Illinois collaborators, and looked for more specific literature to make neighborhood biofuel production and zone heating integral to his design solution

HEIGHT & SAFETY
With a 10' mown turf edge and an artful seasonal mowing program, Warrendale's biomass fields are designed to help mitigate negative perceptions. Depending on rainfall levels, vegetation will stay within 5-10 feet in height and can be mown to create views across neighborhood blocks.

HARVESTING
Biomass harvesting in Detroit is optimal in the month of February when the ground is frozen and soil compaction and root disturbance can be minimized. Silage machinery (common to hay/alfalfa farmers in the area) is used to cut and bale the biomass providing skilled jobs to the area's economy.
Sources: Biomass Farmer / Researcher Interviews

PELLETING, STORAGE & COMBUSTION
Many biomass boiler systems can burn fuel directly, but a compressed pelleting system increases combustion efficiency. The overall energy balance of switchgrass pellets alone is 14.6:1. For every 1 unit of energy input, switchgrass creates 14.6 units of energy.
Sources: REAP: Resource Efficient Agricultural Program, Canada

Landscape science in studio | 157

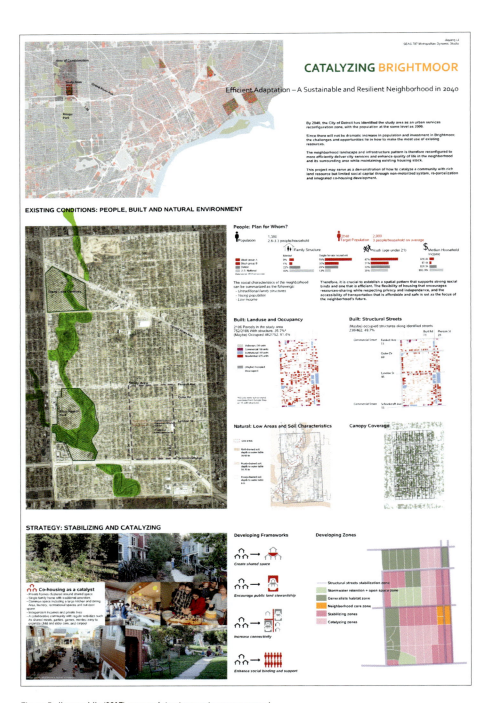

Figure 5 Jiayang Li's (2017) approach to stormwater management observes soil, relief, and vacancy conditions to construct a small piped stormwater system separate from the combined sanitary and stormwater system of the Brightmoor neighborhood of Detroit. This draws directly on the refereed literature and approach we offer from our current research in Detroit (Burton, McElmurry, and Riseng, 2018; Nassauer and Feng, 2018).

Figure 6 Jiayang Li's own investigation of scholarly literature led her to adopt a co-housing approach to new housing construction in a highly vacant neighborhood in Detroit.

production of presentation quality graphics. Consequently, in an iterative evidence-based approach, occasions for producing presentation quality graphics become selected occasions. This approach may provoke students to be more creative and more inventive than if they were to rely more heavily on precedent and presentation, which sometimes leads to mere imitation.

Conclusion: Advancing studio pedagogy to engage science

Bringing active engagement with science into studio pedagogy empowers students with a kind of creative authority that product mastery alone cannot give them. The idea that science empowers creativity is not new (Lyle, 1985b; Nassauer, 2002; Tamminga et al., 2002), but the rapidly growing body of landscape science is inherently new in its content, which is constantly reexamined as part of the conduct of science. To the extent that landscape architecture overlooks this knowledge base, it profoundly limits the capacity that most distinguishes designers from scientists—imagination. To more fully realize the extraordinary potential of landscape architecture to meaningfully affect the future, studio pedagogy must specifically incorporate relevant scientific knowledge, and promote critical thinking about what constitutes evidence that is adequate to inspire and support design decisions. Such a pedagogical evolution emphatically does not discard studio. Rather it employs the opportune structure and project-based learning of studio to further the capacities of students and the credibility of the profession.

REFERENCES

Ahern, J., et al. (2002). Integrating ecology "across" the curriculum of landscape architecture. *Ecology and Design: Frameworks for Learning*. B. Johnson and K. Hill. Washington, D. C. , Island Press: 397-414.

Burton, G. A. J., et al. (2018). Mitigating Aquatic Stressors of Urban Ecosystems through Green Stormwater Infrastructure. *NEW-GI: Neighborhood, Environment and Water Research Collaborations for Green Infrastructure*. J. I. Nassauer. Ann Arbor, Michigan, University of Michigan Water Center: 24.

Cadenasso, M. L. and S. T. Pickett (2008). "Urban principles for ecological landscape design and maintenance: Scientific fundamentals." *Cities and the Environment* (CATE) 1(2): 4.

Felson, A. J. and S. T. A. Pickett (2005). "Designed experiments: new approaches to studying urban ecosystems." *Frontiers in Ecology and the Environment* 3(10): 549-556.

Forman, R. T. T. (2014). *Urban Ecology: Science of Cities*. New York, Cambridge University Press.

Forman, R. T. T. and M. Godron (1986). *Landscape Ecology*. Toronto, Ontario, John Wiley and Sons.

Gobster, P. H. and W.-N. Xiang (2012). "A revised aims and scope for Landscape and Urban Planning: An International Journal of Landscape Science, Planning and Design." *Landscape and Urban Planning* 106(4): 289-292.

John Graham (2016). Working landscapes: Transdisciplinary research on bioenergy and agroforestry alternatives for an Illinois watershed. Doctoral dissertation. University of Michigan. Retrieved from Deep Blue. http://hdl.handle.net/2027.42/133401

Grose, M. J. (2014). "Gaps and futures in working between ecology and design for constructed ecologies." *Landscape and Urban Planning* 132: 69-78.

Grose, M. (2017). *Constructed Ecologies: Critical Reflections on Ecology with Design*. London, Routledge, Taylor & Francis Group.

Hill, K. (2009). "Urban design and urban water ecosystems". *The Water Environment of Cities*. L. A. Baker. Springer: 141-170.

Hill, K. (2018). "Review: Charles Waldheim: Landscape as Urbanism: A General Theory." *Journal of Architectural Education*: 1-11.

Hough, M. (1984). *City Form and Natural Processes*. New York, Van Nostrand Reinhold Company.

Johnson, B. R. and K. Hill (2002). *Ecology and Design: Frameworks for Learning*. Washington, D. C., Island Press.

Lyle, J. (1985a). *Design for Human Ecosystems*. New York, Van Nostrand Reinhold.

Lyle, J. T. (1985b). "The alternating current of design process." *Landscape Journal*. 4(1): 7-13.

McDonnell, M. J. and J. Niemelä (2011). "The history of urban ecology." *Urban Ecology*: 9.

Mostafavi, M. and G. Doherty. (2010). *Ecological Urbanism*. Cambridge, Mass. Harvard University Graduate School of Design.

Nassauer, J. I. (1985). "Bringing science to landscape architecture." *CELA Forum* 5: 5.

Nassauer, J. I. (2002). Ecological science and design: A necessary relationship in changing landscapes. *Ecology and Design: Frameworks for Learning*. B. Johnson and K. Hill. Washington, D. C., Island Press: 217-230.

Nassauer, J. I. (2011). "Care and stewardship: From home to planet." *Landscape and Urban Planning* 100(4): 321-323.

Nassauer, J. I. (2012). "Landscape as medium and method for synthesis in urban ecological design." *Landscape and Urban Planning* 106(3): 221-229.

Nassauer, J. I. and J. Raskin (2014). "Urban vacancy and land use legacies: A frontier for urban ecological research, design, and planning." *Landscape and Urban Planning* 125(0): 245-253.

Nassauer, J. I. and Y. Feng (2018). Different contexts, different designs for green stormwater infrastructure. *NEW-GI: Neighborhood, Environment and Water Research Collaborations for Green Infrastructure*. J. I. Nassauer. Ann Arbor, Michigan, University of Michigan Water Center: 45.

Orff, K. (2016). *Toward an Urban Ecology*. SCAPE, New York, New York : The Monacelli Press.

Pickett, S. T. A., et al. (2013). *Resilience in Ecology and Urban Design Linking Theory and Practice for Sustainable Cities*. Dordrecht, Netherlands, Springer.

Poole, K., et al. (2002). Building ecological understandings in design studio: A repetertoire for a well-crafted learning experience. *Ecology and Design: Frameworks for Learning*. B. Johnson and K. Hill. Washington D. C., Island Press: 415-472.

Spirn, A. W. (1984). *The Granite Garden*. New York, Basic Books.

Spirn, A. W. (2002). The authority of nature: Conflict, confusion, and renewal in design, planning, and ecology. *Ecology and Design: Frameworks for Learning*. B. Johnson and K. Hill. Washington, D. C., Island Press: 29-51.

Star, S. L. (2010). "This is not a boundary object: Reflections on the origin of a concept." *Science, Technology & Human Values* 35(5): 601-617.

Tamminga, K., et al. (2002). Building ecological understandings in design studio: A repetertoire for a well-crafted learning experience. *Ecology and Design: Frameworks for Learning*. B. Johnson and K. Hill. Washington D. C., Island Press: 357-396.

Walsh, C. J., et al. (2005). "The urban stream syndrome: Current knowledge and the search for a cure." *Journal of the North American Benthological Society* 24(3): 706-723.

Wu, J. (2014). "Urban ecology and sustainability: The state-of-the-science and future directions." *Landscape and Urban Planning* 125(0): 209-221.

Wu, J. (2017). "Thirty years of Landscape Ecology (1987–2017): retrospects and prospects." *Landscape Ecology* 32 (12): 2225-2239.

Zube, E. (1986). "The advance of ecology." *Landscape Architecture* 76: 58-67.

Toward a second coast: speculating on coastal values through landscape design studio

Maria Goula, Ioanna Spanou, Patricia Pérez Rumpler

Introduction

The relevance of leisure for contemporary societies as an economic force and complex sociological phenomenon is undeniable.[1] Yet, tourism, especially massive coastal tourist developments, are often considered detrimental to coastal landscapes, especially from a socio-environmental point of view. National strategies, planning procedures and policies, even in the case they address the impacts of the tourist phenomenon, they totally fail to respond to the need for innovative spatial models that involve resort typology, their aggregation patterns and finally the leisure landscape they promote (Barba, Pié, 1996:18; Pié, Rosa, 2013: 7). In fact, the majority of tourist operations are developed with low architectural standards and neglect of the landscape conditions and performances of the coastal sites they occupy (Pié, Rosa, 2013; Goula, 2008). More over, Landscape Architecture— a profession inextricably related to leisure in a broad sense—through designs of open and green space, has been, and still is, an accomplice of conventional resort design internationally.

While almost all important cities in the world have been repurposing and redesigning their urban waterfronts in the past decades, there is still a significant gap in knowledge regarding how to upgrade and innovate mature touristic destinations along the coast, particularly with the evolving climate regime. Consequently, there is a need for critical reflection on the spatial implications of coastal leisure patterns that, strangely, have been overlooked by design programs in general until very recently.[2]

This chapter reflects on the pioneering landscape approach from a 25-year-old studio: Landscape and Tourism: New uses for Old territories, integrated in the Master's of Landscape Architecture in Barcelona.[3]

The course was introduced by one of the most relevant figures in the establishment of Landscape Architecture in Catalonia: late professor Rosa Barba.[4] Its outcome, then and now, is to generate new coastal design strategies by speculating on site-specific landscape values and accordingly provide landscape-based designs for tourism. The coast of Spain and France has been the main focus for the studio experience.

The historical conditions of the Mediterranean sea make it an excellent location for the tourism industry, which bases its practices on a paradigm of coastal stabilization, silencing marine performances, creating land out of water, and considering alluvial flat plains or sand barriers ideal for new leisure landscapes. Due to the establishment of democracy in the seventies in Spain, ecologists and other activists joined together with grassroots political support to preserve the few remaining areas with ecological value in the coast, focusing on wetlands, dunes, salt marshes, etc. Planners, such as Rosa Barba and Ricard Pié, quickly understood that studying coastal dynamics and defending site-specific landscape values were necessary for quality sustainable resort development.

The Mediterranean alluvial plains offer a particularly interesting laboratory for Landscape Architecture students to restore and reshape damaged landscapes by creating mutually beneficial relationships between nature and humans in a self-sustaining way. The course gives students the opportunity to examine the few but still valuable pioneer designs developed in the sixties and seventies,[5] providing thus, a historical perspective of tourist coastal settlements, illuminating the concerns of designers then and now; secondly, it develops a particular focus on revealing what we have called "latent identities" of coastal sites, which have been drained to become farmland during centuries, radically transforming the hydrological cycles of many of these coasts. In fact, the latter is the main focus of this article and it aims to showcase the pertinence of such an approach as a necessary pedagogy, especially in the context of the semi-arid Mediterranean climate, characterized by cold and rainy, dry winters and dry hot summers, which stretches students to deal with strong changing conditions regarding the seasonal inflow of tourists and the hydrological regime.

Coastal landscape design pedagogies

Preservation alone, the main approach of governmental institutions in regard to the coast, has acted to isolate natural areas from human activities. This is no longer a valuable strategy. Natural dynamic systems need to be restored, reconstructed and continuously reinvented (Turner, Jordan, 1993).

Based on this assumption, the course evolves around a series of premises, all related to the performance of responsible programs that allow for new possibilities of complexity and long-term resilience. The main premises are: recover the coast as a variable edge, redefine through design of the intrinsic values of these landscapes as unique result of multiple processes; some latent, others defined by frequent episodes of predictable and unpredictable natural disturbances.

The methodological framework of the notion of second coast

The course initiates a challenging task for students: to reveal the latent space and time qualities of the landscape beyond the shoreline through cartographical research.[6]
This exploration leads to the definition of a suggested question to speculate with, which we intentionally name the search of a second coast (Goula, 2008). The second coast, a site specific and interpretable by each student concept, acknowledges the dynamics and potentials of an expanded hydrological unit and becomes the context and design vehicle for sustainable resorts and their surrounding landscapes (Fig. 1).

A threefold approach defined by discrete research questions has been developed to conduct the second coast speculations:

Recovering and revealing the water cycle

An active consciousness of functional operations determined by the watershed as a whole, although currently not visible and basically interrupted, introduces students to "system thinking" (Waltner-Toews, Kay, Lister, 2008)(Fig. 2). The watercourses that nourish the shore with sediments and water are re-established, the connections from and with the hinterland re-activated; spaces on the waterfront are liberated. In Baix Camp, Tarragona, the students bring to surface water-table salinization and contamination, torrent pattern

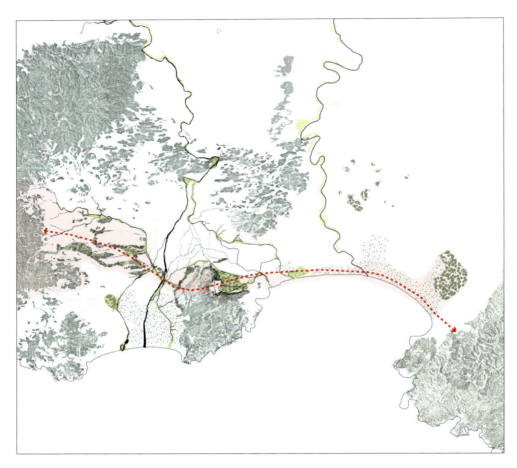

Figure 1 The second coast acknowledges the dynamics and potentials of an expanded hydrological unit and becomes the context and design vehicle for sustainable resorts and their surrounding landscapes.

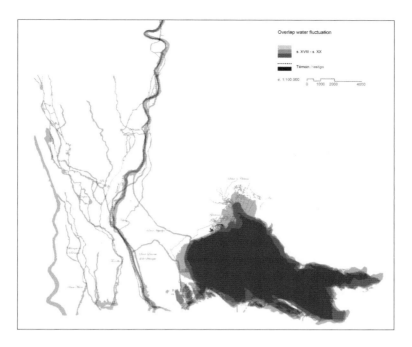

Figure 2 **Overlap of water fluctuation in Baix Camp, Tarragona**

discontinuity, rural abandonment, etc. and, most importantly, by rediscovering all the above as the structural frames of the site (Spirn, 1998), ecological processes get revealed, finally become legible, as apparent fragments of a landscape with a design potential.[4]

In the dry landscape of Baix Camp, where water is scarce and the discussion about it highly political, the second coast becomes the manifestation of a complete water cycle, at the same time, students learn about the interdependence between form and process (Gustavson, 2004).

The second coast not only serves as a locational metaphor for responsible eco-rural tourism in the hinterland, it also becomes a transformative resilient strategy for a more diverse pluri-functional rural landscape for the future.

The introduction of alternative programs to these mainly rural landscapes of the alluvial plains opens real possibilities to regenerate their severely affected by coastal tourism hinterland. Student designs convert torrential creeks to a potential spine for further walkability, detentions and retention of water, and phyto-depuration that coexist with evolved leisure programs, as natural pools and campsites, expanding the territorial offer beyond the beach.[5]

Forcing cartography beyond its conventional constraints

In coastal landscapes where the sea is the primary value, guiding students on one hand, to discovering different expressions of wetness beyond the shoreline and its dynamics in time, and on the other by asking them to reveal alternative to the sea and sun values, ones that emerge from the character of the surrounding heritage and ordinary agricultural landscapes establishes an "expanded" understanding of the idea of value it self.[6]

In this process, representation becomes a main tool of interpretation, varying from the

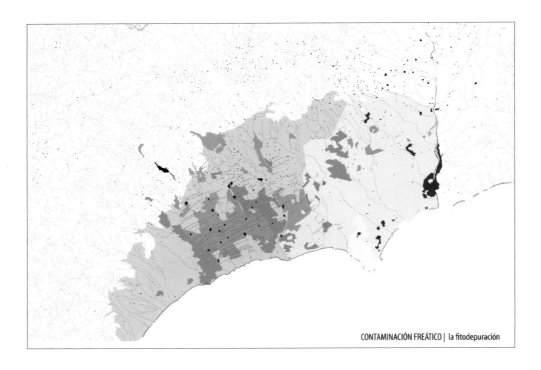

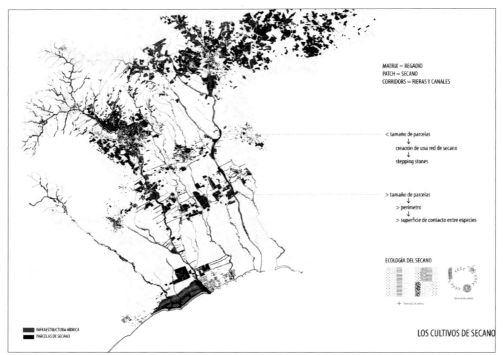

Figures 3 and 4 **In the dry landscape of Baix Camp, the second coast, becomes the manifestation of a complete water cycle.**

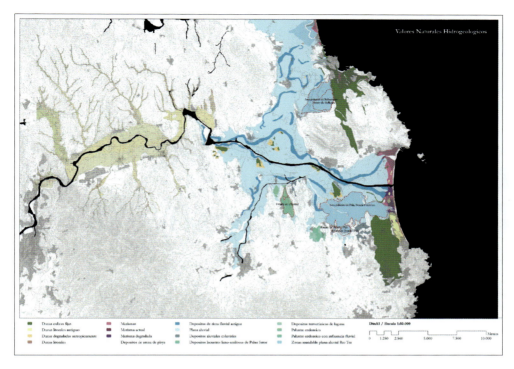

Figure 5 **Hydrogeological values of Toroella de Montgri, Baix Empordà**

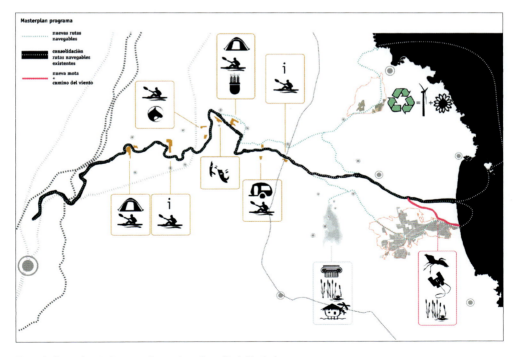

Figure 6 **Alternatives to the sea and sun values, Torroella de Montgrí.**

Figure 7 Images from video by students, to document water traces barely visible in the landscape.

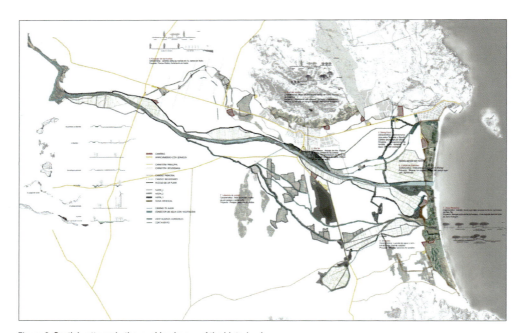

Figure 8 Spatial patterns in the rural landscape of the hinterland of Torroella de Montgrí.

analysis of the historic cartography to variable mappings which reflect the dynamics that shape the coastal landscape. These iterations become deeply projective exercises that induce to a more acute understanding of the landscapes in question.

The integration of historic cartography into GIS for example, becomes not only a culturally sophisticated act of recognizing the past, in the case of the Mediterranean coast, and in particular of the one we examine here: it is a necessary unveiling of what the coast has been and of what it may become. While the geo-referencing of historical maps is often impossible, or not as accurate, the historic maps become a source of inspiration, a potential reality to explore.

The students, through a diachronic analysis of the site, based on historic aerial photos and a detailed analysis of existing topography, indicate the processes of constructing and deconstructing of this landscape through the desiccation of the alluvial plain. They discover water traces, still vaguely perceptible through minimum changes in the landscape topography and the related landscape patterns. The recovery of these lost dynamic forms become the base for their proposal (Fig. 6).

In this sense, the interpretive cartographies are also driven towards a grounded, experiential interpretation of the site, through concepts that reflect the dynamics of perception such as embodied experience and atmosphere (Zumthor, 2006; Böhme, 1993a; 1993b). The mapping process is extended beyond conventional constraints of geolocalization, parameterization and measurement of discrete tangible elements, in order to guide students to rethink the latent values assigned to these ordinary landscapes. Their qualities inform in continuation about landscape patterns, now merged with patterns of experience: landscape involves our body, sustains experience and attracts perception.[7]

Through mapping and video in the form of traveling, students explore the embodied experience of spatial patterns in the rural landscape of the hinterland (Figs. 7 and 8). Under the theme of "rooms" they manifest how the geometry of plots, that become explicit by vegetation buffering the strong wind, and, most of all, its variability in time becomes a juxtaposition of different experiences. Here, the idea of the second coast is defined as a rotation of different management protocols, allowing wetness through vacancy to emerge. This experiential reading of the landscape nourishes also the definition of the strategy, the latter based on the configuration of a sequence of accessible "rooms" of variable character and program.

In a similar approach to the rural hinterland, in this exercise too, the embodied experience of the site leads to the deciphering of rural patterns (Fig. 9 and 10). Working with the necessary precision in order to exemplify the complexity and variety of the agricultural patterns, the students are instructed to go beyond the conventions of scale. Cartography "exemplifies" the meanings of the landscape, independently of the scale of the territory in question. In this project, the precision in the analysis of the landscape agricultural patterns informs the definition of the second coast, as a parallel to the coast agricultural fringe: this fringe denotes a minimum change of slope of the alluvial plain, almost imperceptible in situ, though causing a great impact as far as the disposition and the configuration of the agricultural parcels are concerned. This second coast becomes thus a liminal landscape, a transition from the "coast" to the interior landscape and vice versa.

The project crosses environmental design and embodied experience: the students propose the recovery of an antique lake, in order to increase biodiversity, recover the memory of the landscape, and improve water quality, but also configure a potential node of attraction for visitors (Figs. 11-13). The project takes in tourism as a main activator of the landscape regeneration, and as such, the observer's gaze and experience becomes an equally important programmatic need.

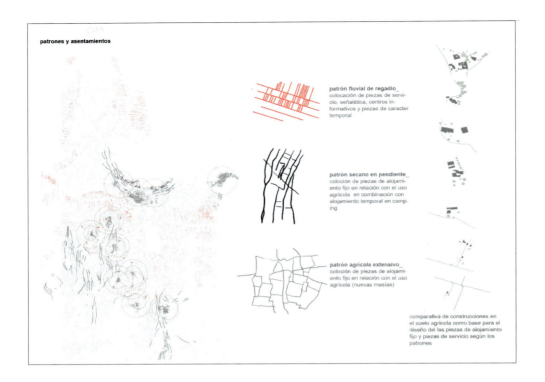

Figures 9 and 10 **Agricultural patterns and second coast at Torroella de Montgrí, Baix Empordà district.**

This experiential reading of the landscape acts as a counterpoint in the process of designing a new landscape narrative, and site-specific modes of embodied experience inform new assemblages, where the reactivation of the ecological system is merged with the design of the experience itself. These narratives perform through a non-linear sequence of specific niches of experience that seek to retain the perceptual attention of the observers and actively involve them in the site regeneration.[8]

Introducing change as an integral part of students understanding the speculation on the second coast.

The intrinsic temporality of Mediterranean climate as well as of the coastal leisure stretches students to deal with strongly changing conditions regarding the seasonal inflow of tourists and the hydrological regime. This singularity becomes particularly interesting when it overlaps with the reality of climate change and sea level rise. Students are instructed to interact with a set of conditions (forces and relations) that produce functioning of the landscape open to predictable and unpredictable change. Design exercises that aim to reveal the latent dynamics of the landscape by applying recent ecological thinking on uncertainty and resilience, taking in tourism as the main activator for change.

In Port Barcarès, Languedoc Rousillon, the second coast is a physical territory (Figs. 14 and 15). Its existing wetness in decline, is a sanctuary for locals, the lagoons face problems of eutrophication and privatization, there is no articulation with the rest of the territory and its water systems. The invented, designed, coastal resort part of mission Racine, as an expression of modernity, more than ever remained incomplete. Students, through vector explorations of the evolution of sediment in the lagoon in the past and in the future, propose to use the dynamics of the water to capture sediment, to adapt to change in the future and as a further step to speculate on new forms of leisure, inhabitation and mixed productivity in the interior shore of Port Barcarès.

New opportunities for old territories

Landscape architecture offers a proactive set of methodologies and tools for a sustainable and responsible regeneration of mature coastal destinations—and not only as an added value of tourism resorts—providing design codes that intentionally interact and revive natural dynamics while sustaining public and tourist use. This perspective becomes a real opportunity for territories in expectation of responsible activation of their economies.

In the realm of teaching, the notion of second coast has proven to be an operative concept that redefines the coast itself, mitigates its impacts by reconnecting it with its hinterland, and improving water quality. Thus, introducing a new design ethos toward overexploited territories that are losing their capacity of attraction.

The way we have occupied our "first coasts" is no longer justifiable. The term "second coast" stands up as a design tactic for a site that should admit both natural processes and responsible human inhabitation, yet requires continual human intervention to avoid its collapse. It certainly implies conceptual links of projective stewardship as suggested by the theories of "Gardenification of Nature" (Janzen, 1997), or the "Second Nature" (Pollain, 1991). These approaches show a different attitude toward the culture-nature polarity, where nature and culture meanings are decoded and grounded within site–specific design iterations.

As Bruno Latour claims in his last book "Facing Gaia" (Latour, 2017), the need of visualizing the earth, through new representations is the only real option beyond modernity to operate in an era of great uncertainty. By facilitating possibilities for multiple conversations (Latour, 2004) between the involved: collectives, lands, waters and species, by helping them emerge, the second coast becomes a necessary theoretical inquiry and a design paradigm, where the coast is re-established as a landscape.

Figures 11–13
Students proposal for the recovery of an antique lake near Torroella de Montgrí, to configure a potential node of attraction for visitors.

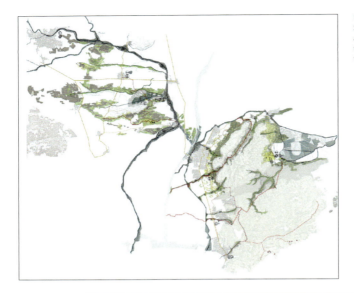

Figure 11

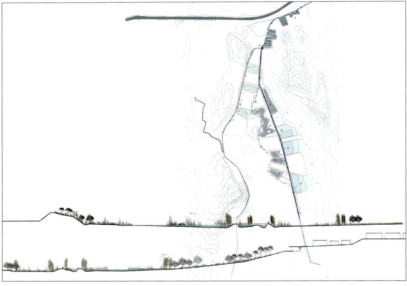

Figure 12

Figure 13

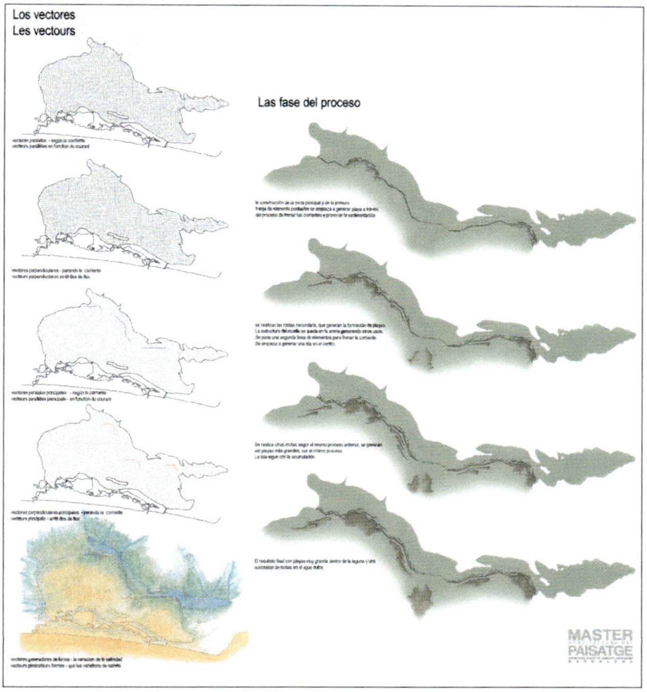

Figure 14

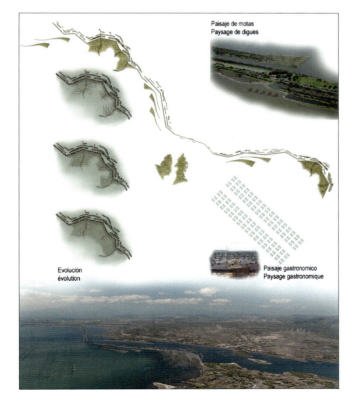

Figure 15

Figures 14 and 15 In Port Barcarés, Languedoc Rousillon, the second coast is a physical territory.

Toward a second coast: speculating on coastal values through landscape design studio | 173

NOTES

1 Since Veblen and his theory of the leisure class, a long list of thinkers have studied the tourist phenomenon. Corbin and Boyer distilled the history of the construction of the seashore as a desirable destination, Urry defined the specificity of the tourist gaze, and MacCannel examined massive tourism relations with hypermodernity.

2 Pié and Barba created the first postgraduate program on tourism and architecture organized by the Chapter of Architects of Palma de Mallorca in1993-4 in Mallorca and 1994-5 in Barcelona (Sijmons bibliographic compilation in 2012, Le Notre Forum, 2013, European Masters in Landscape Architecture EMiLA summer workshop as relevant examples).

3 Master's in Landscape Architecture, MAP, ETSAB, School of Architecture of Barcelona, Fundació Universitat Politècnica de Catalunya. The current title of the studio is second coast (with a varying subtitle, integrated in the module of tourism and landscape. The work shown here focuses on the years between 2011 and 2015, where the concept of the second coast became primary for the development of the teaching approach. Other professors involved in the same teaching period are Ricard Pié, Purificación Díaz, Anna Majoral, Mònica Batalla, (for the video exercise) Panagiotis Angelopoulos 2011, Marcel Pié 2015.

4 As part of the 1993 reform of the master's program, after a successful experience with Ricard Pié, mentioned above. Both architects have shown a remarkable professional trajectory with national awards, studying and defending the improvement of coastal leisure resorts in Spain. Unfortunately their work is only published in Spanish and Catalan, and hopefully this article will help transcend their teaching.

5 Materials of the 20th century history of tourist Architecture, such as Mission Racine, in the south of France, costa Esmeralda in Sardegna, design competitions for La manga del mar menor and Maspalomas, Spain, as well as unique responses from architects of the modern movement, such as Oiza, Coderch, Kandilis, etc.

6 Photography and video have been complementing the basic landscape research within the design studio. Due to the length of the present article we will basically focus on mapping speculations.

7 "It will take more than ecologically regenerative designs for culture to be sustainable, that what is needed are designed landscapes that provoke those who experience them to become more aware of how their actions affect the environment, and to care enough to make changes" (Meyer, E. 2008: 1:6-23).

8 Students think about the design from a variety of scales, understanding each phenomena in the appropriate scale at the first level of analysis, while their second coast mappings are intentionally cartographic exercises in between scales. Such discoveries may be tangible, like a relic or a significant tree or stone, or they may be intangible, like an atmospheric quality.

REFERENCES

Barba, R., Pié, R., eds. (1996). *Arquitectura y turismo: Planes y proyectos* (Barcelona: CRPP, Departamento de Urbanismo y Ordenación del Territorio, UPC)

Böhme, G. (1993a). 'The Space of Bodily Presence and Space as a Medium of Representation', in M. Hard, A. Losch, D. Verdicchio (eds.), (2003). *Transforming Spaces. The Topological Turn in Technology studies.* Retrieved from: www.ifs.tu darmstadt.de/gradkoll/Publicationen/transformingspaces.html

Böhme, G. (1993b). 'Atmosphere as the Fundamental Concept of a New Aesthetics' *Thesis Eleven* 1993: 36

Goula M. (2008). New opportunities for old landscapes. Some concepts on the Mediterranean coast'. in *'scape the International magazine for landscape architecture and urbanism,* No. 2:26 -33

Gustavson, Roland, (2004). 'Exploring Woodland design. Designing with complexity and dynamics' in *The dynamic Landscape. Design, Ecology and Management of Urban Planting,* (London/New York: Spon Press)

Janzen, D. H. (1997). 'How to Grow a Wildland: The Gardenification of Nature', *Insect Sci. Applic.* Vol. 17, No. 3/4

Latour, B. (2017). *Conference Facing Gaia: Eight Lectures on the New Climatic Regime,* 1st Edition

Latour, B. (2004). *Politics of Nature: How to bring the sciences into democracy* (Cambridge, Mass.: Harvard University Press)

Meyer K, E. (2008). 'Sustaining beauty. The performance of appearance: A Manifesto in three parts', *Journal of Landscape Architecture,* Vol. 3, No. 1:6-23

Norberg Schulz, C. (1980). *Genius loci, towards a phenomenology of architecture* (London: Academy Editions)

Pié, R., Rosa, C. eds. (2013). *Turismo líquido* (Barcelona: Editores iHTT-UPC-UMA)

Pollain, M. (1991). *Second Nature, A Gardener Education.* (New York: Grove Press)

Sijmons, D. Chief editor, (2008). *Greetings from Europe. Landscape & Leisure* (Rotterdam: 010 Publishers)

Spanou, I. (2016). 'Experiential mappings: approaching the landscape through atmosphere", in *SPOOL,* [S.l.], Vol. 3, No. 1: 37-56. Available at: http://journals.library.tudelft.nl/index.php/spool/article/view/1101

Spirn, A.W. (1998). *The language of the landscape* (New Haven-London: Yale University Press)

Turner, F., Jordan III, W. (1993). *Beyond Preservation. Restoring and Inventing Landscapes* (Minneapolis: Univ. of Minnesota Press)

Waltner-Toews, D., Kay, J. J., & Lister, N.-M. E. (2008). *The ecosystem approach complexity, uncertainty, and managing for sustainability* (New York, Columbia University Press)

Zumthor, P. (2006). *Atmospheres – Architectural Environments – Surrounding Objects* (Basel: Birkhäuser)

Teaching landscape urbanism in the French context

Karin Helms, Pierre Donadieu

This chapter addresses (1) the historical and cultural background of landscape architecture teaching in France; (2) the development, over time, of the methodology of teaching landscape architecture; and (3) the adaptation of training at Versailles to these objectives.

In the 1930s, urban planning concepts began to enter the teaching of landscape architecture at Versailles. The educational focus shifted away from training in gardening and green space management to educating students as landscape architects and urban planners. This radical change is now embedded in landscape architecture teaching. Knowledge of botany and horticulture has been to some extent superseded by land and earthwork experience, as well as historical and ecological understanding of the site to be converted. Ecological sciences and environmental studies are now related to large landscape dynamic processes, related in turn to climate change, sustainable energy issues, urban agriculture and the problem of urban sprawl.

This significant shift in the focus of teaching has put greater emphasis on the experience of practitioners, as well as on public sector demand. This new approach to teaching was introduced prior to 1945 as part of the training of horticultural students, and it continues to evolve to this day in French landscape architecture schools—the notable example of this being the École Nationale Supérieure de Paysage de Versailles from 1976 onwards— as it adapts to public policy on urban planning and landscape architecture.

As we will demonstrate later on, however, this happy marriage of urbanism and landscape architecture was arrived at independently of the landscape urbanism movement that first appeared in the USA in the late 1990s (Waldheim, 2006).

Changes to teaching at landscape architecture schools

The first French landscape architects/urban planners appeared after the Second World War. In 1972, the French government initiated a landscape research and training lab for innovative landscape planning in the city of Trappes (near Versailles). Between 1972 and 1978, it was known as the Centre National d'Études et de Recherches Paysagères (CNERP). This new type of urban landscape architect was known as a *"paysagiste d'aménagement"*, a landscape planner who used urban and rural economics to inform how they transformed spaces and adapted landscape features. After 1976, this concept of large landscape (from the French *grands paysages*) studies became a touchstone for the newly founded landscape architect graduate programme at the École Nationale Supérieure de Paysage de Versailles (ENSPV).[1] Students were taught mainly by invited professionals, although some academics were carried over from the former horticulture school (ENSHV). The new training programme was developed in two project studios: "André-Le-Nôtre", named after King Louis XIV's gardener at Versailles and directed by Michel Corajoud, and "Charles-Rivière-Dufresny", directed by Bernard Lassus and named after the 17th century artist who introduced the "English garden" to France. This second studio emphasised artistic and conceptual approaches to landscape and garden design, as well as the use of creativity.

The principle of "atelier Le Nôtre" was to privilege the geography of the landscape project site and experimentation. At that time (the 1980s), the instructors, both old and new, were looking to reinvent the function of the landscape architect, which since the Second World War had been reduced to the creation of generic urban green spaces. They focused on the open spaces of housing developments, often neglected both in the 1970s and before this. Residents wanted to improve their living environment by rethinking the outdoor areas around their housing. The training programme's objective was to create unique spaces providing greater dignity to their residents; to inspire these residents to re-appropriate their neighbourhoods, rather than seek to escape them.

Designing large landscapes

The concept of *"grand paysage"* (referring to the geographic scale of the inhabited landscape) and the landscape plan were new themes in teaching. They were introduced in 1961 to the school of Versailles by the landscape architect/urban planner Jacques Sgard (who received his training in urban planning at Versailles and the Sorbonne, as well as at Wageningen University from J. Bijhouver). This tradition was continued by the landscape architect Pierre Dauvergne, who applied it to all scales of urban and rural landscapes, as well as suburban developments or new cities. Teachers of landscape architecture used the same process and approach as on the scale of urban neighbourhoods. They aimed to recover the meaning of places from their geography and history, their grounds and vegetation.

These two scales of intervention, the open space left by architecture in towns and cities and the large landscape of the territory, were adopted and connected without a pre-existing development programme of management. The project process began with the interpretation of a site and its context (historical, ecological, economic, social and so on). No distinction was drawn between urban planning and landscape architecture. The idea was that the inhabitants' and users' perception of the landscape unified the organisation of the neighbourhoods under consideration. The landscape was integral to the structure of the neighbourhood or the territory. There was a complete break with analytical methods of urban or ecological planning. The landscape project process included determining the capacity of a site to receive new elements. So students were trained to be facilitators and negotiators in this process, a role also essential to the designer, whose dialogue with stakeholders was necessarily ongoing.

Later, these new aims of training became part of the pedagogic programmes of other landscape schools created in 1975, 1991, 1993 and 2004 in Angers, Bordeaux, Blois and Lille. So arose what was later called "the French school of landscape design" (Helms, 2017).

This kind of urban planning was not linked to urban regulation or legal aspects of planning but was innovative in establishing landscape design as a prerequisite for urban planning. These new practices anticipated long-term changes by looking at the general dynamics of a territory as well as details (Donadieu, 2009). They established an original discipline of project-based urban planning, previously little explored by urban planners, with the exception of a small number of architects. Its originality was (and remains) the expansion of the usual scale of landscape design (focusing on the garden, for example) to encompass the terrain more globally: at landscape level, neighbourhood-level as well as sidewalk-level. These practical concerns contemplated by practitioners took into account hydrological and plant forms and functions in continuity and relationship between neighbourhoods and municipal districts; respecting the multifunctionality of place, combining recreation and local businesses within the context of public policy on sustainable development.

The concept of the urban landscape

This approach was introduced at ENSP Versailles at the start of the 1970s by Michel Corajoud, from an art school background, and Jacques Simon, a landscape designer. They introduced a radical change to the school's then-current horticultural focus, proposing a vision of the city by "reading the landscape … through the inhabitants", a new way of redefining how we think about locations. They were inspired by Kevin Lynch's work (The image of the city) and collaboration with the urban planning and architecture firm AUA—Atelier d'Urbanisme et d'Architecture (Blanchon, 2015).

Later, after 1985, this teaching method, inherited from the pioneers, was gradually established as part of the school's teaching identity. Studios and landscape architecture courses were oriented towards learning the design process through understanding "layers" and reading what is "already there" as a foundation for future urban, suburban and rural projects. Studio projects varied from open spaces in existing towns to new urban settlements on various types of terrain—for instance, wetlands or post-industrial areas. Scale, too, varied—from large to very large spatial transformation of suburban and rural areas, involving infrastructural or geographic dynamics such as waterways or energy production. The overall issue was space organisation and form (Masboungi, 2001, 2009).

One of the major consequences of this shift in the focus of teaching was the gradual disappearance from the teaching programme of garden-level design and a portion of the technical and scientific knowledge traditionally associated with such projects. Planting design, for instance, was not always a required part of project presentations during studios. Other subjects, such as urban economics and urban planning law, have disappeared from the curriculum and been replaced by the socio-geography of landscapes.

Landscape morphology as structural basis for the project

Understanding and interpreting physical landforms has become fundamental to students' first experience of the site. The design process begins by understanding contour lines, through models, maps, maquettes and historical documents, grounding proposals in the site's specific identity and revealing the spatial capacity of a place to host new settlements. Planting based on the concept of préverdissement[2] and revealing an echo of the landform can then follow. This project method, developed by Michel Corajoud and Jacques Simon, became crucial and defined the future work of French landscape designers such as Gilles Vexlard, Jacques Coulon, Alain Marguerit, Alexandre Chemetoff, Michel Desvigne, Agence Ter's founders and others.

Figure 1
Urban edges at La Réunion, Saint-Paul,
Office: Agence Folléa-Gautier Landscape architects and urbanists.
Project: 1998-2013

The Route des Tamarins is a new highway created over 35 km to open up the coastline. The new road should also be an enabler to connect the towns with their protected natural areas and the farming plots situated on the volcano's slopes. The designers have been educated at ENSP Versailles and their mode of acting is to make the site's unique morphology and hydrography a constant of the draft design by drawing on the landscape's geography and history.

Figure 2
Urban edges at La Réunion, Saint-Paul,
Office: Agence Folléa-Gautier Landscape architects and urbanists.
Project: 1998-2013

With the regional council, the landscape architects have successfully set ambitious landscape orientations for the west coast of the island. At St.Paul the project around the repositioned highway allows the inhabitants to reclaim their living spaces: by re-creating a wetland area which constitutes the identity of the town and by creating two new promenades. Large-scale landscape projects are becoming common working scales for designers in France.

Figure 3 Detail of the flower beds along the new public spaces on the former Port dock. The idea was to literally turn the inhabitants back to their main geography: river Garonne. The new public spaces are an in-between landscape, an entity that connects the historical city to the river. 2005. Atelier R: Anouk Debarre Landscape architect.

Figure 4 Detail of the mirror sequence. The water surface is a leisure moment for children and reflects the sky and the historical buildings of the Garonne dock. Moreover, the water body is situated where once the river was situated, a transposition in design of a former geography element. 2005. Atelier R: Anouk Debarre Landscape architect.

A key document demonstrating this historical shift in the focus of teaching is the "Letter to students" written by Michel Corajoud in 2000.[3] It explains the construction of a landscape project in nine stages, which include brainstorming, exploring in every direction, going beyond limits, working with scale, leaving in order to return, testing project approaches …

At the beginning of his Letter, Corajoud writes: "Allow ideas to bubble up at the start of a project before coming to any conclusions about the design or site. In order to work on a project involving a landscape that you will most likely be unfamiliar with, you will have to overcome a huge knowledge deficit, and ask yourself thousands of questions: What plans have been made for the site? What is it to be transformed into? And who wants these changes?" He goes on to add: "The important thing is to develop a project mindset as early on as possible in order to avoid the hesitation and indecision caused by an overly long preliminary analysis" (Corajoud, 2010, p. 37). Corajoud then describes the various steps involved in producing a draft design. This design process is supplemented by input from lecturers with backgrounds in various technical and scientific fields, who teach the students both inside and outside the studio over the course of their four years of study. Their drafts evolve and develop before being formally presented to course lecturers. In this way, students gain experience in producing increasingly more complex designs before having to respond to a real request in their final year.[4]

One of the main aspects of the design process that students are taught is how to make the site's unique morphology and hydrography a constant of the draft design by drawing on the landscape's geography and history. By doing so, landforms should be revealed, presented and showcased. In this way, the site itself provides the starting point and plan for the design, by taking into account the activities that it is intended or expected the site will eventually be used for (Figs. 1 and 2).

Figure 5 The design of the left river bank along the Garonne runs in sequences on 4.5 km. The large-scale landscape project is subdivided in sequences; still these sequences are smoothly organised. Source: 2000. Competition document Atelier Michel Corajoud and Atelier R: Anouk Debarre Landscape architect.

Landscape urbanism?

Landscape urbanism, according to the definition given in various texts in *The landscape urbanism reader* (Waldheim, 2006) came as a manifesto for some and facilitated breaking down the barriers between disciplines. It was a hybrid of two approaches to organising space —urban design and landscape design—which offered a name for a new mode of practice, and a new potential market. Waldheim (op. cit., pp. 37-53) suggested, "building cities not around architecture but around landscapes" and "making an urbanism of landscape architecture".

Such approaches engage wider scales of practice (for example with l' Agence Ter et Grün Metropole: a master plan for 53 districts across three European countries) or with more complex urban questions (for example l' Agence Michel et Claire Corajoud with a new urban river bank proposal in Bordeaux). Projects such as these involved understanding the landscape on the very long term and revealing hidden geography through the language of flows, continuities of spaces, landscape entities and their systems through artistic interpretation. (Figs. 3-5). There are therefore some similarities, but also some differences, between the ways of thinking about landscape urbanism that surfaced in the USA and those emerging in France around the 2000s. James Corner makes this point in his introduction to M. Desvignes's *Natures intermédiaires* (2004, p. 9): "What is most striking, in this regard, about Desvignes's work is his fascination with the incomplete." It was this generation of landscape architects, trained at the start of the 1980s, that introduced some element of forward thinking to the uncertainty of urban planning (Masboungi, 2011).

This way of thinking about landscape design—as a continuation of the process of constructing landscapes—was incorporated directly into the teaching at ENSP Versailles and other French schools. Students were no longer taught in terms of "composition" (the word had dropped out of use) but in terms of building on the natural landscape. The rules of landscape architecture no longer involved sticking to conventions such as those used to produce certain garden styles, or fixing landscape structures in place. The rules had to, and still have to, be made up as you went along, with each site remaining, or becoming, unique and adapted to its users' needs. Michel Corajoud (2010) said that the project should address the horizon. By transcending the physical limits of the site, fragmentation, segregation and zoning can be avoided (Figs. 6-9).

Figure 6 New urban planning of Strasbourg's former port through a landscape and geographic understanding of the site. Agence Ter in their project "Territoire deux Rives" develop a project that seeks to develop an urban strategy based on the pre-existent landscape base. The Rhine territory is structured by water, declined in all its forms. A set of canals, docks and basins gives form and direction to the urbanisation. Public spaces are deployed along the banks, reinforcing their role as structuring urban connectors. These spaces allow the development of a green landscape structure on a metropolitan scale. Source: Agence Ter competition image 2015.

Figure 7 Detail planning of the new urban planning of Strasbourg. Interconnection between former wetlands, industrial areas and new innovative housing and office areas. Zooming is avoided to enable geographic continuities. Source: Agence Ter 2015.

Figure 8 A new district between the river Rhine and the historical city of Strasbourg. A landscape architect urbanism process to design integrated hidden geographies as founding design elements: hereby a former river arm which becomes the new landscape entity for a housing area.

Figure 9 The project of the Two Banks Territory is the last phase of Strasbourg's ambitious policy to reclaim the spaces of its former port. Starting from the city zones of Heyritz, Malraux and Danube, the project proposes new types of public space; at the same time natural and wild spaces, influenced by the river, are open to offer contextual spaces for the residents.

Teaching landscape urbanism in the French context | 183

Conclusion

For forty years, the training of *paysagistes concepteurs* (landscape architects) in France has evolved and become more established. With public policy taking a more direct interest in landscape issues since the passing in 1993 of a law to protect landscapes, this training combines the tradition of garden art with a new vision for urban design that has been accepted by urban planners. In this way, students learn to support the structuring of landscapes at a range of different scales (in terms of both space and time) as part of the urban planning process. Landscapes and places are built through complex processes—economic, social, legal and environmental.

This shift towards urban planning, which began at Versailles in 1946 and became more evident from 1985 onwards, could also be seen at the four other schools (Angers, Bordeaux, Lille, Blois). It is a shift that has allowed landscape architects to adopt *paysagiste concepteur* as their official title (as regulated by a law passed in 2016), rather than "government-qualified landscape architect", since the French Order of Architects had opposed the use of the term "landscape architect". The result of this is that the professional worlds of the architect, the urban planner and the civil engineer can be separated once and for all from that of the landscape architect, since each of these professions is regulated by law.

The use of drafting and design studios to teach students has gone hand in hand with a change in the types of lecturers working at these schools. It has become more and more common for landscape architects to teach the students about visual art, techniques for producing graphic renderings and the eco-biological and social environments, in addition to training them in the techniques required of a professional landscape architect. They work with artists and scientists, including geographers, historians, anthropologists and philosophers. Over the past forty years, a culture of landscape design has progressively taken the place of civil engineering, urbanism and architecture in spatial planning.

The approach that each school has taken is different, however, with Angers leaning more towards the sciences, and some schools giving a greater emphasis to architecture and urban planning, while others focus more on the social mediation of the governance of projects. Regardless of these differences, all the schools have introduced research labs and doctoral programmes, either concerned with landscape design or linked to other artistic or scientific fields (such as geography, history, political science or ethnoecology). In most cases, however, the desired interaction between studios taught by practitioners and labs taught by researchers has not been achieved.

Since 2000, landscape architects have won the *Grand Prix de l'urbanisme* (an award for urban planning) three times, and in 2018, two landscape architecture firms (Agence TER and Atelier Jacqueline Osty et associés) were pre-selected alongside two urban planners.

REFERENCES

Agence Ter, (2011), *357824 hectares de paysages habités*, (Brussels: Éditions AAM Ante Prima).

Blanchon, B., (2015), "Jacques Simon et Michel Corajoud à l'AUA, ou la fondation du paysagisme urbain", in *Une architecture de l'engagement, l'AUA 1960-1985* Jean-Louis Cohen and Vanessa Grossman (eds.) (Paris: Éditions Carré, Cité de l'architecture et du patrimoine).

Brisson, J.-L. (2000), *Le jardinier, l'artiste, l'ingénieur*, (Arles : Actes Sud).

Corajoud, M. (2010), *Le paysage c'est l'endroit ou le ciel et la terre se touchent*, (Arles: Acte Sud/ENSP).

Davodeau, H. (2008), "Le 'socle', matériau du projet de paysage, l'usage de 'la géographie' par les étudiants de l'École du paysage de Versailles', in Projets de paysage (Versailles: ENSP).

Desvigne, M., Tiberghien, G., Corner, J. (2009), *Natures intermédiaires, les paysages de Michel Desvignes*, (Basel: Birkhäuser).

Donadieu, P. (2009), *Les paysagistes ou les métamorphoses du jardinier* (Arles : Actes Sud/ENSP Versailles).

Helms, K. (2006), 'The Pioneers', in *Landscape Architecture Europe Fieldwork* (Basel: Birkhäuser LAE Foundation) 64-69.

Helms, K. (2013), 'Année André le Nôtre', *TOPOS*, 2013, 23.

Helms, K. (2016), *Learning from M. Corajoud*. Film, 15 minutes, produced by Association L'Atelier Michel Corajoud.

Helms, K. (2017), 'Practice-Based Research in Large Landscape Strategies', in *Design-Based Theories and Methods in PhDs from Landscape Architecture, Urban Design and Architecture* (H. Readers, Prominski and M. Von Seggern édits.).

Helms, K. (2018), The facilitator in anticipary of landscape stratégies, PhD dissertation, RMIT Europe.

Lynch, K. (1960). *The Image of the City* (Massachusetts:The MIT Press).

Masboungi, A. (2001), *Penser la ville par le paysage autour de M. Corajoud* (Paris: Édition de la Villette).

Masboungi, A., Mangin, D. (2009), *Agir sur les grands territoires* (Paris: Le Moniteur)

Masboungi, A. (2011), *Le paysage en préalable, Michel Desvigne, grand prix du paysage* (Paris: Parenthèses).

Siddi, C., Helms, K. (2009), 'Landscape Urbanism on the Mediterranean Coast'. Quartu Sant'Elena (Sardinia: Gangemi Editore).

Waldheim, Charles (ed) (2006) *The Landscape Urbanism Reader*, New York : Princeton Architectural Press.

NOTES

1 This new school was the successor of the CNERP and the Section of Landscape Architecture and Garden Art (1946-1974), which was the part of the École Nationale Supérieure d'Horticulture de Versailles (ENSHV; a horticultural school) that taught landscape architecture.

2 The term *préverdissement* was first used in France in the early 1970s to describe a settlement principle whereby vegetation was planted to prepare the grounds of post-industrial sites for future recreation or other urban programmes.

3 A video was produced from the *Letter to students* by K. Helms in 2016.

4 Regional teaching studios for fourth-year students were introduced at Versailles in 1983 (although this was not the case at other landscape architecture schools). Over the course of six months, the students handle real requests involving public contracts, and are supervised by small groups that include the school's practitioner-lecturers.

Teaching the unpredictable, critically engaging with urban landscapes

Lisa Diedrich, Mads Farsø

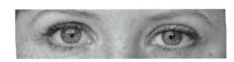

REALMS Crossing academic and artistic realms in teaching. Cover of the documentation of the Thinking Eyes course.

Urbanisation is a global trend, and since industrialisation intervening in the urban realm has increasingly become a task for landscape architects. In Europe landscape architects have developed a strong reputation as professionals of the urban environment, with projects that range from large scale strategic design to small scale urban open space, from publicly driven policies to community initiated designs, from climate adaptive urban structures to urban performance art. Publication of such projects has generated a body of literature about the contemporary practice of landscape architecture, as evident in the IFLA Europe supported book series *Landscape Architecture Europe* (Diedrich et al. 2018, 2015, 2012, 2009, 2006). Still, in times of rapid change of ecological, economic and demographic patterns, which means in times of extremely unpredictable urban futures, the skills, work modes, methods and knowledge of today are often outdated tomorrow. Education of "future-proof" landscape architects, therefore, has to acknowledge that teachers need to prepare their students to tackle situations of a future that cannot be fully anticipated today.

QUESTIONS In light of the "wicked problems" of the 21st century, how can we teach solutions if we do not yet know what knowledge the next generation needs?

RELATIONS Research, teaching and practice in landscape architecture are intimately related yet follow different "game rules". Feedback session in exhibition of final student works.

Consequently, we aim to teach the unpredictable—i.e. the ever evolving complexity of urban landscapes—through engagement in an open-ended learning process[1] that focuses on re-formulating questions and re-defining methodology, instead of posing standard questions and training through traditional methods. We require this engagement to be critical, in the three meanings of the term: we create awareness of sites and situations *at risk*; we search for the *crucial conditions* to intervene in those situations; and we formulate well-argued *positions* that invite for change. This takes us to the margins of our own knowledge and sometimes into uncharted territory, and, we hope, towards innovative teaching practices. To quote the Swiss-German landscape architect Günther Vogt, famous in Europe as a practitioner, practice-based researcher and teacher: "We are more interested in a debate that engages what is going on behind the scenes—the process of fruitful meanderings, of voyages of discovery at the periphery" (Foxley and Vogt 2010: 7).

OMNIPRESENT How to find places you weren't searching for, and qualities you otherwise would have overlooked? Site visit to the Öresund, the central water body linking Copenhagen, Denmark, with Malmö, Sweden.

1 | Crossing lines

Having taught design studios and design research seminars in different landscape architecture programmes in Europe, Australia and the U.S. before meeting at the University of Copenhagen in 2009 and working as colleagues at the Swedish University of Agricultural Sciences in Alnarp (SLU) since 2013, we now strive to combine two approaches typically separated in landscape architecture education: the scientifically inspired approach, with its rigorous methods of observation, interpretation and academic writing, and the artistically oriented approach, with its case-specific and future-oriented speculations through drawing, modelling and exhibiting. These approaches, linked to both research and practice in landscape architecture, come with their normative value imperatives: while science is associated with data, analysis, evidence, truth and "objectivity", design is seen as artistic activity, form finding, craftsmanship and "subjectivity".

The first trend is mostly prominent at science and technology universities (termed STEM disciplines in the Anglo-Saxon context—science, technology, engineering, mathematics); the latter normally rules studio-based curricula (typically taught at art, design and architecture schools). We think clinging exclusively to the one or the other approach is senseless as we need both the scientific and artistic methods if we are to succeed in our attempts to conceptualise the urban landscapes for an uncertain "tomorrow".

This uncertainty urges us to cross the line between the sciences and the arts, between making and thinking, and between conventional and future forms of knowledge generation. We teach what we do not yet know—a pedagogy which for French philosopher, semiotician and critic Roland Barthes (1915-1980) simply corresponds to research (Barthes 1978). Hence we endeavour to teach young landscape architects the mindsets and skills

ITINERARY How to develop an itinerary as a "way to discover" a landscape's particular value? Site visits around and across the Öresund.

WICKED Alternative approaches are needed to tackle today's "wicked" problems as encountered, rather than the particularised "tame problems" of the 20th century. Site visit to the Superkilen project, Copenhagen.

with which we as researchers conduct investigative projects that tackle urban challenges of the 21st century. Relying on German design theoretician Horst Rittel (1977) we conceive of such projects as "wicked problems" that are complex and ill-defined, in need of approaches different from those that addressed the sectorial "tame problems" of the 20th century. This resonates with adopting theories of knowledge beyond conventional scientific beliefs (cf. Moore 2010).

According to many contemporary scholars of the design disciplines, "design thinking" (Brown 2009, Lawson and Dorst 2009, Simon 1996) is particularly apt to transfer to young people the skills and competences they need in the 21st century. Design thinking as a method forwards a different kind of knowledge management, namely one that invokes processes of information selection, acquisition, integration, analysis, synthesis and sharing in the networked environments of the contemporary knowledge society (Noweski et al 2012, Ascher 2009, Nowotny 2008, 2001). It is astonishing that design thinking as a method remains unfamiliar on the ground from which it arose, namely architecture, urban design, and also landscape architecture. As a profession, landscape architecture has so far largely failed to theorise its tacit practice knowledge, leaving the field for exploration by other design disciplines, such as industrial design, which transferred the insight gained to yet other fields, e.g. economics, IT technology and pedagogical sciences.[2]

DANCE Teachers need to prepare their students through confrontation of situations that no one is able to fully anticipate. Student presentation of site qualities delivered as a dance performance.

MEDIA Challenging conventional presentations of site findings through performative media and alternative means of expression.

In landscape architecture there is no scholarly tradition that would explore how practice-based knowledge arises and which methods of enquiry and operation support it, as scholars in landscape architecture have predominantly been active in the science and technology field, and landscape studio teachers have concentrated on teaching the arts of drawing and building projects. Only for a decade or so have landscape architecture and urban design scholars joined in refining the scope of design thinking for the sake of urban landscape oriented design research (e.g. von Seggern 2008, Sieverts 2008). Having emerged since the early 1960s as a poly-paradigmatic field, design research relies neither on an accepted canon nor a repertoire of research practices, methodologies and epistemologies. In SLU's scientific environment we strive to create acceptance for understanding design thinking as a necessary complement to both studio practice and scientific research. We also propose as a basic tenet to accept "design" as an indispensable conceptual and technical activity, beyond definitions as superficial formalisation, for steering the transformation of contemporary urban landscapes. These in turn are understood beyond restrictions of 'green' environments, as both natural and human-made. Consequently, our teaching approach exemplifies the crossing of scientific-technological and artistic realms.

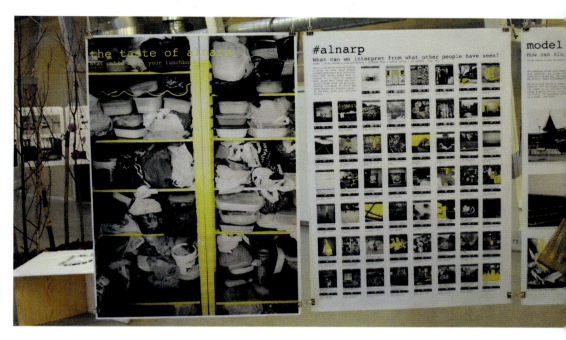

CONCEPTUALISING A combination of scientific and artistic knowledge is needed to conceptualise the urban landscapes of an uncertain "tomorrow". Final student projects exhibited on panels.

2 | Provoking engagement

Teachers can use imaginative course scenarios to provoke critical engagement with urban landscapes. The following two examples stem from two courses devised in 2013 and 2015 at SLU Alnarp:

> "Imagine the procedure for the European-wide EUROPAN competition for young architects (http://www.europan-europe.com) is revised. The EUROPAN cities and juries are fed up with receiving useless architectural fantasies produced by designers who sometimes have not even set foot onto the competition sites. However, on the threshold of 21st century and in view of climate change, shrinking resources, social turbulences and economic uncertainties, the European cities are increasingly in need of innovative approaches for site-specific urban transformation proposed by designers who are able to identify and work with existing site qualities. This is something landscape architects are good at (at least after this course). Consequently, the EUROPAN authorities have decided to open up the competition for teams headed by landscape architects (this is reality), and to restrict the participation through a prequalification stage (this is the course scenario). To prequalify for EUROPAN, one must submit a portfolio comprising of a critical reflection on contemporary site-specific design and one's own approach to site specificity. In addition one must also orally defend one's position to the EUROPAN jury" (Diedrich and Farsø 2013: 3).

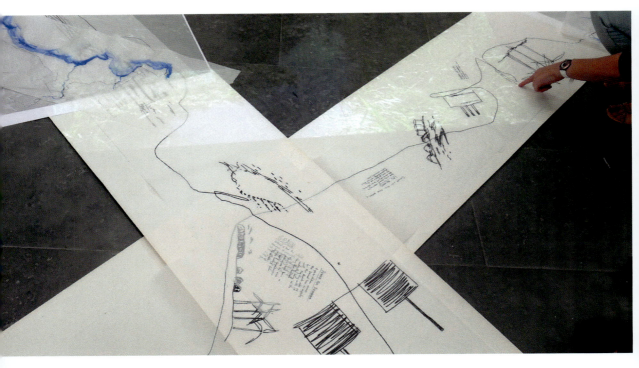

RETHINKING All media are acceptable, both traditional and new ones, but seldom does one medium alone suffice to convey the qualities of landscape. Discussion of student installations and site drawings encountered during fieldwork.

"Imagine the Öresund region had a project to develop a hiking trail to experience its particular landscapes and raise the awareness of inhabitants and visitors for particular beauties, histories, conflicts and change in the Öresund urban landscapes. What would the trail look like? Which sites would it include and how could their specific (and unique) values be communicated? Wouldn't increased public awareness of the Öresund's specificities lay the foundation for a more sustainable development? In this course, students will explore the Öresund region through transecting travels in order to propose particular sites to be included into the itinerary of a discovery path of the Öresund region. The experience of hiking through strange landscapes full of stories and opportunities sharpens the minds of those involved for site qualities beyond the officially accepted touristic highlights. It caters to an appreciation of existing site conditions and for a revision of value systems and concepts of landscape beauty—from such a public awareness of landscapes 'as found', new design concepts can arise" (Diedrich, Lee and Farsø 2013: 3-4).

3 | Design as a thinking medium

The first scenario, of an elective Master of Science (MSc) course of ten weeks, was named the 'Thinking Eyes' in reference to the similarly termed section in the *Journal of Landscape Architecture*, which presents research that is not only written but also drawn, painted, built, or in short: expressed in whatever medium best conveys new problem framing and paths towards knowledge. The second scenario, entitled "Öresundsect", was run as a joint MSc/PhD summer course during two weeks in the context of the Travelling Transect research of Gini Lee and Lisa Diedrich (Lee and Diedrich, 2019) aimed at doing fieldwork while also conceptualising and codifying it.

TRACKING Design is an indispensable conceptual and technical tool for the transformation of contemporary urban landscapes. Site visit to derelict sites at Nyhamnen, Malmö's harbour.

Both courses were conceived to enable students to immerse themselves into urban realities in order to capture qualities in the field in scientific and artistic ways, as well as to take critical distance towards these sites through literature study, reflection in seminars, academic writing and artistic exhibition. We do not claim that our teaching of practice-based and theory-oriented components is radically novel. However, these components are seldom taught in entanglement, within one and the same course, and even less so in adopting a critical perspective to both designing projects and thinking about project design. We invite students to explore, practically and theoretically, what is *critical*: what they perceive at *risk* on a site, what they think are its *crucial conditions* for instating change, and how they formulate a well-founded *position* supporting that change.

Critical distance and enquiry

Literature was at the start of both courses. In the Thinking Eyes, the students were asked to read professional articles about contemporary landscape architecture as well as academic writings about site theory. They then had to choose a nearby contemporary design work, become acquainted with its context and history through archive research, then visit it, interview the designer, and write a critique. In the much shorter Öresundsect course, instead of doing a written critique students discussed the readings with invited authors in seminar sessions, and PhD students had to hand in an academic paper within a month after the course. In both courses, the enquiry into theoretical literature was linked to the enquiry into concrete design works or sites slated for design interventions. This enabled students to realise that theory, design and site could not be considered as absolute givens but are always subject to discussion and evaluation in a humanities-inspired study. Learning outcome: critical reflection enables students to complement intuitive project design by a reflected design of the methods with which to apprehend their urban landscapes.

POSITIONING Exhibition of site findings and discussions with peers enable students to develop a critical position towards sites slated for design, professional design works and theoretical literature. Mid-crit exhibition with guest teachers.

IMMERSE Urban landscapes require bodily immersion to capture qualities in both scientific and artistic ways; their interpretation requires critical distance through the study of literature, academic writing and artistic exhibition. Students sorting through site samples and thoughts, in studio.

DESELECTED Regular reviews and changing presentation modes encouraged the students to select, de- and re-select materials gathered on site, a process that helps them to define the most appropriate modes of expression for their research questions. Deselected material on studio floor.

Immersion and intentional serendipity

On-site fieldwork complemented the off-site literature study. In the Thinking Eyes, the students were asked to explore their campus, in the outskirts of Malmö, close to the coast, and surrounded by multiple land uses: a large park, agricultural fields, motorways, country roads, train tracks and scattered built-up terrain ranging from shopping centres and industrial areas to 1960s housing estates and garden city districts. In the Öresundsect, we sent the students out to the same site, to "transect" it along a line from various starting points towards the coast and into the Öresund, the water body between Sweden and Denmark. This provided students with the common experience of walking along a specific route identified on a map that revealed insight into the site's qualities and conflicts. Students also understood that individual discoveries turned out to be different for everyone, and that it was exactly this "biased" difference that raised the next research question.

In the following stage the students were split into groups to define various transects from the Swedish side to the Danish side of the Öresund and to deviate from the defined pathway in order to find what they did not search for—it may seem paradoxical but referring to French urban studies scholar Francois Ascher (2009) this serendipity was intended in that it enabled discoveries that otherwise may have been overlooked. *Learning outcome: Scientific rigour allows students to define methods and scope of site scrutiny, and artistic freedom enables students to embark on deviations during site scrutiny to capture the unexpected and include it into the enquiry.*

IMPRESSIONS Arts-based methods help in grappling site-specific qualities and future-oriented speculations. Drawing, modelling and mini-exhibition of first impressions and samples from site, in studio.

Mediation and epistemic transfers

As findings needed to be transported from the field into the studio in both courses, the students were asked to use a mix of tools stemming from both scientific and artistic exploration: containers and bags for sampling; note books for sketching, notes and statements from interviewees; and smart phones for positioning and itinerary tracking, photographing, filming, recording sound, and for other measurements. These tools would then serve to process the immediate discoveries into mediated findings that could be communicated to those who had not been on-site and then processed into more elaborate expressions through studio work. By changing the media of presentation each week (e.g. handing in drawings, then a film, then a model, then a narrative, then an advertisement poster for that story, then an installation in space), we encouraged the students to select from the collected site material the most relevant findings and media for transfer into a design project, and to motivate their choices. This spurred critical thinking, about how to use different media, what arguments those media would best support, and why.

All students found it hard to combine the two intellectual levels: to express their concrete findings in artistic media while also reflecting what principles these media would forward to the meta-level of design research and knowledge generation. However hard it was, student course evaluations classified these epistemic transfer operations as the most rewarding learning experience.[3] *Learning outcome: transfer from on-site to off-site is never without inherent bias; the media used delimit or allow findings and insights, and the meta-reflection about media spurs critical thinking and evidence-based chain of arguments.*

REFLECTION Students present and proactively discuss their interpretations of the site and resulting designs with an external jury composed of design practitioners and authorities. Exhibition and final student crit in studio.

Insight and decisions

In both courses we asked students to present their final works in the form of an exhibition. In the Thinking Eyes course the students had to propose a strategic design for Alnarp Campus, and in the Öresundsect course students had to develop a landscape narrative about the Öresund region from which design interventions could be derived. The exhibition included all media used during the course, supplemented by an oral presentation by students for invited critics in the exhibition. The exhibition proved to a suitable academic evaluation format that conveyed evidence from the field to support elaborate statements about site qualities and their development into design. *Learning outcome: Site qualities and site-specific design decisions benefit from artistic expression and scientific rigour alike, enabling the public that has not necessarily been on site to understand the arguments of the site researcher/designer and to engage critically with her/his societally relevant position.*

ENGAGEMENT Teachers engage in a learning process that focuses on reformulating questions and redefining methodology. The special exhibition environment stimulates discussion.

4 | Design thinking for unpredictable futures

Design thinking as a conceptual basis for education offers structure to a process in clearly defined steps, without putting a straitjacket on the way in which each step is performed and on the nature of the outcomes the whole endeavour intends to produce. As a method-driven teaching model, design thinking transcends both scientific and artistic traditions. Scientific approaches, prevalent in scientific universities such as SLU, tend to shape educational content according to a "masterplan": data-driven analysis produces clearly defined but sectorial outcomes and little critical reflection about the interrelations of these outcomes with the complex whole of urban landscapes and their future. Artistic approaches, familiar in art and architecture schools, tend to repeat the Beaux Arts "master model": a master's (the teacher's) intuitive approaches to a problem are adopted by the students and steer the process of making scenarios for imagined futures, and this intuition-driven training hinders the tacit knowledge of the "making" being raised onto a level of "thinking" from where insights can be offered as research outcomes. Design thinking-based teaching inflicts academic rigour while leaving freedom for intuition and interpretation. It involves the "making" as much as the "thinking". It is universal while bearing the capacity to be performed ever differently with respect to the specific conditions of a site, a time, a culture. Finally, it is faster than conventional scientific research, and it is more intelligible than typical artistic production. Speed and evidence are *critical* for the forthcoming generation's capacity to tackle urban challenges, including those that are unpredictable today. All sorts of knowledge are needed, and even more urgently needed are methods for how to combine forms of knowledge in transdisciplinary ways. Urban landscapes present a real-world laboratory, and education can serve as experimental research. Our pedagogical experiments confirm what Belgian architect Julian De Smedt noted: "Rather than a definitive direction, our agenda is a definite attitude—of eagerness, enthusiasm, and optimism, of criticality and concern, of fun and inquiry. It is a directive, a motivation to act, at times without clear knowledge of where our agenda will lead" (De Smedt 2009: 1-2).

INSIGHTS How to convey site qualities gathered through personal bodily immersion to an audience that has not been on site? Narrating site experiences in a real scale exhibition.

TAKE-AWAYS Formulating problems in whatever medium best conveys paths towards knowledge. Final exhibition as a takeaway installation.

NOTES

1 To convey this learning process the term "learning outcomes" is used in the following text. Formulating "learning outcomes" is a means to describe the aims of a teaching unit, with respect to the intended increase in knowledge, competences and skills for a course student. Currently built into curricula at SLU and at many universities internationally they reflect a tendency in contemporary pedagogical research to better describe nature, content and intent of training units within a curriculum, and to make progression and evaluation schemes more transparent to colleagues and students. In this chapter the term is used metaphorically to express what the authors themselves have learnt when conceiving, carrying out and evaluating their courses, but also what prompts generalisation and transfer into concrete learning outcomes of forthcoming courses of the same intent.

2 Design Thinking is a method designers use to imagine and realise projects. It describes an iterative process consisting of 5 steps: Empathise, Define, Ideate, Prototype and Test. Design thinking programmes have been run in renowned universities such as Stanford's d.school in the U.S. (https://dschool.stanford.edu), or the Hasso Plattner Institute Potsdam in Europe (https://hpi.de/en/school-of-design-thinking.html).

3 This was clearly conveyed by one exchange student: "This was my first module at SLU Alnarp and quite possibly the best module I have ever taken. I have never worked so hard (I seem to say that every time I do a new module, but this time I really mean it) nor have I been pushed so hard, nor has *so much* been *demanded* of me. The same goes for the rest of my peers. Despite this, or maybe because of this, the Thinking Eyes module was the highlight of my academic year(s). Theory (which I feel is so missing from design education today), literature, design critiques, presentation skills, layout, art, conceptual models, scale models, collage, film, exhibition development and presentation were all key elements of the course. We touched upon all of the above and learned something new (for the first time, or perhaps developed upon existing skills). Thoroughly the most rewarding course I have ever done (…)" (http://peripateticisland.blogspot.com, 8 Jan 2014).

VALUE How to revise value systems and concepts of landscape beauty? Installation about the specific landscape qualities of SLU's Alnarp Campus.

GALLERY Invited critics participate in a full day of floor talks with students in an art gallery-like environment. Student projects encompass various media, both analogue and digital.

REFERENCES

Ascher, F. (2009), *L'age des métapoles* (La Tour d'Aigues: L'Aube)

Barthes, R. (1978), *Lecon. Lecon inaugurale de la Chaire de Sémiologie littéraire du Collège de France* (Paris: Seuil)

Brown, T. (2009), *Change by Design. How Design Thinking Transforms Organisations and Inspires Innovation* (New York: HarperCollins)

De Smedt, Julian (2009), *Agenda* (Barcelona: Actar)

Diedrich, L. et al. (2018, 2015, 2012, 2009, 2006), *Landscape Architecture Europe* (Basel: Birkhäuser/Wageningen: Blauwdruk)

Diedrich, L. and Farsø, M. (2013), *Thinking Eyes. Show me your site specificity* (Alnarp: SLU), unpublished course documentation

Diedrich, L., Lee, G. and Farsø, M. (2013), *Öresundsect. Appropriating site qualities in the Öresund urban landscape* (Alnarp: SLU), unpublished course documentation (download https://oresundsect.wordpress.com/)

Foxley, A. and Vogt, G. (2010), *Distance and Engagement. Walking, Thinking and Making Landscape* (Baden: Lars Müller Publishers)

Lawson, B. and Dorst, K. (2009), *Design Expertise* (Oxford: Elsevier)

Lee, G. and Diedrich, L. (2019), Transareal excursions into landscapes of fragility and endurance: a contemporary interpretation of Alexander von Humboldt's mobile science. In Braae, E. and Steiner, H. (eds) *Routledge Research Companion to Landscape Architecture* (London: Routledge)

Moore, K. (2010), *Overlooking the Visual. Demystifying the Art of Design* (London: Routledge)

Noweski, C. et al. (2012), Towards a paradigm shift in education practice: developing twenty-first century skills with design thinking. In Plattner, H. et al. (eds) *Design Thinking Research* (Berlin/Heidelberg: Springer)

Nowotny, H. and Scott, P. and Gibbons, M. (2001 [2004]), *Re-Thinking Science. Knowledge and the Public in an Age of Uncertainty* (Cambridge: Polity Press)

Nowotny, H. (2008). Designing as Working Knowledge. In Seggern et al. (eds) *Creating Knowledge. Innovationsstrategien im Entwerfen urbaner Landschaften* (Berlin: Jovis), 12-15.

Rittel, H. and Webber M. (1977), *Dilemmas in a general theory of planning* (Stuttgart: IGP)

Seggern, H. v, Werner, J., and Grosse-Bächle, L. (eds) (2008), *Creating Knowledge: Innovationsstrategien im Entwerfen Urbaner Landschaften* (Berlin: Jovis)

Sieverts, T. (2008), Improving the Quality of Fragmented Urban Landscapes—a Global Challenge! In H. v Seggern, J. Werner and L. Grosse-Bächle (eds) *Creating Knowledge. Innovation Strategies for Designing Urban Landscapes* (Berlin: Jovis)

Simon, H. (1996), *The Sciences of the Artificial* (Cambridge: MIT Press)

200

LANDSCAPE HISTORY AND THEORY

Traditionally topics such as history and theory, which are not usually directly associated with education for planning or designing interventions in the landscape, usually tend to be taught in more conventional forms of teaching such as lecture courses or seminars. Here too the use of studio teaching format represents a break with this tradition.

In this section three different approaches to addressing three different aspects of landscape history (and theory) are presented. The themes dealt with here are cultural landscapes, historic landscape design and the history of urban open space. Constructing landscape biographies, working with archival sources and drawing cross-sections are the main methods employed to address the themes concerned.

A collection of photographic records of historic landscapes provided the inspiration for a programme of repeat photography as a means of identifying the transformations which had taken place in the intervening timespan. Bruno Notteboom and Pieter Uyttenhove have used this photographic project as a means of constructing biographies of the landscapes concerned. Students were involved in this process of knowledge production through interviews with specialists on, and users of, the landscapes concerned.

Another collection of a different type forms the basis for the second contribution in this section. This archive of work by Austrian landscape architects from the 20th century provided the basis for considering how it could be made use of in teaching contexts as well as for research. Ulrike Krippner, Lilli Lička and Roland Wuck explain the various ways in which this archival resource has been integrated into a wide range of forms of research-based landscape architecture teaching.

History teaching permeates through different parts of the landscape architecture programme run by the National School of Landscape Architecture at Versailles. The teaching methods described in Bernadette Blachon's chapter are based on preparing and analysing sections at different scales through selected parts of the urban fabric in order to highlight the mutual interrelationships between buildings and open spaces. The objects for study are provided by housing schemes planned and designed within the Paris region from the beginning of the 20th century until today.

Recollecting Landscapes:
teaching and making landscape biographies

Bruno Notteboom, Pieter Uyttenhove

One of the challenges of teaching landscape is how to address the vernacular landscape: the ever-changing landscape that is shaped through an accumulation of day-to-day alterations by people who live and work in it. It is much easier to focus on what J.B. Jackson has called 'political landscapes': landscape archetypes, coherent designs determined by power, ideology or religion (Jackson 1984). The formation of these landscapes can be explained as the result of a succession of interventions by one or more identifiable *authors* (the Jeffersonian grid, the picturesque park, the highway system, the urban square, the ecological corridor et cetera). But how do we teach students how to read landscapes in a context in which authorship is not so easily identifiable, in which a myriad of actors is at play, 'designing' the landscape from below as well as from above? In D.W. Meinig's seminal essay collection *The Interpretation of Ordinary Landscapes* (1979), geographer Marwyn Samuels coined the term 'landscape biography' as a way of understanding the role of individuals and particularities in the development of landscapes over time. Such a landscape biography would avoid generalizations by including individual experience and narratives (Samuels 1979). The idea of the landscape biography was recently brought back to the attention by heritage researchers who want to give a voice to history, memory and relevant societal actors when thinking about the future development of the landscape (Bosma & Kolen 2010, Kolen et al. 2013).

This chapter deals with Recollecting Landscapes, an on-going rephotographic survey documenting a century of landscape transformation in Flanders that can be considered as such a biographic project. It aims at redirecting our attention to the gradual transformation of landscapes, authored by its inhabitants as much as by designers, planners, engineers or policy makers (Notteboom & Uyttenhove 2018). Focusing on sixty landscapes photographed in the early twentieth century, 1980, 2004 and 2014, the project gives an insight into the mechanisms of landscape transformation between large-scale interventions and everyday changes: the continuous re-allotment of agricultural land; sprawling habitation and economic activities; the construction of infrastructure large and small; nature destruction, preservation and expansion; informal and temporary occupation of residual spaces et cetera. Through a series snapshots spread out in time and space, Recollecting Landscapes records the evolution of one of the most densely urbanized regions in Europe, a rural-urban continuum shaped by a shared but often conflicting authorship. In contrast to maps, (re)photographic images prove to be an outstanding medium to understand the complexity of the contemporary (urban) landscape. The landscape image is created by an embedded viewpoint of the photographer (and the viewer) and includes details that are lacking in the codified map.

Recollecting Landscapes is not only a tool to teach students (and the audience at large) about landscape by explaining its evolution, it is also co-produced with students. The foundations for the project were laid in the early 1980s by the National Botanic Garden of Belgium and the Belgian Nature and Bird Sanctuaries, who published a commented rephotography of sixty landscapes, a selection out of a series of landscapes photographed in the early twentieth century by Jean Massart, professor of botany at the Université Libre de Bruxelles (Free University of Brussels) (Vanhecke et al. 1981). The initial rephotography aimed at demonstrating the decline of biodiversity, mainly due to the upscaling of agriculture and the disappearance of small-scale landscape elements. Hence the images were exclusively interpreted by specialists in the field of botany. The two most recent rephotographic stages (2004 and 2014), on the contrary, originated in a different disciplinary context and field of interest. Guided by Labo S, the Laboratory for Urbanism of Ghent University and initially supported by the Flemish Architecture Institute, the scope of the project broadened to a general interest in all aspects of landscape transformation, including architecture, landscape architecture, urban planning and infrastructure, but also vernacular ways of dealing with the landscape by non-designers: small-scale agricultural amenities, gardens and spontaneous developments such as vegetation on wastelands (Fig. 1). The research resulted in two books (one in Dutch after the rephotography of 2004 and one in English after the most recent rephotography) (Uyttenhove et al. 2006, Notteboom & Uyttenhove 2018), two exhibitions and a website (www.recollectingland-scapes.be) communicating the research in Dutch as well as in English.

The student as producer of knowledge

Although for docents these media provide a useful aid in ex-cathedra landscape (history) classes, the exchange of knowledge works in two directions: students have also been involved in the production of information generated by the images. Over a period of more than a decade, research seminars and master theses helped to actively produce the knowledge base created around the expanding series of images of Recollecting Landscapes.[1] In the research seminars, groups of students each focused on one specific landscape, which they were asked to address from two angles. A first angle was the perspective of the specialist: among others, biologists, agricultural scientists, policy experts, urban planners and designers were interviewed, explaining the transformation visualized in the image series. The second angle was that of the users: students went on the spot to talk to inhabitants, farmers and passers-by, revealing the micro-histories and narratives attached to specific places. For example, in the case of a landscape that was transformed from a productive agricultural landscape into a recreational landscape by the owner of a manege, interviews with inhabitants brought to the fore problems of 'visual appropriation' of the landscape.

Figure 1
Opwijk, small farmstead
Jean Massart (1911)
Georges Charlier (1980)
Jan Kempenaers (2003)
and Michiel De Cleene (2014)

The series illustrates the evolution of a relatively poor agricultural village to a village of commuters. A part of the orchard was replaced by an open storage shed, next to a manure heap covered with plastic and car tyres. This type of 'messiness' is typical for small agricultural businesses which remained small and diversified over time, and contrasts with the 'sanitization' of those business that expanded and specialized. Today, the house is replaced by a new construction, and the barn will soon be demolished to enlarge the garden.

Figure 2
Zonnebeke (Geluveld), Oude Zonnebekestraat
Jean Massart (1911)
Georges Charlier (1980)
Jan Kempenaers (2003)
Michiel De Cleene (2014)

A row of trees disappears after the two World Wars and the post-war process of upscaling of agriculture, a process that made many landscape elements disappear. Recently, a wealthy businessman bought the land in order to establish a manege. He replanted the trees and planted hedges, which blocks the view and divided the land both visually and physically.

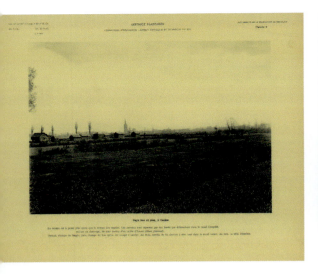

Figure 3 Eeklo
Jean Massart (1911)
Georges Charlier (1980)
Jan Kempenaers (2003)
Michiel De Cleene (2014).

Agricultural evolutions keep altering the landscape. The labour-intensive flax cultures of the early twentieth century (we see labourers on their knees in the distance) have made place for pasture land, alternated with maize that blocks the view. In the more recent stages, vegetation became more diverse, visualized for example the by reed in between the maize and the meadow). This change is driven by a less extensive grazing on the meadows itself, as kettle-breeding becomes a more industrialized and hence more indoor-based activity.

Figure 4 **Klemskerke**
Jean Massart (1908)
Georges Charlier (1980)
Jan Kempenaers (2004)
Michiel De Cleene (2014)

Massart photographed a landscape at the inland edge of the dunes, characterized by intensive cultivation on parcels with poor soils. The landscape is divided by hedgerows that served as windbreaks, were a source of firewood and kept the blowing sand away from the fields. This landscape was gradually taken over by mass tourism as the owners of the farm sold their land. The houses on the foreground illustrate a typically Belgian dwelling culture that is based on private home-ownership and a self-building and renovating economy.

Figure 5 Antwerp (Lillo),
right bank of the river Scheldt
Jean Massart (1904)
Georges Charlier (1980)
Jan Kempenaers (2003)
Michiel De Cleene (2014)

The Galgenschoor is historically a muddy area, flooded in the event of heavy seas. Today it is a protected nature reserve in the harbour of Antwerp. Changes at the horizon (shrouded in mist in the last image) reveal the massive development of infrastructure over the last century, in the form of harbour infrastructure and a nuclear power plant. The two recent images also show the continuous battle against reforestation as part of the nature management plan of the nature reserve, which will become part of an ecological network throughout the harbour, which is now under development.

The reluctance towards fences and hedges were in this case considered as too invasive in the open landscape. This is an interesting finding which actually goes against the general assumption that beautification by 're-hedging' is what people want (Fig. 2). The interviews were complemented by other sources that further developed the landscape biographies, ranging from publications and archives of local history associations, over geographical atlases, to a broad array of literature on the social, cultural, economical and agricultural development of the landscape under study. The resulting biographies were summarized in the books and on the website in the form of captions accompanying each photo-set. In addition, in a series of master theses, the landscape biographies of a selection of landscapes was further substantiated. These played a prominent role as more elaborate case study chapters in the books.

An advantage of this method of teaching is its capacity to activate the student in the sense that (s)he also produces, and not only consumes knowledge. However, this is also the case when writing a paper in a 'classical' landscape history class. More important, perhaps, is that working with photographic images as a first 'entry' into the landscape, and working with interviews of both experts and inhabitants make students aware of the complexity of landscape transformation and its authorship. During the process of making the biography, students step literally in and out of the landscape and alternate an embedded social, cultural and emotional experience of the inhabitants with the more distant experience of the expert. Another reason why this method can contribute to landscape teaching is that it works cross-scale, from the detail to the extent of the landscape as a whole, and beyond to the global scale. Being asked to interpret each element within the frame of the photographic image, students become aware of the effects of the entanglement of micro and macro stories. For example, an image series of the fields near Eeklo that shows in detail the specific consequences of evolving cultivation and cattle-breeding methods, and changes in agricultural areas over time, constitutes an entry to a broader understanding of agro-economical evolutions in the region (Fig. 3). Or in the series shot in Klemskerke, the story of a family farm and the gradual sell-out of its land embodies the macro-history of the rise of consumption society, the democratisation of recreation and its effects on the Belgian coast in the course of the twentieth century (Fig. 4).

Trying to conceptualize what kind of instrument for knowledge production the Recollecting Landscapes books and website can be, we refer to Stefano Boeri's concept of the 'eclectic atlas' (Boeri 1998) as an instrument of gathering different types of information: photographic, textual, maps, schemes, sections et cetera. However, these case studies differ methodologically from the eclectic atlases, in the sense that Recollecting Landscapes starts in the first place from (series of) photographic images, to address the map only as a secondary source of information. If we consider Recollecting Landscapes from the perspective of the landscape biography, it is a biography that looks to both the past and the future: the record of the visual transformation of the landscape over time, allows students also to think prospectively, and not only in terms of a historical biography of the landscape. Understanding the mechanisms of landscape transformation and the role of different actors therein makes it possible to project future images of this unwritten scenario of the landscape. In several research seminars, students were asked to project a future image of the landscape, based on the preceding stages, which resulted in an imaginary continuation of the photo series and even films (Figs. 5 and 6). This prospective position helps students to explore their role as a designer in a landscape that is on the one hand determined by sudden, planned interventions, but on the other hand seems to produce itself without the help of any designer. In this sense Recollecting Landscapes not only creates a knowledge base for students, but is also a pedagogical project that develops new forms of education in between research and design.

Figure 6 Students in 2004 created a future image that predicts the further urbanization and development of the nuclear plant along the river Scheldt near Antwerp, along with a domestication of nature and infrastructure.

Figure 7 Excursion to the Belgian coast, guided by Jean Massart (1912). Source: Massart J. (1912). 'La 50e herborisation de la Société Royale Belge de Botanique. Sur le littoral Belge.' Bulletin de la Société Royale Belge de Botanique (51): 70-185.

Figure 8 Analogue photographic material in the 'archive' volume at the Recollecting Landscapes exhibition of 2006-2007.

Figure 9 Digital photographic material, documentary films and website inside the 'classroom' volume at the Recollecting Landscapes exhibition of 2006-2007.

Crossing the walls of the classroom

Recollecting Landscapes was developed within the walls of academia. However, the multiple media and forums that were involved in its presentation and discussion aim at fostering a dialogue with society. The project led not only to two books and a website. Also two exhibitions, accompanied by lectures and debates, (one in the contemporary art museum SMAK in Ghent in 2006-2007, and one in deSingel International Arts Campus in Antwerp in 2015, hosted by the Flemish Architecture Institute), propelled the work of students and researchers into society. Historically, this dialogue between science and society was encoded in the project from the early start. The image archive of biology professor Jean Massart, that lies at the basis of this project, was developed as a scientific as well as a pedagogical tool. The large-scale (30x40 cm) plates of his photographic album Les aspects de la végétation en Belgique (Massart & Bommer 1908, 1912) provided a didactic and systematic overview of the Belgian geobotanical regions. Massart used them primarily for university teaching; however, they were also used in the context of secondary education, particularly in agricultural schools. Massart, from a humble background himself, was active in popular education by means of numerous lectures all over the country and by special university courses at the ULB aimed at the middle and working classes.[2] Apart from his scientific atlases, he published numerous popularizing books, articles, tourist guides and similar material. He was also one of the first botanists of his generation who pleaded for the observation of living organisms in their environment, and he preferred to send everyone who followed his classes on the terrain for direct observation (Fig. 7).

The popularizing goal was continued in the first rephotography in 1980. The first rephotographic book, which preceded the actual Recollecting Landscapes project and was published by the National Botanic Garden of Belgium and the Belgian Nature and Bird Sanctuaries (Vanhecke et al. 1981), was accompanied by a series of photo-exhibitions in cultural centres all over the country. In the most recent exhibitions, curated by Labo S, the research material produced by students and researchers was also made accessible on different levels (Figs. 8 and 9). The familiarity of the images of vernacular landscapes as such proved to attract a large crowd. However, for those visitors who wanted to dive deeper into the landscape biographies, documentary films were on display, and also the website could be consulted in the exhibition. We argued before that Recollecting Landscapes moves back and forth between different archetypical spaces of knowledge production, storage and display, both inside and outside of academia: the archive, the exhibition space and the classroom (Notteboom 2011). Perhaps we should add a fourth space: the landscape itself, in which students and researchers are immersed in the materiality of the landscape, considering it as a palimpsest that is the result of actions by different types of actors. Sending students out of the classroom into the landscape transforms them from passive consumers into active producers of knowledge (and eventually, designers). However, even with the integration of contemporary technologies such as a website, a challenge remains for a project such as Recollecting Landscapes and also for landscape teaching and research in general. Indeed, the creation of landscape biographies and spaces of knowledge production should open up to other voices than those of teachers, researchers, students and specialists: voices from outside of academia of those who actually shape the landscape and induce both vernacular and political landscape transformations.

REFERENCES

Boeri, S. (1998), 'The Italian landscape: towards an "eclectic atlas"', in G. Basilico and S. Boeri Stefano (eds.), Italy. Cross Sections of a Country (Zürich: Scalo).

Bosma, K., Kolen, J. (eds.) (2010), Geschiedenis en ontwerp. Een handboek voor de omgang met cultureel erfgoed (Nijmegen: Uitgeverij Vantilt).

Jackson, J.B. (1984), 'A Pair of Ideal Landscapes', in Jackson, J.B. Discovering the Vernacular Landscape (Yale University Press: New Haven Conn.).

Kolen, J., Renes H. and Hermans, R. (2013), Landscape Biographies: Geographical, Historical and Archaeological Perspectives on the Production and Transmission of Landscapes (Amsterdam: Amsterdam University Press).

Massart, J. and C. Bommer (1908), Les aspects de la végétation en Belgique. Les districts littoraux et alluviaux (Brussels, Jardin Botanique de l'État / Ministère de l'Intérieur et de l'Agriculture).

Massart, J. and C. Bommer (1912), Les aspects de la végétation en Belgique. Les districts flandrien et campinien (Brussels, Jardin Botanique de l'État / Ministère de l'Intérieur et de l'Agriculture).

Notteboom, B. (2009), 'Ouvrons les yeux!' Stedenbouw en beeldvorming van het landschap in België 1890-1940 (doctoral dissertation) (Ghent: Ghent University).

Notteboom, B. (2011), Recollecting Landscapes: Landscape Photography as a Didactic Tool', Architectural Research Quarterly 15/ 1, 47-55.

Notteboom, B., Uyttenhove, P., et al. (2018), Recollecting Landscapes. Rephotography, Memory and Transformation 1904-1980-2004-2014 (Amsterdam: Roma Publishers).

Samuels, M. S. (1979), 'The Biography of Landscape. Cause and Culpability', in Meinig, D.W., The Interpretation of Ordinary Landscapes (Oxford: Oxford University Press).

Uyttenhove, P. (ed.), Vanbelleghem, D., Van Bouwel, I., Notteboom, B., Debergh, R. and Willequet, B. (2006), Recollecting landscapes: herfotografie, geheugen en transformatie 1904-1980-2004 (Ghent: A&S/Books).

Vanhecke, L., Charlier, G. et al. (1981), Landschappen in Vlaanderen vroeger en nu. Van groene armoede naar grijze overvloed (Meise / Brussels, Nationale Plantentuin van België / vzw Belgische Natuur- en Vogelreservaten).

www.recollectinglandscapes.be

NOTES

1 Research seminars and master theses guided by the authors at the Department of Architecture and Urban Planning of Ghent Uyniveristy, with the exception of one research seminar guided by Bruno Notteboom in his course Landscape Urbanism at KU Leuven, Faculty of Architecture.

2 Within the framework of the so-called Extension de l'Université Libre de Bruxelles, a people's university organized by the ULB (Notteboom 2009: 83-84).

Learning from history:
integrating an archive in landscape teaching

Ulrike Krippner, Lilli Lička, Roland Wück

Landscape architecture is a hugely complex profession to teach and learn. Practical skills as well as spatial and artistic understandings go along with a deep knowledge of society, culture, science, engineering, and the landscape. Teaching and learning is about changing the student's conceptions of the world (Ramsden 2003), which correlates with Dianne Harris's understanding of recent landscape history as a history of landscapes with multiple spatial, social, and process-related contexts (Harris 1999).

This paper discusses the potentials of integrating an archive of landscape architecture into landscape teaching and research. Although still in progress, this archive provides very valuable material and data on Austrian landscape architecture of the twentieth century, which we use in selected courses, ranging from undergraduate to postgraduate level. A close examination of recent landscape projects, principles, techniques, and discourses fosters a comprehensive perception of the contemporary landscape architecture and its challenges.

The teaching–research nexus

At the Institute of Landscape Architecture (ILA) at the University of Natural Resources and Life Sciences (BOKU), Vienna, teaching is understood as a collaborative process between students and tutors. Students are encouraged and guided to extend their curiosity and to develop their own appetite for enhancing their experience, skills, and knowledge. This aim goes along with the university's principle of stipulating a strong connection between research and teaching, which includes learning by research as well as learning about research and learning research outcomes (first-hand).

According to Hughes (2005: 15), research-guided teaching and research-guided learning are related to one other 'context-specifically'. Scholars, tutors, and students address similar questions concerning the multifaceted structure of the profession. This nexus could be a clue to advancing knowledge. The most common perception of the teaching–research nexus is the transfer of findings to students, but Healey (2005) and Roberts (2007) show that the relationship is more complex and offers strategies that are either student-focused or teacher-focused and put their emphasis on either research content or research processes (Fig. 1).

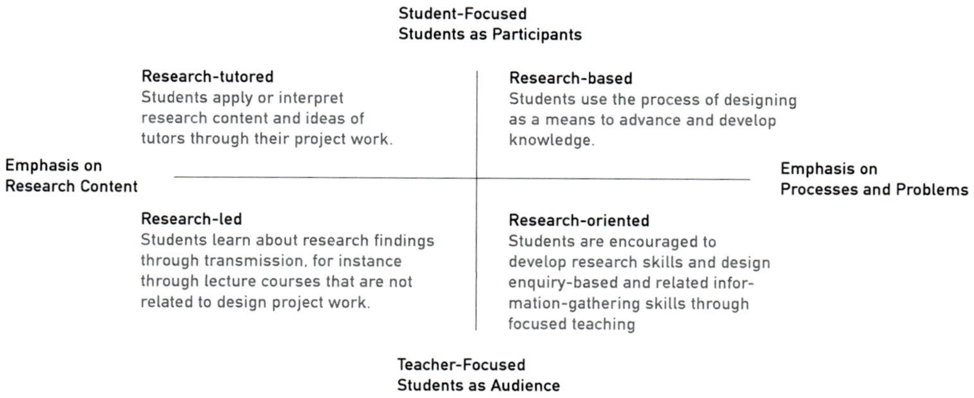

Student-Focused
Students as Participants

Research-tutored
Students apply or interpret research content and ideas of tutors through their project work.

Research-based
Students use the process of designing as a means to advance and develop knowledge.

Emphasis on Research Content

Emphasis on Processes and Problems

Research-led
Students learn about research findings through transmission, for instance through lecture courses that are not related to design project work.

Research-oriented
Students are encouraged to develop research skills and design enquiry-based and related information-gathering skills through focused teaching

Teacher-Focused
Students as Audience

Figure 1 Roberts's design-focused version of Healey's model of the teaching-research nexus. (Roberts 2007: 16)

In the field of landscape architecture both teaching and research deal with designed landscapes and their historic record and importance. Other issues to be tackled are designs and designers, their personalities, approaches, and techniques, since, as Mareis states, 'the focus of an epistemological design analysis is no longer traditional design criteria such as "form" or "function". Instead design practices, objects, tools, institutions, and designers themselves become central components in a complex epistemic structure' (Mareis 2010: 11–12). This shift is similar to the development in landscape history that today addresses questions of 'how, why and by whom landscapes were created, constructed, used, perceived, received and how they were related to wider social, political and cultural forces' (Dümpelmann 2011: 627). This supports the overall intention to encourage a holistic understanding of landscape architecture as a continuous process—a process in which contemporary interpretations of landscape projects form the basis for future developments.

Using LArchiv as a tool for teaching

This understanding motivated us to establish the Austrian Landscape Architecture Archive (LArchiv) in 2007 in order to collect, analyse, and discuss documents and data on the Austrian landscape history of the twentieth and twenty-first centuries. An analogue collection covers plans, written documents, photos, prints, and slides relating to projects by Albert Esch, Josef Oskar Wladar, Friedrich Woess, and the firm KoseLička. We also have a unique collection of manuscripts, images, drawings, and photos, which Friedrich Woess designed and made during his thirty-five years of teaching at BOKU Vienna. As Woess was the key person fostering and implementing landscape architecture on the academic level, his collection can give a valuable insight into the development of academic training in Austria during the twentieth century. A digital inventory contains data concerning training, professional organizations, historical publications, and work assignments as well as individual biographies (Fig. 2). In our globalized world, digital databases seem to be an appropriate means to gather scattered information and make it commonly available.

We strive to use the archive as an innovative teaching tool in order to foster exploration and a comprehensive understanding of landscape and its design. As part of this aim, we have formulated three goals to be achieved by intertwining research activities—archival

LArchiv

ANALOGUE COLLECTION	DIGITAL INVENTORY
Albert Esch (1883–1954)	530 biographies of landscape architects
Josef Oskar Wladar (1900–2002)	1,435 landscape projects
Hans Grubbauer (1900–1974)	1,410 publications
Eduard Maria Ihm (1904–1971)	50 training institutions
Viktor Mödlhammer (1905–1999)	78 professional organizations
Gertrud Kraus (1915–2013)	
Friedrich Woess (1915–1995)	
Hermann Kern (1935–2017)	
KoseLička (1991–2016)	

Figure 2 **Structure and scope of LArchiv (as of 15 September 2017).**

work, historical research, and interpretation—with the teaching of landscape architecture and design (Fig. 3): first, to raise awareness about historical continuity by enhancing students' knowledge of pioneers in the field and their biographies and work as well as an understanding of landscape history and discourse; second, to improve skills and knowledge relating to techniques, styles, assignments, and archival work; and third, to increase accessibility and encourage students to consult an archive and integrate history into the everyday working processes of landscape architecture. While raising awareness of landscape history is an overall goal in all courses, efforts to communicate the other two objectives are adapted to the character and level of education. Classes at different levels focus on one or the other item in accordance with the students' experience in and understanding of landscape architecture and history.

Moreover, we carefully select adequate teaching strategies from the fourfold model of the teaching–research nexus in order to respond to the students' evolving knowledge (Fig. 1). Undergraduate courses face the challenge of communicating a broad load of basic knowledge in a short time and thus mainly follow research-led strategies. In contrast, graduate and postgraduate courses offer opportunities for actively integrating students into the research process and for using research-based and research-oriented strategies.

Courses integrating LArchiv as a tool for teaching

Ten years after the first attempts to set up LArchiv, we have now established a solid archival structure and compiled a remarkable amount of material and data. Originally conceived merely as a tool for research, we have now started to integrate LArchiv into our teaching. Courses in landscape history only start in the master's programme at BOKU Vienna. Nevertheless, we aim to introduce landscape history and the archive into undergraduate courses at a very basic level too. It is, of course, the best strategy to involve as many instructors as possible in order to raise awareness, regardless of whether they are offering a lecture or seminar.

Even for research-led teaching strategies, an archive provides thorough information on projects and landscape architects when preparing field trips, design courses, or lectures on landscape architecture and history. Data retrieved from an archive can even be used for project-based learning in classes that are not obviously connected to history, like CAD or

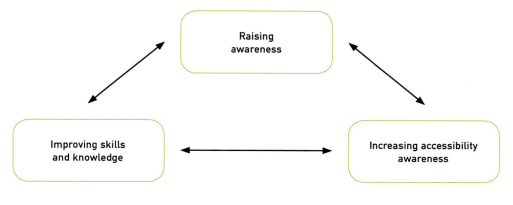

Figure 3 **Goals for intertwining teaching with historical research activities.**

Goals for intertwining teaching with historical research activities	Undergraduate courses		Master courses			Postgraduate
	CAD	Thesis	Drawing courses	Restoration and management	Thesis	PhD thesis
Raising awareness	X	X	X	X	X	X
Improving skills and knowledge	X	X	X	X	X	X
Increasing accessibility		X		X	X	X

Figure 4 **Courses integrating LArchiv as a tool for teaching.**

design classes. Working on modern or postmodern landscape projects that are now in danger of being destroyed or redesigned can be a challenge for landscape design courses. In addition to these content-focused strategies, an archive may be used for research-oriented teaching to help impart skills and knowledge relating to archival work and may also be employed for the analysis of projects and personalities and the development of educational content as a means to inculcate a comprehensive understanding of the profession.

So far we have adapted a number of courses, which effectively work with archival material and/or use the digital inventory as a research tool for gathering data on the Austrian landscape architecture of the twentieth century (Fig. 4).

Drawing courses in the undergraduate and master programme

In our undergraduate courses on computer-aided design (CAD), we need projects to work on: these are seen as 'working knowledge' according to Helga Nowotny (2008), who transferred Pickstone's definition (2007) from the humanities to landscape design. For example, the CAD advanced course teaches students to apply CAD in different stages of the design process (presentation plans, technical plans, sections, technical details, planting

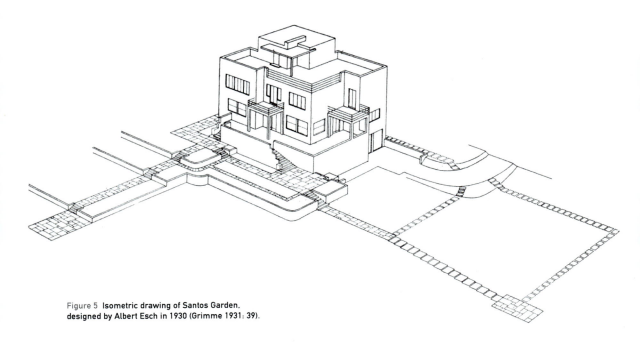

Figure 5 Isometric drawing of Santos Garden, designed by Albert Esch in 1930 (Grimme 1931: 39).

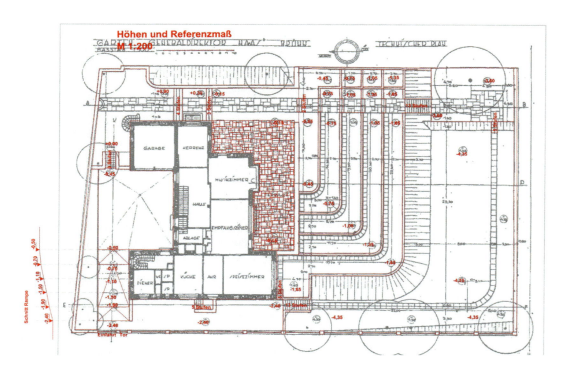

Figure 6 Technical plan of Haas Garden, designed by Albert Esch in 1930 (Grimme 1931: 39) with red reference lines, which we added to help students decipher the historical drawing.

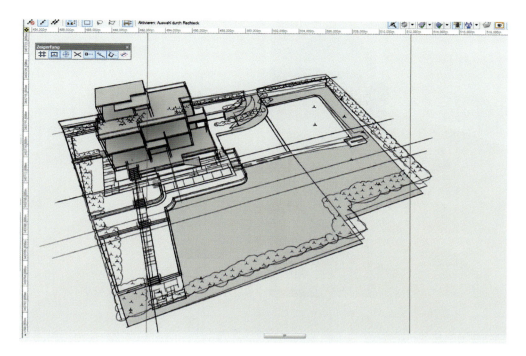

Figure 7 Computer-aided 3D plan of Santos Garden (drawing: Vigil Peer, 2017).

Figure 8 Computer-aided presentation plan of Santos Garden (drawing: Vigil Peer, 2017).

Figure 9 **Students at a drawing course, 2017.**

plans). Instead of working on well-known contemporary projects, like the Highline in New York, we provide plans from landscape architects like Albert Esch or Josef Oskar Wladar, who offer a varied oeuvre for us to draw on. We start every project by vectorizing and digitizing hand-drawn plans, which we overlay with plans of the site using open-source data maps (Figs. 5 to 8). This requires precise observation of the material, because the graphic style and the meaning of the signs must be decoded. Sometimes there is a need for interpretation or explanation, in discussion with the teacher, because the plans do not show all the necessary information (Fig. 6). This involves comparison and analysis, which might then lead to an expanded understanding of the project's context.

Following a similar research-led strategy, in spring 2017 Thaïsa Way used archive material in her guest course on drawing in order to 'explore and understand the role of drawing in the emergence of landscape architecture as a practice and a profession' (Way 2017). In the drawing sessions, students of the master's programme examined and analysed in detail a variety of plans and perspectives produced by Albert Esch, Josef Oskar Wladar, and Friedrich Woess (Fig. 9). Students were asked to reflect on the author's intention and to copy sections in the author's style. They were also to sketch and interpret sections in their own style. Adding colours, patterns, shades, or people to the historical drawings animated the students to think about drawing as a tool for visualization and representation (Figs. 10 to 12). Discussions in class explored questions of style and personal handwriting as well as of material, techniques, and colouring for both the landscape architects and the students. At a time when many designers only draw digitally, examining handwritten plans and perspectives through sketching encourages the students 'to inquire into the role of research in drawing and design thinking' (Way 2017).

The location of LArchiv at our institute ensures quick access to material and makes its implementation in the courses very easy. Awareness starts with the process of studying the biographies and works of local landscape architects, whom students do not usually find in international publications. Working out the technical details from other periods and comparing them with today's standards deepens our understanding of the materials, the tools of the trade, and the profession. Archives in the professional context also allow research to be carried out on the impact of international trends at the local level.

Exploration and analysis in master courses

As mentioned above, we teach landscape history courses in the master's programme.

We have a rich research experience when it comes to recent Austrian history, ranging from the 1920s to the 1960s. Research results have been transferred into LArchiv, so that we can now draw on this data and material in our landscape history courses. However, faced with the challenge to communicate the entirety of landscape history from ancient to modern times in one semester, we can only work on a research-led basis, communicating our research findings in intensive ex cathedra lectures (Fig. 13).

The methodological strategy shifts from being teacher-focused to student-focused for a course on historic landscape preservation and management. We have recently redrafted the aim and didactic programme of this course, which will start in spring 2018. Within the new concept, students will focus on post-World War II landscape architecture in Austria in order to learn about recent trends, projects, and design attitudes. Besides this, they will experience and test a tool for identifying the landscape heritage, a field manual on landscape architecture of the 1950s and 1960s compiled by a German research team (Butenschön et al. 2016). After a general introduction to landscape architecture of the 1950s and 1960s, students will be asked to identify landscape projects of that time in major towns near their family home using the field manual (Fig. 14). Students will explore, classify, and assess projects and contextualize them by using information on Austrian landscape architecture of that time (biographies, projects, discourse, publications) provided by LArchiv. In turn, the students' findings will be included in the inventory of landscape projects in Austria, and thus help to advance and develop knowledge.

Nowadays post-World War II landscape projects are in great danger of slow decay, clandestine destruction, or redesign (Bredenbek 2013: 9–10). We want to engage the students in a comprehensive discussion on the cultural assessment of these landscapes, and their development and management, in order to understand the professional roots, attitudes, and principles underlying them and to raise awareness of the cultural value of these sites.

Archival research within theses

A collection of data and documents further develops the research–teaching nexus, as Healey suggests (Healey 2005: 78). Following a research-based strategy, LArchiv operates as a pool to generate research questions for theses on several levels. A recent bachelor thesis investigated the history of the Blindengarten, designed by Josef Oskar Wladar and Viktor Mödlhammer in 1958 in Vienna (Figs. 15 and 16). The student retrieved data from LArchiv to contextualize the historical project and gained experience of archival and field research in order to assess the status quo in comparison with the historical design.

At an advanced level, students contribute significantly to research when they uncover material that is so far unedited. The collection of a professional landscape architect provides documents and other archival proofs to trace down, analyse, and describe the development of the profession across a working lifetime. The core focus is on the historical continuity of changes in work and contexts. In her PhD thesis, Anja Seliger sorted, classified, and examined the collection of Josef Oskar Wladar, spanning the period from the 1930s to the 1980s (Fig. 17). This is of mutual benefit to both the archive and the student: the student adds a thoroughly inventoried and analysed set of archival material to the archive and contributes new findings to landscape history, while also gaining experience of archival work, which has increasing relevance in landscape practice and research (Powers and Walker 2009: 105). The three learning outcomes of this research-based process are achieved almost as a side effect: the threshold for consulting an archive is done away with; an awareness of historical continuity is generated by the PhD student and enhanced by publications; and the student becomes a skilled archival worker.

Figures 10, 11 and 12 **Analyses of Josef Oskar Wladar's design of the Spritzer Garden, 1937 (drawings: Rita Engl, 2017).**

Figure 13 Jewish cemetery at Vienna's Central Cemetery, designed by Helene Wolf in 1928 (Architektur und Bautechnik. 17/5: 70).

Figure 14 Spa garden in Baden designed by Viktor Mödlhammer in 1967.

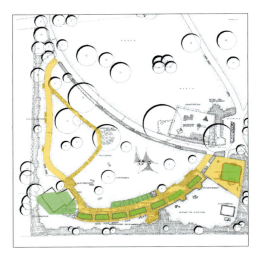
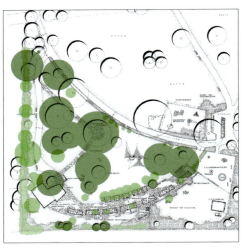

Figure 15 Survey of paving and architectural structures at Blindengarten, Vienna, designed by Josef Oskar Wladar in 1958 (Bachelor thesis, Jennifer Fischer, 2015).

Figure 16 Survey of vegetation at Blindengarten, Vienna, designed by Josef Oskar Wladar in 1958 (Bachelor thesis, Jennifer Fischer, 2015).

Figure 17 Freeway, Schnarrendorf section, designed by Josef Oskar Wladar in 1957 (LArchiv, Archive of Austrian Landscape Architecture, University of Natural Resources and Life Sciences BOKU, Vienna).

Conclusions

These first attempts to integrate LArchiv into teaching are promising. Students and instructors were enthusiastic about exploring the material and landscape history of twentieth-century Austria. In investigating historical documents and data, students learn about local history and experience the complex structure of landscape architecture in the context of sociopolitical developments and trends in culture and art. This engagement fosters an understanding of the social impact of the profession. Moreover, classes encourage the students to reflect on their own design attitudes, techniques, and styles.

Integrating LArchiv into teaching seems to be an appropriate way of raising students' awareness of landscape history and the profession of landscape architecture, of improving skills and knowledge and making the task of working with archival material more accessible. This strategy is suitable for students—as well as for teacher-focused courses. Our experience of this approach encourages us to further strengthen the teaching–research nexus and to integrate LArchiv into our teaching in accordance with Ramsden's insight that learning is about changing students' conceptions of landscape architecture and history.

REFERENCES

Bredenbeck, M. (ed.)(2013), *Grün modern – Gärten und Parks der 1950er bis 1970er Jahre: Ein Kulturerbe als Herausforderung für Denkmalpflege und Vermittlungsarbeit* (Bonn: Bund Heimat und Umwelt in Deutschland BHU).

Butenschön, S., et al. (2016), *Öffentliche Grünanlagen der 1950er- und 1960er-Jahre: Qualitäten neu entdecken; Leitfaden zum Erkennen typischer Merkmale des Stadtgrüns der Nachkriegsmoderne* (Berlin: Universitätsverlag TU Berlin).

Dümpelmann, S. (2011), 'Taking Turns: Landscape and Environmental History at the Crossroads', *Landscape Research* 36/6: 625–40.

Fischer, J. (2015), Der Blindengarten im Wertheimsteinpark. Der Umgang mit historischen Gärten der Nachkriegszeit, unpublished bachelor thesis (University of Natural Resources and Life Sciences BOKU Vienna).

Grimme, K. (1931), *Gärten von Albert Esch* (Vienna: Winkler).

Harris, D. (1999), 'The Postmodernization of Landscape: A Critical Historiography', *Journal of the Society of Architectural Historians* 58/3: 434–43.

Healey, M. (2005), 'Linking Research and Teaching: Disciplinary Spaces', in R. Barnett (ed.), *Reshaping the University: New Relationships between Research, Scholarship and Teaching* (Maidenhead: McGraw-Hill/ Open University Press), 67–78.

Hopstock, L. and Schönwälder, K. (2013), 'Gedächtnis einer akademischen Disziplin', *Stadt+Grün* 62/2: 34–39.

Hughes, M. (2005), 'The Mythology of Research and Teaching Relationships in Universities', in R. Barnett (ed.), *Reshaping the University: New Relationships between Research,*

Scholarship and Teaching (Maidenhead: McGraw-Hill/ Open University Press), 14–26.

Karn, S., Nater, B., and Schubert, B. (2012), '30 Jahre Archiv für Schweizer Landschaftsarchitektur', *Anthos* 51/2: 8–11.

Mareis, C. (2010), 'Entwerfen – Wissen – Produzieren: Designforschung im Anwendungskontext', in C. Mareis, G. Joost, and K. Kimpel (eds.), *Entwerfen – Wissen – Produzieren: Designforschung im Anwendungskontext* (Bielefeld: transcript), 9–32.

Nowotny, H. (2008), 'Designing as Working Knowledge', in H. Seggern (ed.), *Creating Knowledge: Innovation Strategies for Designing Urban Landscapes* (Berlin: Jovis), 12–15.

Pickstone, J. V. (2007), 'Working Knowledges before and after Circa 1800: Practices and Disciplines in the History of Science, Technology, and Medicine', *Isis* 98/3: 489–516.

Powers, M. N. and Walker, J. B. (2009), 'Twenty-Five Years of Landscape Journal: An Analysis of Authorship and Article Content', *Landscape Journal* 28/1: 96–110.

Ramsden, P. (2003), *Learning to Teach in Higher Education* (New York/London: Routledge/Falmer).

Roberts, A. (2007), 'The Link between Research and Teaching in Architecture', *Journal for Education in the Built Environment*, 2/2: 3–20.

Way, T. (2017), Drawing and the Emergence of Landscape Architecture, unpublished syllabus (University of Natural Resources and Life Sciences BOKU Vienna).

Teaching the history of urban open space using a multi-scale approach

Bernadette Blanchon

Introduction

This module is part of the humanities department; it includes lectures in landscape architecture and urban history, reading reference books and group tutorial works which is mainly developed in this paper and called here 'History Workshop'. The aim of the module is to provide students with references relating to landscape urbanism, to raise awareness of the role and potential of the dimension of history for current issues in order to provide them with the skills to deploy such data in their own projects.

History teaching on the ENSP curriculum

Our module intends to give priority, in terms of content, method, and tools, to links with the teaching of project training (studios). The link between theoretical and practical teaching becomes explicit during group tutorial work (the History Workshop), which, through thematically orientated re-drawing of the studied sites, aims to provide an enlightened understanding of the issues of landscape practice. Up to the present, however, the studios have not worked in direct partnership with the module and it is the student's responsibility to draw connections between history teaching and project teaching.

Teaching history through 20th-century case studies
Case studies between practice and research

Deciphering historical and contemporary achievements is a means of understanding the translation of ideas into concrete projects, at different periods of time. Teaching history through case studies allows the student to apply to a specific site a number of the themes, topics, and concepts presented during the lectures focusing on iconic cases. The lectures themselves employ the same methods and address case studies that bridge the gap between research and practice. The module is based on representation in plans and sections, using similar means to those mobilized in the studio project. Exploring topical questions through case studies provides food for thought to students as a concrete introduction to the historical dimension of contemporary issues.

Modern landscape architecture: a history misconstrued in France

Focusing on 20th-century works aims at embracing the modern period into a historical approach. Today, in France, this period is insufficiently addressed in heritage matters and still has to fight against certain a priori. If this is changing in architecture, in landscape architecture, however, it is far more difficult to step out from garden art history to urban landscape architecture and thus to the recognition of 20th-century work. We believe it is impossible to separate buildings from landscape architecture when considering a residential district, a fact important to impress upon young future professionals.

A global approach: architecture and landscape, project and analysis

Our approach is based on a 'reversed' vision of the site based on open spaces (often incorrectly treated as 'empty'), in contradistinction to an approach usually centred on construction. Students are thus asked to focus on qualities that usually go unnoticed. Likewise, we are also opposed to the 'black potatoes syndrome', when buildings, indicated as blurry spots, are excluded from the landscape, thus reducing landscape architects to agents for greening. By observing neighbourhoods in the context of their outdoor spaces, by reading architecture through its links with the land and the surroundings, it is our intention to show the potential of a global vision, embracing both buildings and landscape, for the management and transformation processes of these neighbourhoods—as well as of most urban sites.

Describing places: elements of vocabulary

Description is directly linked to the ability to observe precisely what is being described (Dutoit, 2008); but it is also connected to the knowledge gained about what is perceived (see below). Describing something means being able to recognize and name it. The deeper one's knowledge, the more one requires accurate words to describe things. In fact, the process is back-and-forth process between observation and learning (about space, history, facts, ideas etc.) It is vocabulary that makes it possible to bring out the links between ideas and spaces. In this module we endeavour to provide students with the means to describe and name the elements of both architecture and landscape architecture. It also forms part of the link between lectures and case-study work. Drawing is supplemented by written material. Though this is often difficult to enforce, we insist that every design has a signification which can be expressed in a title: every drawing must have a meaningful caption summing up the idea (and not only 'cross-section A-A1'). We also ask for brief texts outlining the general aim.

Theoretical basis for the approach: between writing and reading

Description as experience of the place and feedback

We base our approach on a historical (or retrospective) knowledge nourishing a prospective description (focusing on what can be useful for future projects).[1] According to Swiss geographer Corboz, description is an intentional, problematized act (only efficient regarding a question or objective), engaging a relationship between the subject and its object. In 'Description between reading and writing' (Corboz, 1995) he details a 'reading' operation extending the 'writing' exercise of design, 'a "passageway" between the world as reading and the world as writing' (Corboz, 2001: 252). The two extremes he indicates (radical ecology and the CIAM—he notes this opposition is near caricature) both deal with landscape matters and the post-war period. On the one hand, in radical 'ecologism', all-powerful land and its local qualities dictate every action, while the dimension of the project for transformation is sidelined; on the other hand, modern urbanism tends to exclude any understanding of site and it is the almighty project that takes command.

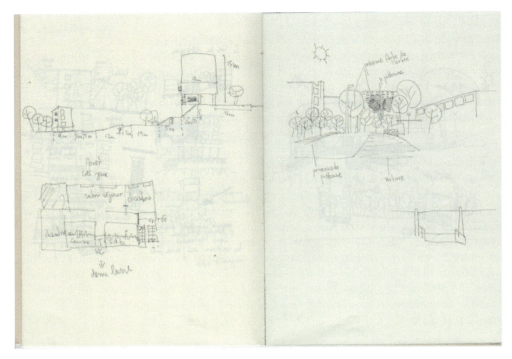

Figure 1 Initial sketches and on-site notes. La Butte Rouge,
Chatenay-Malabry, 2011-12, students: S. Bertrand,
H. Carpentier, S. Cathelain.

Corboz explains how the ability to see, and thus include elements in the description, is related to the 'cultural horizon' of the person describing: 'It is impossible to observe without having an idea of what one is observing. This idea identifies with the subject's expectations or, more generally, his/her culture' (Corboz, 2001: 253). It is then necessary both to widen knowledge through lectures and provide it with a concrete underpinning through description work.[2]

Description as a narrative reflecting history(ies) and uses of a place

In the field of anthropology, Clifford Geertz's work concerns 'thick' description (Geertz, 1973) and questions the limits between description and interpretation. His studies integrate the historical dimension and usage over a multitude of strata and cultures involved in the public space. Even if the module is too brief for students to establish connections with inhabitants and local managers, this is an aspect that appeals to them, and several groups find it beneficial to get involved in narrative approaches to the site, including their perception of its uses and practices.

Graphics discourse as critical reading

We also supplement our teaching activity by our work on the JoLA editorial team (2006-2014) for the section Under the Sky, dealing with the critical reading of completed works (Blanchon, 2016). Though graphic discourse was mainly deployed in the Thinking Eye section, we experimented fruitful issues in Under the Sky, such as the 'thick section approach' inspired by Geertz's 'thick description', developed with students at University

Figure 2 Drawings, La Maladrerie, Aubervilliers, 2016-17, students: O. Fouché, A. Touboul.

of Washington (Way, 2013: 37; Blanchon, 2016: 70), as a creative use of constructing sections inspired by the historical background. We also refer to the idea of the 'Thinking Hand' (Pallasmaa, 2009), through which a single drawing can express and create ideas in a synthetic way better than pages of words.[3] Means and issues of representing strata of historical layers is part of an on-going reflection in the field of landscape architecture (Cosgrove, 1999; Treib, 2008).

The multi-scale method
A multi-scale approach through space and time

We address open-space urban history using examples of housing developments designed from the beginning of the 20th century to the present day that represent various stages in the creation of the urban fabric. Both description and analysis embrace buildings and exterior spaces in a joint approach using a range of scales: that of the site and land; that of the neighbourhood structured by its open spaces (parks, squares, streets, gardens...), and finally the details and spatial 'devices' that articulate the buildings between each other and with the ground and the sky (thresholds, steps, gutters...; vegetal structures of every variety; porches, windows, balconies...). At every level we aim to explore a variety of time-scales from the present day to the original site. Questions concerning scale consistency are addressed, the objective being to zoom back and forth from one scale to another.

Figure 3a Multi-scale sections, Suresnes, 2014, students:
B. Rigal, L. Poirier, A. Munoz, C. Beau Yon de Jonage.

Figure 3b Section, Square Jean Allemane, La Butte Rouge,
Chatenay-Malabry, 2016, students: C. Durand, L. Provost.
'A site between forest and national road: main public spaces
of the district, on the lowest parts, following the course of a
former stream'.

Figure 4 District scale; section, Seine Rive Gauche, Paris,
2011, students: S. Bertrand, H. Carpentier, S. Cathelain.
(see also Fig. 20b)

Figure 5a Territorial scale, Contour lines, geographical
transects and topographical block. Theme: limits and fringes,
Verneuil 2014. Students: J. Thau, M. Sivré, F. Suss,
A. Schneider.

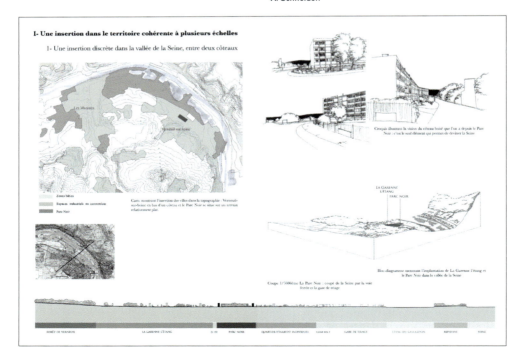

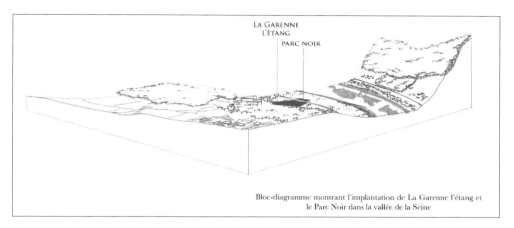

Figure 5b **Territorial scale, Three-dimensional block, Theme: limits and fringes, Verneuil 2014. Students: J. Thau, M. Sivré, F. Suss, A. Schneider. 'Le Parc noir [the dark park]: A former castle park and hunting wood'.**

From intuition to maps and sections

Matters begin with an intuitive global approach: strolling about the site and making observations in an informal and receptive manner. Students immerse themselves in the atmosphere of the place, reproduce sensations and 'clues', features of the materiality of the space, through, for instance, sketching and photography (Figs. 1 & 2). Then students, in groups of four, focus on a central theme that will run as a red thread to reduce complexity and prevent students embarking on lengthy monographs. They explore the selected theme on site following three levels of reading: territory, district, practices /physicality. For this, the preferred tool is the section. Sections represent the most eloquent means of reflecting these relationships, providing a tool for testing continuities and connections (Figs. 3a, 3b & 4). Moving from one scale to another makes it possible to question the consistency of the design on various levels of reading. This transcends the administrative or private-public limits to follow the everyday travel of the inhabitants, who physically oscillate from outside to indoor private spaces.

At the territorial scale we can redefine the scale or theme of the project, including it in a geographical and urban context and addressing its connection to the surroundings. We use maps with contour lines and geographical profile sections (Figs. 5a, 5b, 6a & 6b).

On the district level we can represent the ground strata as a shared common space. We start with a master plan of the neighbourhood noting trees and open spaces; we use aerial views and earlier planning states (Fig. 7). Each group focuses on a more precise ground plan associated with selected sections (Fig. 8).

On the scale of practice and physicality we show the materiality (details, materials…) of the place. We rely on the notion of 'spatial device', defined as a group of elements in the space whose assemblage contributes to its characterization. This offers a guide as to the sections that require detailed, close-up attention. These 'spatial devices' can be comprise plants, or concern levelling or the relationship between buildings—such as threshold and porches (Figs. 9 to 17, notably 16 and 18d, 19d, 19e). The selected 'devices' can be used in combination to describe the site, as well as the period, region, or designer—with assistance from the teaching team. They are then connected to the signification of the location (Francis, 2001:19).

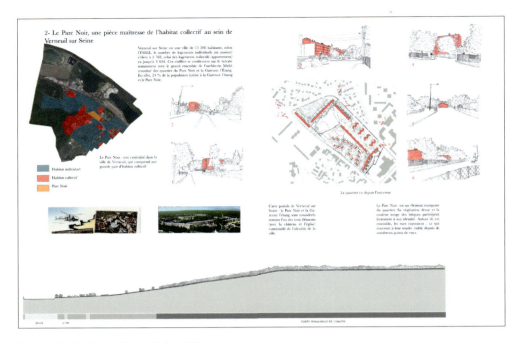

Figure 6a **Territorial scale. Theme: limits and fringes.**
Verneuil 2014. Students: J. Thau, M. Sivré, F. Suss, A. Schneider.

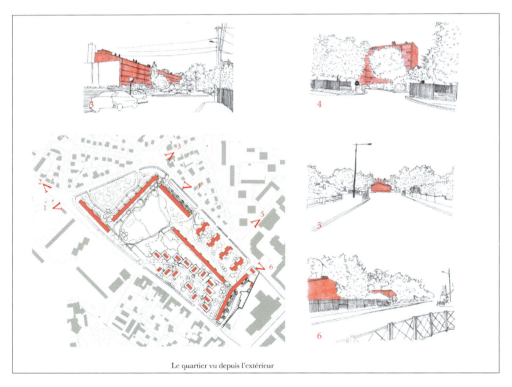

Figure 6b **Territorial scale. Theme: limits and fringes.**
Verneuil 2014. students: J. Thau, M. Sivré, F. Suss, A. Schneider.
(zoom) The district seen from the surroundings.

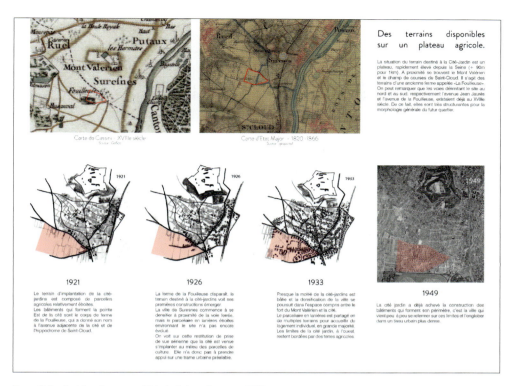

Figure 7 **Territorial scale zoom on historical steps, Suresnes, 2014.**
Students: B. Bouan, A. Costeramon, E. Desmeules, A. Gu.
'From a agricultural plateau to the Garden city'
(about the same place see also Fig. 3a)

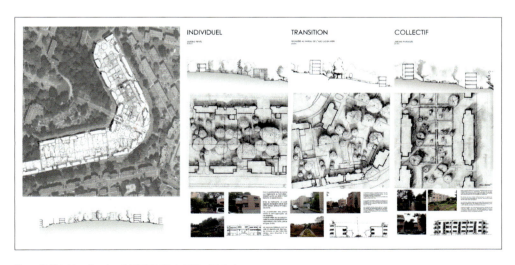

Figure 8 **Neighbourhood and detail scale; master plan and section, La Butte Rouge, Chatenay-Malabry, 2016, students:** E. Fernandez Martinez, E. Morillon, J. Feig. The main axis, between two blocks: individual housing and private gardens / collective housing and allotments.
(about the same place, see also Figs. 1, 3b & 20a)

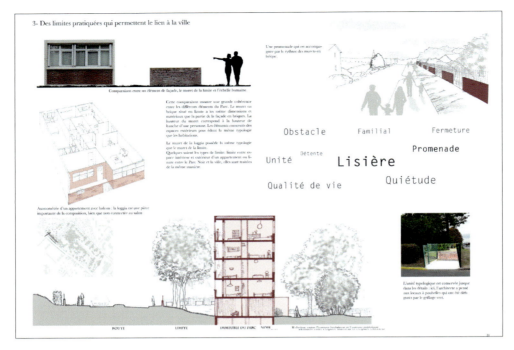

Figure 9 Detail scale, fringes and limits, thresholds. Verneuil, 2014, students: J. Thau, M. Sivré, F. Suss, A. Schneider. 'Verneuil, le Parc noir: Vegetation as articulation and smooth transition between the limits of the district and the buildings'.

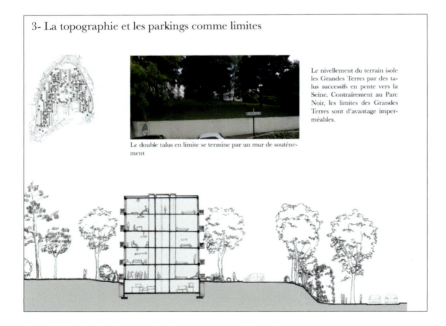

Figure 10 Detail scale, fringes and limits, comparison with Verneuil, 2014, students: J. Thau, M. Sivré, F. Suss, A. Schneider. 'Marly les grandes terres : Vegetation and topography as protection and closure between the limits of the district and the buildings'.(Comparison between Figs. 9 and 10: Vegetation as limit, different levels of porosity).

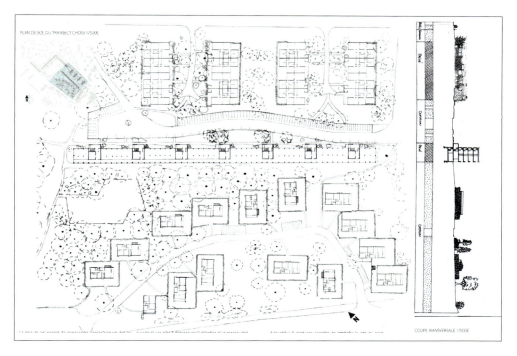

Figure 11 Detail scale; housing types, Map, Verneuil, 2014,
students: F. Gormotte, R. Goven, T. Ropion, E. Vazzanino.
'A mix of typologies'.

Figures 12 and 13 Detail scale; housing types, Map, Verneuil, 2014,
students: F. Gormotte, R. Goven, T. Ropion, E. Vazzanino.
'A mix of typologies'.

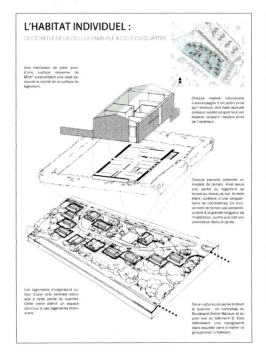
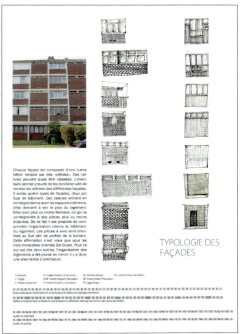

Teaching the history of urban open space using a multi-scale approach | 235

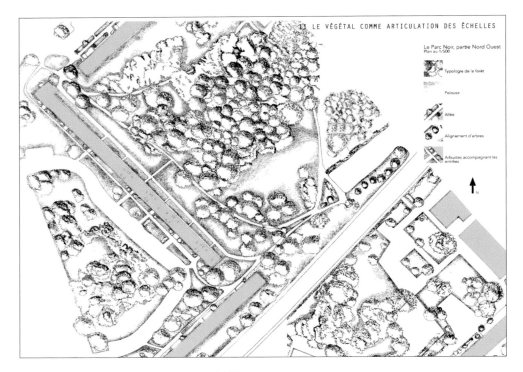

Figure 14 District scale; map of vegetation, Verneuil, 2014, students: C. Bento, O. Malanot. 'Traces of a former wood, between clearings for play and forestry mood for rest'.

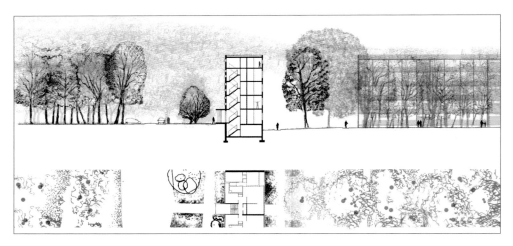

Figure 15 Detail scale; map and section, vegetation, Verneuil, 2014, students: C. Bento, O. Malanot. 'Vegetation as articulation between spaces'.

Figure 16 Detail scale: 'Sketches of different entrances', vegetation, Verneuil, 2014, students: C. Bento, O. Malanot.

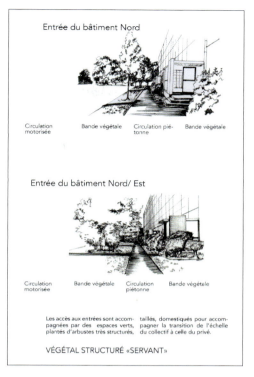

Figure 17a Theme: vegetation map, Boisfort, Bruxelles, 2016, students: E. Lapleau, L. Richard. Species are chosen for their ability to define spaces.

Figure 17b Theme: vegetation, section, Boisfort, Bruxelles, 2016, students: E. Lapleau, L. Richard. Entrance in the footpaths and 'heart' of block.

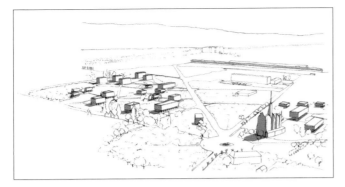

Figure 18a Renault-Flins district: from a leisure site near the Seine (garden city and Paris Beach) to a working site. Students: GR 11 (Un habitat qui produit un paysage qui dialogue avec le territoire [The design of the district produces a landscape connected with the large scale territory]) students: L. Gascon, S. regal, J. Robin, M. Zago.

Figure 18a, b, c, d Aubergenvile-Elisabethville, Flins a modern district for a industrial company, B. Zehrfuss, architect (1951-1954). 2014 (from territorial scale to detail scale).

Figure 18b, c Renault-Flins district. Car factory and housing for employees. Map and section: a wide open space. students: L. Gascon, S. regal, J. Robin, M. Zago.

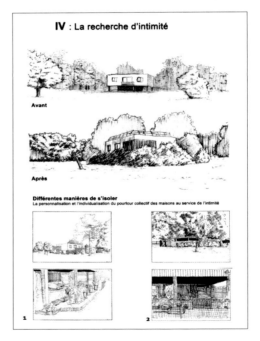

Figure 18b

Figure 18d Renault-Flins district. Vegetation Before/After. Photo Reconduction (same place, 50 years later). Looking for privacy. Evolution of usage under the stilts. Appropriation in individuals / closing in collective housing. Students: GR 9, K. Barthalay, S. Jung, A. Rankebrandt, G. Rouchier. (Habiter l'espace ouvert: l'espace collectif au détriment de l'intimité? [Living in the open space: the collective space to the detriment of intimacy?])

Figure 18d

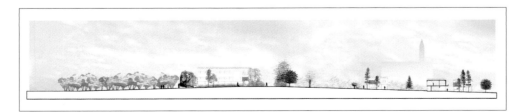

Figure 18c

238

Investigation: surveys and archives in reconstructing the different phases of the site

We are necessarily interested in investigation, in surveying through interviews with various actors, through archival work, in order to reconstruct the different phases of a project: current, original, and intermediary, as well as the site prior to the project.

'An in-depth survey and its archival study reveals the unexpected steps, surprises, forgotten points, changes in implementation, where essential parts of a project often lie' (Blanchon, 2016: 69). It makes it possible to form a standpoint as to the appropriateness and nature of the maintenance. Due to time constraints, access to archives can be a difficult task, unless prepared for upstream. This too forms part of the preparatory work undertaken by the teaching team. As far as possible, we show students what work in an archive consists in so that they can undertake it later on their own—for example in their thesis work the following year.

A selection of case studies reflecting the 20th-century urban fabric in Greater Paris

Locations: Our main study sites represents episodes in the Grand Paris urban fabric, involving landscape issues on different levels: interwar garden cities (La Butte Rouge at Chatenay-Malabry, Stains, Suresnes …); major post-war housing districts (Meudon-la-Forêt, the Cité de la Plaine at Clamart, Sarcelles-Lochères, Les Bleuets at Creteil…), sometimes recently rehabilitated; contemporary neighbourhoods, such as the Zones d'Aménagement Concerté (ZAC) [Joint development zone], from the 1980s that started to involve landscape architects as team coordinators (Villejuif, ZAC des Hautes Bruyères…), and more recent 'eco-districts' (Boulogne, ZAC Trapèze, Paris Seine Rive Gauche…).

This choice was made according to two criteria: the interaction between the interventions of architects and landscape designers in this type of operation, and the accessibility of the site for students. Students will be required to return on site on their own for visits, surveys, and measures. The site's interest should also be readily appreciable: some may be of singular interest from a research point of view but less attractive for students (extensively reconfigured, for instance).

'Making of': When choosing a new site we make an initial study of its situation and supposed interest with regard to the issues and themes addressed by the studios. Since our case studies always concern housing districts, their selection also has to take into account the authorization and requirements of its inhabitants and administrators. The teaching team[4] visits the site, establishing contact with owner associations or representatives, as well as with designers and authors of earlier research work and studies. A search also takes place for archives and future projects. Preparations are then made for an initial on-site visit by the students.

Main themes: Students deal with themes characterizing the landscape project process and representing the main steps in describing a completed work. These concern landscape as an art of articulation, between the pre-existing situation and the work described, between geography and current setting, between building and outside space, between people and the land, both horizontally and vertically. Most of the time, the themes are similar for the different case studies: limits, fringes, and urban scale (Figs. 5a, 6a, 6b, 9 & 10); typologies and buildings (Figs. 11, 12 & 13); vegetation and green structures (Figs. 14, 15, 16, 17a & 17b); topography and land modelling, or water management…

Final production: The final presentation takes the form of a vertical concertina A3 sketchbook (carnet chinois, Chinese book or Leporello), allowing both exhibition (Figs. 22 & 23) and notebook presentation (Figs. 20a, 20b, 21a & 21b). The pdf or notebook is provided the site contacts and owners, though little feedback is received, except from the Association des cités jardins d'Ile de France [regional garden-city association], connected with the MUS (Musée d'Histoire urbaine et sociale) [museum for urban and social history].[5]

Figure 19a Créteil, Les Bleuets, A fan shape opened towards the urban landscape. Mineral and vegetation strata. Students: J. Gatier, M. Negron, L. Clermontonerre, T. Calvet. (Vegetation)

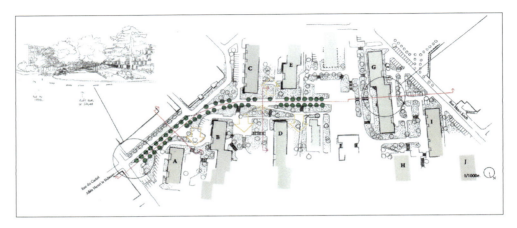

Figure 19b Créteil, Les Bleuets, Master plan around a planted mall: a fan shape, a slight difference. Students: H. Bouju, Q. Debenest, C. Délegue, A. Hopquin.

Figure 19c Créteil, Les Bleuets, Section, expressive modernity. Students: L. Braouch, M. Lefebvre, M. Nedelec, M. Ruffin.

Figure 19a, b, c, d Créteil, Les Bleuets, Brutalism architecture and naturalistic landscape. P. Bossard architect (1959-1962). 2012 (District and detail scale)

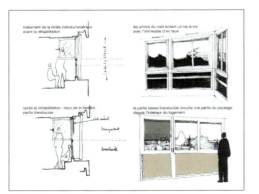

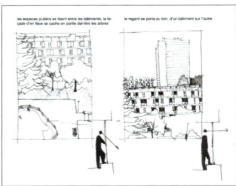

Figure 19d, e Créteil, Les Bleuets, Details. Mastering the design for life inside and views towards the landscape. Students: L. Braouch, M. Lefebvre, M. Nedelec, M. Ruffin.

Efficiency in comparison

Focusing on specific themes allows both monographic presentations and thematic comparisons between different case studies. Finally each group is also asked for a comparison with another neighbourhood, whose selection must be justified. The aim is to place the theme, or an aspect of the theme or site, into perspective. 'The comparative dimension explores either several projects at different scales at the same geographical area, or diverse cases about a similar theme, thus widening the question addressed'. In fact the module offers wide potential for comparison, thereby helping students define their own approach better.

Between different themes on a single site (four groups per site)

Certain documents will be produced jointly for the different groups on a given site (situation, the main figures involved, the history of the project, master plan, etc.), since it is necessary to avoid repeating these elements. Through this common material (on the geographic and urban level and on the master-plan level), however, students have to think of the best way to express the issues of their own theme, each group probably employing different material for sections, ground plan, and the practice/physicality level.

Between different sites around one theme (three groups per theme)

This kind of comparison can prove very fruitful. We use a thematic exhibition of the work in progress for an intermediary presentation. It is highly efficient, since students can observe how colleagues deal with a similar question. Different ways of understanding the same theme emerge, ranging from more conceptual to more technical. This considerably improves the student's understanding of their own intentions and, with the help of the teaching team, makes it possible to point out the evolution of a theme at different historical junctures. The differences between several case studies better reveals the specificities of each case studied. Students progressively understand the theme at different stages of the project or within differing contexts (by way of types, for instance).

Comparison with another completed work, neighbourhood, reference work or school project site

Finally each group (the attempt to involve every student individually proved unwieldy) has to put in perspective an aspect of its study with another case chosen by the students themselves (Fig. 9, 10, 20a & 20b). This can be historical or contemporary, preferably distinct from the focus of their area of study. The acceptance of sites that have not been visited always throws a debate, but, at this stage, the tendency is to do so, in order that foreign cases can be addressed. Students are instructed to explain why the comparison is revealing. They are also invited to compare with the site or some element related to their on-going studio project, but they rarely manage to do so. We ask for this other work to be chosen early enough to be tested and deciphered at least roughly so they are able to use it for a back-and-forth reflection in their study. If students do this, we can better provide help even for the choice, but very often they take matters in hand too late. No excessive pressure is applied since we see this as a personal resource that should afford pleasure.

Openings and limits: the module's role and efficiency

Links with other teaching methods

Our ambition is to explore means of developing links between teaching in history and project. Some students tried out the method in the studio workshop, leading them to focus on inside-outside relationship in their master-plan district project, but this was in the way of an experiment. To show the potential of this global vision in the management

Figure 20a Folding A3 'Chinese' sketchbook La Butte Rouge, Chatenay-Malabry, 2011.
students: S. Bertrand, H. Carpentier, S. Cathelain.

Figure 20b Folding A3 sketchbook, Seine Rive Gauche, Paris, 2011.
students: S. Bertrand, H. Carpentier, S. Cathelain.

Figure 20a & 20b Comparison between Natural ground (Fig. 20a: Garden city La Butte Rouge 1930-1960) and Artificial ground (Fig. 20b: Seine Rive Gauche , contemporary district, 1991-2011). Physical continuity (Fig. 20a: Garden city La Butte Rouge 1930-1960) / Visual continuity (Fig. 20b: Seine Rive Gauche, contemporary district, 1991- 2011). At different scales: open collective spaces (1930-1960, garden-city district, Fig. 20a) / Private spaces with limited access and fences for the new 'open blocks' (only visual continuity, contemporary district, Fig. 20b).

and transformation processes of these neighbourhoods, it needs to be introduced in the teaching structure. Another fruitful aspect is the issue of representation addressed independently from a project design workshop: specifically focusing on plants and vegetation and the land. It implies expanding contacts with the ecology department.

Other schools/other paths

In most architecture schools, history courses are separate from the exercise of design. Most of the time there is little open-space history in a general curriculum in architecture or landscape architecture. History tends to be disconnected from project teaching.[6] In fact the kind of training we are describing is better developed in specific courses focused on heritage matters at the Master 2 level.[7] A survey of this question requires a more specific study than a single paragraph can offer. Given the length of our training programme (L2, M1, M2) and of this module, such brief exercises can concentrate a number of objectives and raise awareness about a large range of skills (such as designing trees in concrete situations for instance).

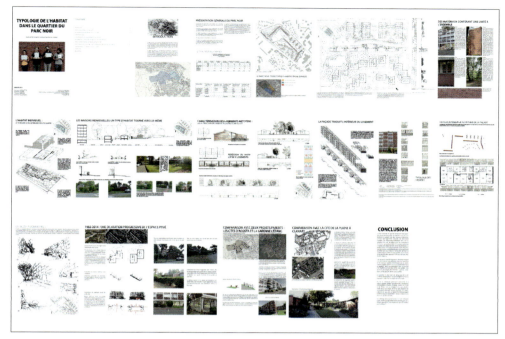

Figure 21a **Full submission, Verneuil, 2014, Theme Housing types.**

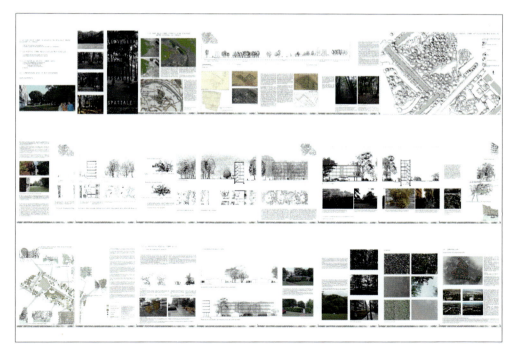

Figure 21b **Full submission, Verneuil, 2014, Theme Vegetation.**

Figure 22, 23 The Chinese book is deployed for exhibition and final presentation. The 'Chinese book' folded can be read like a note-book and easily stocked.

Though often modest, these essential open spaces act as a focus of communal daily life, anchoring the neighbourhood in history and geography. Drawing attention to their importance and the issues they represent as social spaces can inform the specific skills called for in design and management and how they impact on the formulation of commissions and economic issues. We conclude that they are a source of lessons to be observed, examined, and evaluated. They provide references for thinking about housing neighbourhoods in the city today, where common spaces and public spaces are tending to disappear, and where maintenance issues are changing and integrating sustainable development challenges. Thus, we introduce thematic issues that we believe likely to be taken up by students in their master thesis the following year.

Acknowledgements

I am grateful to Denis Delbaere (ENSAP Lille), Olivier Gaudin (ESNP Blois) and Stéphanie de Courtois (ENSA Versailles) for their interest in providing information concerning history teaching at their school.

NOTES

1 See the projects by Swiss architect Georges Descombes, in Lancy or for the river Aire (Descombes, 1988; Marot, 1999).

2 Art critic Daniel Arasse (Arasse, 2000) also combines detailed, direct observation of the work with the creative use of knowledge, providing insightful examples of new and convincing readings of familiar masterpieces.

3 Georges Farhat's work, on Le Nôtre, showing how project skills can change the vision of history (Farhat, 2003), and about the site as a 'living archive' (Farhat, 2011), also reflects our objectives.

4 The teaching team: involves two assistants, reflecting the range of skills required. One is a landscape architect, the other is a doctoral student (or young PhD) trained in architectural and urban history. Another landscape architect joins the intermediary and final presentations, so two 'architect-landscape architect' pairs can be formed when needed (including me as trained architect). Assistants from 2010-2018: Nathalie Levy, François Moreau, Simon Cathelain, (landscape architects). Caroline Alder, Vanessa Fernandez, Federico Ferrari, Denyse Rodriguez-Tome, Pauline Lefort, Alexandro Panzeri (architects & PhD fellows)

5 Sited near Paris in Suresnes (92), a municipality incorporating a sizable garden city, the museum sometimes offers to host our students' work in-between major exhibitions.

6 Such as in Lille ENSAP (Ecole Nationale Supérieure d'Architecture et de Paysage) and Blois (Ecole de la Nature et des Paysages).

7 Such as the course 'Jardins historiques, paysage, patrimoine' [Historical gardens, landscape and heritage], offered at the neighbouring School of Architecture in Versailles (ENSAV). There, history is embedded with in-depth case diagnosis. The training is not meant for designers however, but to raise awareness about the issues arising from such projects in all kinds of involvement.

REFERENCES

Arasse, D. (2000), On n'y voit rien, descriptions, [There's nothing to see: descriptions], (Paris: Denoël).

Blanchon, B., (2016), 'Criticism: the potential of scholarly reading of constructed landscapes. Or the difficult art of interpretation.' *Journal of Landscape Architecture,* 10th anniversary issue, 10/2: 66-71.

Blanchon Bernadette, Delbaere Denis, Garleff Jorn, (2010), 'Le paysage dans les ensembles urbains, 1940-1980', [Landscape in post-war housing complexes], in *Les grands ensembles,* (Paris: Carré), 206-239.

Corboz A. (2001), 'La description: entre lecture et écriture', [Description, between reading and writing], in Le territoire comme palimpseste et autres essais, [Land as palimpsest and other texts] (Paris: L'Imprimeur), 249-258. Original text: (1995) 'La descrizione tra lettura e scrittura', 2° convegno di urbanistica; 'La descrizione', Prato, 30 March–1 April. Published in (2000) Faces 48: 52-54. (Unpublished in English)

Cosgrove, D. (1999), ed., *Mappings,* (London: Reaktion Books)

Descombes, G. (1988), *Shifting Sites, il territorio transitivo, presented by Tironi Giordano,* (Rome: Gangemi editore).

Dutoit, A. (2008), 'Looking as Inquiry, Drawing the Implied Urban Realm', in M. Treib (ed.), *Drawing / Thinking: Confronting an Electronic Age,* (London: Routledge), 148-159.

Farhat, G. (2003), 'Optique topographique: la grande terrasse de Saint-Germain-en-Laye' [Topographical optics: the Grande Terrasse at Saint-Germain-en-Laye], in various authors, Le Nôtre, un inconnu illustre? (Paris: Monum, Éditions du Patrimoine), 122-135. (Proceedings of the ICOMOS International Conference, Versailles and Chantilly, October 2000)

Farhat, G. (2011), 'Archives et paysage: du site comme agent historique' [Archives and Landscape: site as historical agent], *Colonnes,* N° 27, June: 52-55.

Francis, M., (2001), 'A Case Study Method for Landscape Architecture', *Landscape Journal,* 20:15-29.

Geertz, C. (1973), 'Thick description: towards an interpretive theory of culture', in *The Interpretation of Cultures: Selected Essays,* (New York: Basic Books), 2-30.

Marot S. (1999), 'L'art de la mémoire, le territoire et l'architecture', *LeVisiteur,* 4: 115-176.

Pallasmaa, J. (1996), *The Eyes of the Skin,* (New Jersey: John Wiley & Sons).

Pallasmaa, J. (2009), *The Thinking Hand,* (New Jersey: John Wiley & Sons).

Treib, Marc (2008) *Representing landscape architecture* (London: Taylor Francis).

Way, T. (2013),'Landscapes of Industrial Excess: A Thick Sections Approach to Gas Work Park', *JoLA, Journal of Landscape Architecture,* 8/1: 28-39.

APPENDIX

ABOUT THE EDITORS

Karsten Jørgensen

is Professor of Landscape Architecture in the School of Landscape Architecture at the Norwegian University of Life Sciences, Norway, and holds a Dr.-Scient. degree from NMBU, 1989, in landscape architecture. He was Founding Editor of JoLA – the *Journal of Landscape Architecture* – 2006–2015. Karsten Jørgensen has published regularly in national and international journals and books. In 2016 he edited the volume *Mainstreaming Landscape through the European Landscape Convention* (2016) together with Tim Richardson, Kine Thoren and Morten Clemetsen, and in 2018 he edited *Defining Landscape Democracy* (2018) together with Shelley Egoz and Deni Ruggeri.

Nilgül Karadeniz

is Professor of Landscape Architecture at Ankara University, Turkey. Her teaching and research interest focuses on participatory landscape planning and recently on landscape biography. She has been an editorial board member of SCI-expanded journals. She was Secretary General (2006–2009) and Vice President (2009–2012) of ECLAS. She is a founding member of the LE:NOTRE Institute and she chaired the Institute between 2016 and 2018.

Elke Mertens

is Professor of Landscape Architecture and Open Space Management at the Hochschule Neubrandenburg – University of Applied Sciences, Germany. She holds a Dr.-Ing. degree from the Technical University in Berlin (1997) in landscape architecture. Elke Mertens has been active in the LE:NOTRE Thematic Network as well as in ECLAS as member of the executive boards. She served as general secretary of the Institute from 2016 to 2018 and has been co-chair of the German Hochschulkonferenz Landschaft (HKL) since 2014.

Richard Stiles

is Professor of Landscape Architecture in the Faculty of Architecture and Planning at Vienna University of Technology, Austria, having studied biology and landscape design at the Universities of Oxford and Newcastle upon Tyne and having previously taught at Manchester University in the UK. His teaching and research interests focus on strategic landscape planning and design in urban areas. He is a past President of the European Council of Landscape Architecture Schools and was Coordinator of the European Union co-funded LE:NOTRE Thematic Network in Landscape Architecture for 11 years, during which time he was closely involved in preparing recommendations for landscape architecture education.

AUTHORS' BIOGRAPHIES

Maria-Beatrice Andreucci
PhD, IFLA Advisory Circle. Landscape architect, economist. Research Professor of Environmental Design, Planning, Design, Technology of Architecture Department, 'Sapienza' University of Rome. Through extensive international research, her work contributes to an evolving framework, bridging the professional fields of sustainable architecture and urban design, with the interdisciplinary subject of landscape economy. Co-chair of the EU-WHO funded research Eklipse − Urban and peri-urban green & blue spaces and human mental health; leader of the WG Urban Economies and Welfare, Urban Europe Research Alliance (UERA); and Management Committee member of the EU funded research COST Action CA15206 Payments for Ecosystem Services − PESFOR-W.

Bernadette Blanchon
is a certified architect, Associate Professor at Ecole Nationale Supérieure de Paysage in Versailles, research fellow at LAREP (Laboratoire de Recherche en Projets de Paysage), after a collaboration at Alexandre Chemetoff's office, "Bureau des Paysages". Her teaching and research work mainly focuses on urban open spaces, following two main axes: the development of landscape architecture during the post-war era − including the contribution of women − and the critical analysis of completed works. A founding editor of the academic journal *JoLA, Journal of Landscape Architecture*, she developed the Under the Sky section, for critical reading of works, from 2006 to 2014.

Marco Casagrande
born 1971, graduated from the Helsinki University of Technology Department of Architecture in 2001. He was a partner with Sami Rintala before establishing his current Casagrande Laboratory. From the early stages of his career Casagrande started to mix architecture with other disciplines of art and science landing with a series of ecologically conscious architectural installations around the world. Casagrande is Professor of Ecological Urban Planning in the Taiwan based Tamkang University. Casagrande has been teaching in 65 academic institutions in 25 countries and realized more than 70 works in 14 different countries. His widely published works have been exhibited five times in the Venice Architecture Biennale (2000, 2004, 2006, 2014 and 2016) and in a number of other exhibitions. He is the laureate of the European Prize for Architecture 2013, Committee of International Architecture Critics CICA Award 2013 for conceptual and artistic architecture and UNESCO & Locus Foundation's Global Award for Sustainable Architecture 2015.

Lisa Diedrich
studied architecture and urbanism in Paris, Marseille and Stuttgart, journalism in Berlin, and landscape architecture at the University of Copenhagen, where she received her doctoral degree. She currently works as a Professor of landscape architecture at the Swedish University of Agricultural Sciences in Alnarp/Malmö, directing the research platform SLU Urban Futures. She is also editor-in-chief of the professional book series Landscape Architecture Europe (*Fieldwork / On Site / In Touch / On The Move / Care Create Act*) and co-editor-in-chief, with Harry Harsema, of *'scape* the international magazine for landscape architecture and urbanism.

Pierre Donadieu
is a distinguished Professor of Landscape Sciences at the École Nationale Supérieure de Paysage (ENSP) Versailles, where he has taught since 1977. He established a master's programme in theory and understanding of the design process for pre-doctoral students, "Théories et démarches du projet de paysage", with the Université Paris Pantheon-Sorbonne and AgroParisTech (University Paris-Saclay).

Mads Farsø
born 1978, studied Geography (MSc) and Landscape Architecture (PhD) at the University of Copenhagen and is accredited practitioner (MDL) running his studio Farsø Have. Mads is Programme Director of Studies for the 5-year Landscape Architecture programme at the Swedish University of Agricultural Science, near Malmö, where he is also Assistant Senior Lecturer focused on landscape architectural values, media and film. He co-founded and led the Copenhagen Architecture Festival (CAFx) 2014-2017, and has recently initiated the research collaborative platform Surroundings Lab, which explores new media and theory − related to landscape architecture − that expresses ambient values of everyday surroundings.

Maria Goula

PhD, 2007 UPC, is currently an Associate Professor at the Landscape Architecture Department, Cornell University and an adjunct researcher at the Institute for Research Habitat, Territory and Tourism, Universitat Politecnica de Catalunya and University of Malaga, developing research on coastal tourism, especially in regard to the interpretation of leisure patterns and coastal dynamics. Foundation member of the International Landscape Architecture Biennial in Barcelona since 2000. Leader, with Jamie Vanucchi, of the "Upstate Archipelago" team Cornell University. The design team is one of the finalists for the "Reimagining the New York Canals" international design competition July 2018.

Karin Helms

is a landscape architect and founder of the firm Karin Helms, Paysagiste Sarl (1993–2002). She is Associate Professor in Landscape Architecture, responsible for international relations, at the École Nationale Supérieure de Paysage (ENSP) Versailles. She established the European Master in Landscape Architecture: EMiLA, run by five universities/schools (www.emila.eu). She has been a French State Advisor in Landscape Architecture since 1999. Her studies include large-scale research on landscape architecture in rural and suburban areas. She is currently undertaking a practice-led research PhD at RMIT Europe (Barcelona). She was awarded a Marie Curie EU grant through the ADAPT-r programme (2015–2016).

Susan Herrington

is Professor and Chair of the Landscape Architecture programme at the University of British Columbia, Canada. She teaches landscape architecture, environmental design and architecture students. Herrington regularly teaches histories of landscape architecture, theories in landscape architecture, vertical studios and core studios. She recently published Landscape Theory in Design.

Adnan Kaplan

is a Professor in the Department of Landscape Architecture at Ege (Aegean) University, İzmir, Türkiye (Turkey). His research interests span a variety of planning and design topics including urban resilience, blue-green infrastructure, urban public open spaces, coastal wetlands and visual impact assessment.

Ulrike Krippner

is a Senior Researcher at the Institute of Landscape Architecture at BOKU Vienna. She holds a PhD in landscape architecture and teaches landscape history. Her research and writings concentrate on the profession's history of the 20th century, on women in landscape architecture, and on post-World War II landscape architecture.

Lilli Lička

is a Professor of Landscape Architecture at BOKU Vienna. Her projects focus on public open spaces, housing, heritage sites and urban parks. She co-curates an online-collection on contemporary Austrian landscape architecture and heads the LArchiv, Archive of Austrian Landscape Architecture. She was principal of koselicka 1991–2016 and opened LL-L Landscape Architecture in 2017.

Bettina Lamm

Associate Professor, University of Copenhagen. Lamm's research addresses the interaction between urban environment and lived life in the public realm. She studies through practice and theory how temporary interventions, play design and art installations can facilitate social interaction in public space and reframe the urban landscape. Lamm is co-author of the book *Playable* that investigates the relation between, play, art and public space. She runs the practice based research project Move the Neighbourhood that explores collaborative design and construction methods in urban environments. She leads the Urban Intervention Studio where students build 1:1 interventions into landscapes in transformation.

Joan Iverson Nassauer

is Professor of Landscape Architecture at University of Michigan, School of Environment and Sustainability, and Co-Editor-in-Chief, Landscape and Urban Planning. She works in the field of ecological design. She develops design proposals to improve ecosystem services, and uses social science methods to learn how human experience affects and is affected by landscapes. A Fellow of the American Society of Landscape Architects (1992) and a Fellow of the Council of Educators in Landscape Architecture (2007), she was named Distinguished Scholar by the International Association of Landscape Ecology (IALE) (2007) and Distinguished Practitioner of Landscape Ecology (1998) by US – IALE.

AUTHORS' BIOGRAPHIES

Bruno Notteboom
is doctor of urban and regional planning and Associate Professor at the Faculty of Architecture of KULeuven, Belgium. Before, he was Assistant Professor at Ghent University and the University of Antwerp, and visiting scholar at University of California Berkeley. Notteboom's current research focuses on landscape analysis and design from a cultural landscapes perspective, and on the position of the designer between science, society and politics, both from a historical and a contemporary perspective. His most recent book, *Recollecting Landscapes. Rephotography, Memory and Transformation 1904-1980-2004-2014* (with Pieter Uyttenhove, 2018), deals with landscape transformation in Flanders.

Patricia Pérez Rumpler
graduated from Landscape Ecology and Landscape Planning (BOKU, Vienna, 1995) and holds an MLA from UPC, Barcelona, 1997. She started her professional work career as a researcher in CRPP (Center of Research and Landscape Projects ETSAB) directed by Rosa Barba. From 2000 on she has been working for the Department of Landscape Architecture in the Diputació de Barcelona (Regional Public Administration). Together with her main professional activity she carries out an academic activity as Adjunct Professor in the course: Landscape and Tourism (Master in Landscape Architecture UPC), develops editorial work and professional collaborations with several Architecture and Landscape Architecture studios.

Peter Petschek
Born 1959 in Bamberg, Germany. 1979 to 1985, studied at the Technical University of Berlin, Germany (Dipl.-Ing. Landscape Planning). 1985 to 1987, studied at Louisiana State University, USA (Master of Landscape Architecture). 1987 to 1996, worked at various landscape architecture firms in the USA, Germany and Switzerland. Since 1991, Professor at the HSR— University of Applied Sciences Rapperswil, Landscape Architecture Degree Program, with the main focus on site design and digital terrain modelling.

Heike Rahmann
is a landscape architect and urban researcher at RMIT University. Her research explores the intersection of landscape, technology and contemporary urbanism with focus on design practice and theory. She has two co-authored books published including *Landscape Architecture and Digital Technology: Re-conceptualising Design and Making* (with Jillian Walliss 2016).

Shannon Satherley
is a Registered Landscape Architect, and Senior Lecturer in Landscape Architecture at Queensland University of Technology in Brisbane, Australia. Her work focuses on the intersection of creative arts and landscape architectural design practice.

Ioanna Spanou
PhD Architect and landscape architect. Her PhD thesis Mapping Atmosphere: rehearsals in Mediterranean landscapes received the UPC's Extraordinary Doctorate Prize. Adjunct professor in the Department of Urbanism and Regional Planning DUOT – ETSAB – UPC. Coordinator of the Department of Urban Analysis in Barcelona Regional, Urban Development Agency.

Carl Steinitz
is the Alexander and Victoria Wiley Professor of Landscape Architecture and Planning Emeritus at Harvard Graduate School of Design, and Honorary Professor at the Centre for Advanced Spatial Analysis, University College London. He began his affiliation with the Harvard Laboratory for Computer Graphics and Spatial Analysis in 1965. In 1984, the Council of Educators in Landscape Architecture (CELA) presented Professor Steinitz with the Outstanding Educator Award for his "extraordinary contribution to environmental design education" and for his "pioneering exploration in the use of computer technology in landscape planning". He has been honoured as one of Harvard University's outstanding teachers. Professor Steinitz is principal author of *Alternative Futures for Changing Landscapes*, (2003), and author of *A Framework for Geodesign* (2012). He has lectured and given workshops at more than 170 universities, and has several honorary degrees.

Roxi Thoren
is an Associate Professor of Architecture and Landscape Architecture and Director of the Fuller Center for Productive Landscapes at the University of Oregon (USA). Her research focuses on the integration of productivity into landscape architectural design, including research and design projects around agriculture, forestry and power.

Pieter Uyttenhove
is full Professor at Ghent University and was Head of the Department of Architecture and Urbanism until 2014. He studied at KU Leuven and Institut d'urbanisme de Paris, and made his doctorate at the École des Hautes Études en Sciences Sociales, Paris. His current research deals with landscape representation, knowledge and the city; history and theory of urbanism. He published in numerous national and international periodicals, and is author of *Marcel Lods: Action, architecture, histoire* (2009), co-author of *Labo S works 2004-2014* (2014), and co-editor of *Recollecting Landscapes* (2018), among several other books.

Koray Velibeyoğlu
is an Associate Professor at the Department of Urban and Regional Planning, Izmir Institute of Technology. The main foci of his research are urban design, knowledge management, local asset-based development, nature-based solutions, urban ICT policy-making and smart cities. He can be contacted at korayvelibeyoglu@iyte.edu.tr

Anne Margrethe Wagner
Assistant Professor, University of Copenhagen. Anne's scholarly work focuses on urban transformation processes and public space within contemporary urban planning and design practice. In particular, it considers temporary uses and short-term interventions in the context of redevelopment of urban landscapes. Wagner is co-author of the book *Playable* that investigates the relation between, play, art and public space. She is part of the research project Move the Neighbourhood, investigating the relation between co-design of urban public spaces and current planning and design paradigms. Anne co-teaches the Urban Intervention Studio course where students build 1:1 interventions into landscapes in transformation.

Jillian Walliss
works in the Landscape Architecture programme at the University of Melbourne where she teaches landscape theory and design studios. She has published widely on digital design and landscape architecture, with more recent work exploring data driven design methodologies which engage with the challenges of designing for a warming climate.

Carola Wingren
has held an artistic professorship in Landscape Architecture since 2003, and is orientated towards landscape architecture and its methodologies, landscape identity and aesthetics. She investigates the act of design in relation to landscape changes, caused by climate or cultural changes. Her approach is partly based on artistic methods (also from other disciplines), where she lets her own positioning confront other researcher's approaches in a transdisciplinary explorative process.

Roland Wück
is a Senior Lecturer at the Institute of Landscape Architecture at BOKU Vienna. He teaches site design and construction in studios on Bachelor and Master level and has a focus on computing applications and advanced technologies in computer aided design.

INDEX

Note: page numbers in italic type refer to Figures; those in bold type refer to Tables.

1:1 installations 3, 5, 61, 62, 63, 66
3-D model/digital model 68
3-D visualizations 130

Aalto University, Finland, SGT (Sustainable Global Technologies) research centre 8–9, 14
abstraction, in dance movement workshop 28–29
accumulation of pollutants 74; see also pollution
acid mine drainage 33, 33
acupuncture see "green acupuncture"; Urban Acupuncture
"adaptive" architecture and urban design 104
Adobe 69, 70
aesthetic philosophy 30
Agence Folléa-Gautier 179
Agence TER 178, 181, 182, 184
aging community 155, 156–157
agriculture: organic urban farming 5; Overlook Field School 31, 32, 39, 40; re-allotment of agricultural land 203
Aitken, Steph 91, 92

Alexander 62
All Aboard the Arbutus Corridor Facebook page 87
Alliance Grain Terminal Limited 88
Alnarp Campus 196, 199
"alternating current of design" 152
alternative diagrammatic solutions 124
Alvaker, Karolina 19
Andersson, Thorbjörn 81
Andreucci, Maria-Beatrice 95, 104–119
Angelopoulos, Panagiotis 174n3
Angers 178, 184
animals, co-creating with 34, 35
anthropogenic age 136, 140
"anticipatory" path 123, 123
Antwerp 210, 211; Lillo 208
Arbutus Corridor project 81, 82, 83, 83, 84–85, 86–89, 87, 88, 89, 90, 91–92, 92, 93
art installations: as research inquiry 31, 33; see also Overlook Field School
'art of inquiry, an' (Ingold) 41
artistic methods, in dance movement workshop 28–29
Ascher, Francois 195
Asgeirsson, Gudni Brynjolfur 64
assessment, in the ReGenerate Studio 42, 46
assumptions, sequence of 124
Aubergenvile-Elisabethville 237
Aubervilliers 229
auditory collage of sounds, Arbutus Corridor project 86
Austrian Landscape Architecture Archive (LArchiv) 215–217, 216, 217, 218–219, 220, 220–221, 222–224, 225

Bachelard, Gaston 30, 41
Bachelor of Landscape Architectural Design, RMIT University 69
Baix Camp, Tarragona 165
Barba, Rosa 162, 163, 174n3
Barca Bertolla 117
Barcelona 162, 164, 166, 167, 168, 170, 172, 174n2, 174n3
Barrows, Howard 105, 118
Barthalay, K. 238
Barthes, Roland 189
Batalla, Mònica 174n3
bats 91, 92
Bayrakli 138, 145
Beau Yon de Jonage, C. 230
behaviour, in digital design 69, 73, 74, 75, 78
Bélanger, P. 140
Belgian Nature and Bird Sanctuaries 203, 212
Bento, C. 236, 237
Bermuda, 1982, case study 124–125, 125, 126–129
Bertrand, S. 228, 230, 242
beta-testing laboratory 89, 91
BIM (Building Information Modeling) 95, 96, 97–98, 98

biodiversity, integrating in the built environment 105

biofuels production 154, 155, 156–157

bio-urban growth 15

bio-urban healing 14

bio-urban organism 15

bio-urban restoration 8

Biourbanism 9, 14

bio-walls 105

Blanchon, Bernadette 201, 226–245

Blois 178, 184, 244

blue infrastructure 121, 138, 140, 143, 146, 149

bodily experience: value of 28;
see also dance movement workshop

Boeri, Stefano 209

Boisfort 237

BOKU (University of Natural Resources and Life Sciences) 214, 215, 216; *see also* LArchiv (Austrian Landscape Architecture Archive)

Bonnemaison, Tamara 86, 91–92, 93

Bordeaux 178, 181, 184

Bornova 138, 140

Bornova stream 137, 138, 143, 144; micro-basin 138, 139, 140, 143–144, 144, 146, 148

Bossard, P. 240

Bouan, B. 233

Bouju, H. 240

Braouch, L. 240

brief iPhone film, Arbutus Corridor project 86

Brightmoor neighborhood, Detroit 158

Brisbane Powerhouse 42, 43, 44, 45, 46, 47, 48, 48–49, 49, 50, 51, 52, 52–53, 53, 54

Bromell, Larsola 20

Buchanan, R. 43

Bue, Cæcilie Andrea 64

Building Information Modeling (BIM) 95, 96, 97–98, 98

Burre, Theresa 65

CAD classes 216–217, 217, 218–220, 220

Cadenasso, Mary 153

Calvet, T. 240

Campos, Joan 65

Canada: Arbutus Corridor project 81, 82, 83, 83, 84–85, 86–89, 87, 88, 89, 90, 91–92, 92, 93

Canadian Pacific Railway 83, 86, 87

Canfield, Tess 130–131

Carpentier, H. 228, 230, 242

Casagrande, Marco 2, 3, 4–15, 56

Castilla La Mancha, Spain, 2006-7, case study 131

Castrejon, Anibal Figueroa 130

Catalonia, Spain 162

Cathelain 228, 230, 242, 245

Cenci, Consuela 117

Centre Nationales d'Études et de Recherches Paysagères (CNERP) 177

Charlier, Georges 204–208

Charman, Audrey 40, 40

Chatenay-Malabry 228, 230, 233, 239, 242

Chen Cheng-Chen 14

Chinese Culture University Department of Architecture 5

choreography 16, 17, 23, 28;
see also dance movement workshop

Civil 3D 99, 101, 103

Clermontonerre, L. 240

climate change: climate-change adaptation 104; climate-change mitigation 104, 109; and coastal tourism 162

CNC routed model 70

CNERP (Centre Nationales d'Études et de Recherches Paysagères) 177

coastal erosion dance movement workshop 18, 19, 21, 23, 24, 25, 26, 27

coastal landscapes/landscape design 163, 163, 165, 165, 166–168, 169, 170, 171, 172–173

coastal leisure 162, 171

collaboration, and the Urban Intervention Studio 57

collaborative studio 122–124, 123; Bermuda, 1982, case study 124–125, 125, 126–129; Castilla La Mancha, Spain, 2006-7, case study 131; team organisation and project management 133–134; Technical University of Lisbon workshop, 2008 131, 132, 133; Tepotzotlan, Mexico, 2004-5, case study 130; Zona Industriale Padova (ZIP), Italy, 2006-5, case study 130–131

collective Local Knowledge 14

collective mind 4

"commedia dell'architettura" 4

computational design 68; *see also* digital design

concrete visualization 28

contemporaneity 34, 37

contour lines 97, 99, 178, 230, 231

Corajoud, Michel 177, 178, 180, 181, 181

Corboz, A. 227–228

Corner, James 80, 181

Costeramon, A. 233

Coulon, Jacques 178

'creative inhabitance' (Ingold) 43

creative landscape inhabitance teaching strategy, ReGenerate Studio (Queensland University of Technology) 43, 44, 45, 46, 47, 48, 48–49, 49, 50, 51, 52, 52–53, 53, 54

creativity 2, 3, 46; creative studio process 146; ReGenerate Studio 42, 43, 46, 53

Créteil 239, 240

cross-disciplinary dialog 9

cross-scale learning 148

Cupelloni, Luciano 111, 113, 115

Dachau-Schlessheimer canal 115

Dalsgaard, Katrine 64

dance movement workshop 2, 18, 19, 20, 21, 23, 24, 25, 26, 27; discussion of 27–29; students' course evaluations 23

"dancing through the landscape" 17

data, in digital design 68, 69, 70, 73–74, 75, 78

Dauvergne, Pierre 177

David, Daniel 68

Index | **253**

Davis, Bryn 40, 40

De Cleene, Michiel 204–208

de Courtois, Stéphanie 244

De Smedt, Julian 197

Debenest, Q. 240

deductive logic 123, 124

Delbaere, Denis 244

Délegue, C. 240

Delphi technique 124–125, 126–127, 131, 133

Derska, Marta 65

design charrettes 121, 140; IFLA 2016 World Congress International Student Charette 117, 118

design ethic 41

design methods: "THE design method" 123

design options 125

design process 3, 16, 34, 66, 69, 81, 154; Digital Design 68–69, 73, 74, 78; ReGenerate Studio 42, 43, 49

design "sandwich" 132

design strategies 140, 162; collaborative studio 123, 124, 125, 131, 132, 133; Green Infrastructure (GI) 95, 104, 109

Design Techniques, Master of Landscape Architecture, University of Melbourne 69–70, 71, 72, 72–73

design thinking 3, 30, 66, 121, 190, 198n2, 220; corporate 148; digital design 68, 70, 78; regional 138, 140, 142, 143; for unpredictable futures 197

'designerly thinking' 69

Desmeules, E. 233

Desvignes, Michel 181

Detroit 158, 159

Di Sante, Giada 106, 108, 115, 117

'dialogue with the materials of the problem' 69

Díaz, Purificación 174n3

didactic methodology 56

Diedrich, Lisa 81, 121, 186–199

digital adaptations 125

digital design 2, 3, 68, 78; data and simulation 73–74, 75, 76, 77, 78; foundational workflows 69–70, 71, 72, 72–73; as a parametric pedagogy 68–69

digital design pedagogy 69; see also digital design

digital grading 96, 99, 100, 103; see also grading

digital models 68, 69, 70, 71, 72; DTM (Digital Terrain Model) 98, 98, 99

digital tools 155

"dispose" phase of design 52, 153, 154

Doherty, Claire 30, 34

Donadieu, Pierre 121, 176–185

double-blind peer-review research 151–152

Doughty, H. A. 42

drawing: drawing and photo exercises, Urban Intervention Studio 58; drawing courses 217, 217, 218–220, 220; see also sketches/sketching

DTM (Digital Terrain Model) 98, 98, 99

Durand, C. 230

eclectic atlas 209

École Nationale Supérieure de Versailles (ENSP Versailles) 177, 178, 179, 181, 226

ecological knowledge 150–151

ecological turn in landscape science 150, 154

ecologically sustainable urban development 4

ecosystem services 104, 109

educating "conductors" 122, 133, 134

Eeklo 206, 209

Elinder, Frans 64

Ellsworth, E. A. 46

embodied knowledge 29

ENSP Versailles (École Nationale Supérieure de Versailles) 177, 178, 179, 181, 226

environmental awareness 28

environmental science 151

Environmental Technical Design 95, 104–105, 107, 115, 118; teaching and learning in PBL course units 106–107, 107, 108, 109, 110–115, 115, 116–117

'Environmental Technological Sustainability' course unit 107, 117, 118

Esch, Albert 215, 216, 218, 220

EUROPAN competition 191

event-in-progress, place as 37, 39, 40, 38

evidence-based design 118

ex-cathedra landscape 203

experimentation 57, 177; ReGenerate Studio 42, 43, 46, 48

explorative artistic methods 28

"exploratory" path 123, 123, 124

Facebook: Arbutus Corridor project 87

Farsø, Mads 121, 186–199

Feig, J. 233

Fernandex Martinez, E. 233

field trips 123, 216

fieldwork, in Overlook Field School 31, 32, 33, 33, 34, 35, 36, 37, 38, 39, 40, 40–41

finding (Girot's Four Trace Concepts) 80, 83, 89, 90, 91, 92

"first coasts" 171

First generation cities 14

First Nations, Canada 86

'first nature' 140

Flanders see Recollecting Landscapes project

Flemish Architecture Institute 203, 211

Foldager, Kasper 64

Follies theme, Urban Intervention Studio 59

forestry, in Overlook Field School 34, 36, 37, 38, 39, 40

formal imagination 30, 41

Forman, Richard T. T. 153

former industrial sites 43, 56, 59, 178

Fouché, O. 229

founding (Girot's Four Trace Concepts) 80, 83, 91–92, 92, 93

Four Trace Concepts (Girot) 3, 80, 81; Arbutus Corridor project 81, 82, 83, 83, 84–85, 86–89, 87, 88, 89, 90, 91–92, 92, 93 fourth nature 138, 140

France: landscape architecture 227; landscape architects 81; landscape urbanism 121, 176–178, 179, 180, 180–181, 181–183, 184

Free University of Brussels (Université Libre de Bruxelles) 203

French Order of Architects 184

Froh, Emma 36, 37

Fundació Universitat Politècnica de Catalunya 174n3

Gardarsson, Vivica 62

Garden city La Butte Rouge 228, 230, 233, 239, 242

Gascon, L. 238

Gatier, J. 240

Gaudin, Olivier 244

Geertz, Clifford 228

geography 16, 27, 140, 151, 239, 244; collaborative studio 122, 123; landscape urbanism, French 177, 178, 179, 180, 180, 181, 184

Germundsson, Tomas 29

"getting started" 122, 123, 123

Ghent University 203

GI (Green Infrastructure) 95, 104, 105, 138; teaching and learning in PBL course units 106–107, 107, 108, 109, 110–115, 115, 116–117

Girot, Christophe 3, 69, 80–81, 83, 86, 89, 92; see also Four Trace Concepts (Girot)

GNSS (Global Navigation Satellite Systems) 97–98

Goldsworthy, A. 48

Gormotte, F. 235

Gottlieb, Martha 64

Goula, Maria 121, 162–175

Goven, R. 235

grading, and rainwater management 97, 98, 99, 100, 101, 103

"grand paysage" 177

graphical communication methods 28; see also representational techniques

Grasshopper 69, 70, 72

"green acupuncture" 20

Green Infrastructure see GI (Green Infrastructure)

green roofs 96, 105

'greening the grey' 109

Grose, Margaret 150–151

grounding (Girot's Four Trace Concepts) 80, 83, 86–88, 87, 88, 90, 91, 92

Gu, A. 233

Guandu flood plains of Taiwan 9

guerrilla landscape urbanism 2

Hafeniuniversität 56

Halprin, Anna 16

Halprin, Lawrence 16, 28

Harris, Dianne 214

HCMC (Ho Chi Minh City), Vietnam, pollution study 73, 74, 75

Healey, M. 214

heat: digital design studies 73–74, 75, 76, 77, 78

Helms, Karin 121, 176–185

Helsingborg 20, 21

Helsinger 64

heroic leap 124

Herrington, Susan 2, 3, 80–93

Hill, Kristina 151, 153

Hines, Patty 39, 40

history teaching 226; 20th-century case studies 226–227; multi-scale method 228, 229, 229, 230–231, 231, 232–238, 239, 240, 241–242, 242, 243, 244, 244; theoretical basis for 227–229

'History Workshop' 226; see also history teaching

Ho Chi Minh City (HCMC), Vietnam, pollution study 73, 74, 75

Höganäs 23, 24, 25, 26

Hopquin, A. 240

Hsieh Ying-chun 5, 8

HSR University of Applied Sciences Rapperswil, Switzerland 96, 99, 100, 101, 102, 103

Hughes, M. 214

Human Hotel, The 56

Husselr, Edmund 80, 86

identifying the preferences 125

IFLA Europe 187

IFLA International Federation of Landscape Architects: IFLA 2016 World Congress International Student Charette 117, 118

IMLA International Master in Landscape Architecture 106, 108

in situ: Urban Intervention Studio 56, 57, 58

inclusive urban design 104, 109

inductive logic 123, 124

industrial sites, former 43, 56, 59, 178

Ingold, Timothy 30, 41, 43, 46

inhabitance see creative landscape inhabitance teaching strategy, ReGenerate Studio (Queensland University of Technology)

initial designs 31, 125, 129

installations: ReGenerate Studio 43, 46, 49, 50, 52, 52; see also 1:1 installations; site-based art installations; site-specific design installations, Urban Intervention Studio

Institute of Landscape Architecture (ILA), University of Natural Resources and Life Sciences (BOKU) see LArchiv (Austrian Landscape Architecture Archive)

integrating biodiversity in the built environment 105

integrative pedagogy 148

interdisciplinary collaboration 152

interdisciplinary co-operative learning 105, 107

interdisciplinary landscape project education see regional landscape project studio

interfaces 61

International Society of Biourbanism 9, 14

interventions: operational and tactical 149; as transformative agents 61

Index | 255

iPhone film, Arbutus Corridor project 86

İzmir 121, 140, 143

İzmir Bay 138, 139, 143

İzmir metropolitan city 121

Jackson, J. B. 202

Jacobsen, Linnea Carlov 62

Jensen, Kristine Wallin 65

Jepson-Sullivan, Andrew 39, 40

Jiayang Li 153, 158–159

Johnson, Bart 151

Journal of Landscape Architecture (JoLA) 192, 228

Jung, S. 238

JUT Foundation for Arts and Architecture 9, 14

Kahn, Andrea 58

Källman, Paulina 21

Kang Min-Jay 5

Kaplan, Adnan 121, 136–161

Kau, Justin 34, 35

Kempenaers, Jan 204–208

Kinder Morgan Vancouver Wharves 88

Kjeldsen, Marlene 64

Klemskerke 207, 209

knowledge: knowledge management 190; new knowledge building 4, 9, 14; students as producers of 203, 209

Køge Harbor 57

Kondolf, G. M. 148

KoseLička 215, 216

Krippner, Ulrike 201, 214–225

Kwoon, Miwon 58

La Réunion 179

Labaro Prima Porta 111

Laboratory for Urbanism, Ghent University 203

Lamm, Bettina 2, 3, 56–67

landing (Girot's Four Trace Concepts) 80, 83, 83, 84, 86, 91, 92

Landscape and Tourism: New uses for Old territories studio 162

landscape architects 120, 221; French 177, 183, 184

Landscape Architecture and Urbanism research group, *University of Copenhagen* 56

landscape architecture schools: France 176, 177; North America 81

landscape biography 202, 209

landscape complexity 122

landscape design 28, 46, 49, 53, 123, 151, 155; coastal landscapes 162–163, 164, 165, 165, 166–168, 169, 170, 171, 172–173

landscape ecology 151

landscape history 201, 209, 214, 215, 216, 221, 225; LArchiv (Austrian Landscape Architecture Archive) 215–217, 216, 217, 218–219, 220, 220–221, 222–224, 225; Recollecting Landscapes project 202–203, 204–208, 209, 210, 210, 211, 211–212

landscape infrastructure 136, 138, 140, 142, 146, 147, 149

landscape morphology 178, 179, 180

'landscape performance' 109, 119n4

Landscape Scenographies theme, Urban Intervention Studio 59, 64

landscape science 150–151, 159; bringing into studio 152–153, 154, 155, 156, 157, 158; implications for landscape architecture teaching 154–155; importance of for learning and practice 151–152

landscape transformation 202–203, 209, 212

landscape urbanism 2, 81, 226; French context 121, 176–178, 179, 180, 180–181, 181–183, 184

Landschaftspark Duisburg-Nord 43

Lapleau, E. 237

LArchiv (Austrian Landscape Architecture Archive) 215–217, 216, 217, 218–219, 220, 220–221, 222–224, 225

Lassus, Bernard 177

"latent identities" of coastal sites 163

Latour, Bruno 171

Latz, Peter 43

learning outcomes 193, 195–196, 198n1, 221; ReGenerate Studio 3, 42, 43, 46, 70

Lee, Gini 192

Lefebvre, M. 240

leisure landscapes 163

Le:Notre Landscape Forum 2017 108

Leo-Kong Channel 9

Lewis, P. H. 140

Lička, Lilli 201, 214–225

Lille 178, 184

Lindholm, Gunilla 81

Linnros, Fanny 22

Local Knowledge: Taipei City 8, 14, 15

local stakeholders: Urban Intervention Studio 57, 58, 61, 63, 66

location, in site-based art installations 34, 35, 36

Lund, Natasja 64

Lyle, John 152

Lynch, Kevin 178

Lyon, P. 42

MA (Millennium Ecosystem Assessment) 104

Madsen, Simon 64

Majoral, Anna 174n3

Malanot, O. 236, 237

Malmö 19, 20, 188, 193, 194

Manzer, Deanne 87, 87

mapmaking 59

Mareis, C. 215

Marguerit, Alain 178

'market-driven development' 136, 138, 145, 149

Marx, Karl 41

Massart, Jean 203, 204–208, 210, 211–212

Massey, Doreen 41

Master of Landscape Architecture, University of Melbourne 69, 73

material imagination 30

mature coastal tourist destinations 171

meaningful learning 105, 107

mechanisms of landscape transformation 203, 209

Mediterranean sea 121, 162–163, 169, 171

Meining, D. W. 202

Melbourne: heat study 73–74, 75, 77;
see also University of Melbourne

Metropolitan Design Dynamics studio,
University of Michigan 153

Meyer, Elizabeth 81

Meyers, Shelby 37, 39

micro-urban settlements 15

Millennium Ecosystem Assessment (MA) 104

mind maps 138, 142

mockups 61, 62

Morillon, E. 233

'movement and experience' workshop 23

"movement through the landscape" 16, 17

movement workshops 17, 18, 19, 20, 20, 21, 22, 23

multidisciplinary teams 115, 122

multiple scales, Arbutus Corridor project 91

multi-scalar context 136, 138, 139, 140, 148

multi-scale method of teaching history
228, 229, 229, 230–231, 231, 232–238, 239, 240, 241–242,
242, 243, 244, 244

Munich 106, 108

Munoz, A. 230

Nantou County 5

narratives 43

Nassauer, Joan Iverson 120, 150–161

National Botanic Garden of Belgium 203, 212

National Taiwan University: Department of Anthropology 9;
Department of Social Building 5; Department of Sociology
9, 14

Natural Capital 104, 105

Nature as Agriculture 143

Nature as Green/Blueways 143

Nature as History 143

Nature as Recreation 143

Nature as Urban Development and Housing 143

'nature' types 140

nature-based solutions 104, 109

'nature-urban' transect 138, 143

Necessary Digressions exercise, Arbutus Corridor project 86

Nedelec, M. 240

Negron, M. 240

Neuman, M. 146

new knowledge building 4, 9, 14

Ní Neíll, Rionach 24, 29

Nichini, Thomas 64

Nomeros Valley 138, 143

nominated topographical operation 70

non-linear workflows 69, 78

Notteboom, Bruno 201, 202–213

Nussbaum, B. 43

Nyhamnen, Malmö 193

on-going rephotographic survey 202;
see also Recollecting Landscapes project

on-site: Urban Intervention Studio 57, 59, 61, 66

on-site fieldwork 194

Open Form 15

open meetings, Bermuda case study 124

operational interventions 149

Opwijk 204

Öresund/ Öresundsect course, SLU Alnarp
188, 189, 192–195, 196

organic urban farming 5

Osborn, Brian 69

Osty, Jacqueline 184

Overlook Field School
31, 32, 33, 33, 34, 35, 36, 37, 38, 39, 40, 40–41

Oxman, R. 68–69

paper-based design 69

Paracity 12, 13, 15

parametric design process 68, 69

parametric modelling 68–69, 70

parametric pedagogy, digital design as 68–69

parametric processes of design 69, 73, 78

parametric techniques 72

Parco del Roncajette 130

Paris 201, 230, 238, 239, 242

Patamia, Chiara 117

PBL (Problem [or Project]-based Learning) 115, 118;
Green Infrastructure design
106–107, 107, 108, 109, 110–115, 115, 116–117

peer-review research 151–152

peer-to-peer learning 73

Pennsylvania: coal mining industry 40; Overlook Field
School 31, 32, 33, 33, 34, 35, 36, 37, 38, 39, 40, 40–41

Pérez Rumpler, Patricia 121, 162–175

performance: ReGenerate Studio 43, 45, 46, 48, 49

permeable paving 96, 105

Petschek, Peter 95, 96–103

Pettinari, Jessica 111

'phenomenal art' 33

phenomenological approach 58

phenomenological tradition 58

phenomenology 80, 86

photography: drawing and photo exercises, Urban Intervention Studio 58; on-going rephotographic survey 202

physical models 70, 70, 72, 125

Pickett, Steward 153

Pié, Ricard 163, 174n2, 174n3, 174n4

Piercy, Gini 37, 38

Pihooja, Katherine 83, 87, 87, 89, 91

Pirri, Guglielmo 113, 117

Pitt, Shannon 84, 86

Index | 257

place: as an event-in-progress 37, 39, 40, 38; visitor's perception of 33

planning methods: "THE planning method" 123

'poetic creation' 30

Poirier, L. 230

political landscapes 202, 212

Pollack, Kyle 37, 39

pollution: digital design studies 73–74, 75, 76, 77, 78

Poranski, Colin 37, 39

Port Bacarés, Languedoc Rousillon 171, 173

post-industrial sites 43, 56, 59, 178; see also Arbutus Corridor project

post-World War II landscape projects 221

power industry, in Overlook Field School 31, 32, 33, 33, 34, 35, 40, 40

Prahm, Nanna Kontni 64

problem identification 122

Problem [or Project]-based Learning see PBL (Problem [or Project]-based Learning)

project submission 143

"propose" phase of design 152, 154

prototyping 30, 74, 75, 78

Provost, L. 230

public discussion, of dance movement workshop 28

public, the, identifying the preferences of 125

'quiet distillation,' in sited art 34

Rahmann, Heike 2, 3, 68–78

railway sites see Arbutus Corridor project

rain gardens 105

rainwater management 95, 96–97, 103; and BIM (Building Information Modeling) 95, 96, 97–98, 98; and grading 97, 98, 99, 100, 101, 103; HSR site engineering education 96, 99, 100, 101, 102, 103; sustainable urban drainage systems 96, 105, 109; see also stormwater management

Ramsden, P. 225

Rankebrandt, A. 238

re-allotment of agricultural land 203

real-time data in digital design 68, 69, 73, 78

Recollecting Landscapes project 202–203, 204–208, 209, 210, 210, 211, 211–212

Recovering Landscape: Essays in Contemporary Landscape Architecture (Corner) 80, 81

recovering landscapes 80, 81

Refshaleøen 59, 60, 62, 63

Regal, S. 238

ReGenerate Studio (Queensland University of Technology) 42–43; creative landscape inhabitance teaching strategy 43, 44, 45, 46, 47, 48, 48–49, 49, 50, 51, 52, 52–53, 53, 54

regional design thinking 140, 142, 143

regional landscape context 136, 137, 138, 140, 142, 143, 148, 149

regional landscape project studio 136, 137, 139, 139, 1149; application of 140, **141**, 143; basic concepts and terms 138, 140, 142; outputs 143–146.144, 145, 146, 147, 148, 148

'region-urban-local' hierarchical order 138

re-naturing 138, 140, 143

'Re-naturing: Healing the Cities' project 138

Renault-Flins district 238

rendered panoramic views 70, 71

representational techniques 22, 28; coastal landscapes 165, 169; digital 68, 69, 81

research 150; double-blind peer-review research 151–152; teaching-research nexus 214–215, 215; see also landscape science

research-based, interdisciplinary project studios 149

resilient architecture 104, 109

resort design 162

Revit 101, 103

Rhinoceros (Rhino) 69, 70, 70, 72

Richard, L. 237

Rigal, B. 230

'riparian city' concept 144, 145, 147–148

Rittel, Horst 189

River Urbanism 9

RMIT University 68, 70, 72; Bachelor of Landscape Architectural Design 69

Roan Ching-Yueh 5, 8

Roberts, A. 214

Robin, J. 238

Rome 111, 113

Rosengård, Malmö 19

Rouchier, G. 238

Ruffin, M. 240

Ruin Academy, Taipei 9, 10, 11, 14

Saccone, Delfina 117

Salman, Eliza 106, 108

Samuels, Marwyn 202

'Sapienza' Università di Roma see Environmental Technical Design

Satherley, Shannon 2, 3, 42–55

scale 229, 231, 239, 241

scenarios: collaborative studio 124, 130

Schmitke, Chelsea 88, 88, 90

Schneider, A. 230, 231, 232, 234

Schön, Donald 69

School of Architecture, Fundació Universitat Politècnica de Catalunya 174n3

science: and skepticism 150; see also landscape science

Scott, Heather 88, 88, 90

sea level rise dance movement workshop 18, 19, 20, 21, 23, 24, 25, 26, 27

second coast 121, 163, 165, 169, 171

second generation cities 15

second nature 140

sections 220, 226, 229, 230, 231, 231, 232, 233, 236, 237, 238, 240, 241

Seine Rive Gauche 239, 242

Sell, Andrew 153, 154, 155–157

"sensitivity-test" 124

sensual experiences, and sited art 34

sequence of the assumptions 124

Sgard, Jacques 177

SGT (Sustainable Global Technologies) research centre, Aalto University, Finland 8–9, 14

Sharky, Bruce 99

Simon, Jacques 178

simulation, in digital design 68, 69, 73–74, 75, 76, 77, 78

site conditioned sculpture 33–34

site, in site-based art installations 34, 35, 36

site planning: creative landscape inhabitance 46, 53; ReGenerate Studio 42

site-based art installations, Overlook Field School 3, 30, 31, 32, 33, 33, 34, 35, 36, 37, 38, 39, 40, 40–41

site-specific design installations, Urban Intervention Studio 56–58, 58, 59, 59, 60, 61, 62, 63, 63, 64, 65, 66

situated art, Overlook Field School 30, 31, 32, 33, 33, 34, 35, 36, 37, 38, 39, 40, 40–41

situations, and sited art 34

Sivré, M. 230, 231, 232, 234

"size and scale" 124

skepticism, and science 150

sketches/sketching 220, 228, 231, 237, 239, 242; *see also* drawing

Smith, Keri 58

Smithson, Robert 41

sociology 14

Sørensen, Helene Bruun 64

Spaces and Interfaces theme, Urban Intervention Studio 59

'space-time compression' 41

Spain 174n4, 174n5; Castilla La Mancha, 2006-7, case study 131; coastal landscape design 162, 163, 164, 166, 167, 168, 170, 172

Spanou, Ioanna 121, 162–175

'spatial device' 231

Spatial Dialogues theme, Urban Intervention Studio 59

Spencer, Rachel 36, 37

spot elevations 97, 99

sprawling habitation 203

stakeholders, local, Urban Intervention Studio 57, 58, 61, 63, 66

Steinitz, Carl 120, 122–135

STEM (science, technology, engineering, mathematics) subjects 189

Stone, Jillian 36, 37

stormwater management 96, 154, 157, 158; *see also* rainwater management

Strasbourg 182, 183

strategic approach 58

student managerial roles, collaborative studio 133

students, as producers of knowledge 203, 209

students' authorship 122

studios: *nonsite* of 41; research-based, interdisciplinary project studios 149; studio gap 57; *see also* collaborative studio; regional landscape project studio

Superkilen, Copenhagen 189

Suresnes 230, 233, 239

Suss, F. 230, 231, 232, 234

sustainable resort development 163

sustainable urban drainage systems 96, 105, 109

Svennson, Morten Gosta 62

Svensson, Jitka 29

swales 96, 97, 99, 103

Switzerland, rainwater management *see* rainwater management

'SWOT matrix' 109

system color 132

tactical interventions 149

tactical urbanism 56

tactile collage of found objects, Arbutus Corridor project 86

Taipei Basin 9, 14

Taipei City Government 4, 8, 9; Department of Urban development 14

Taiwan 2

'talk back' 69

Tamkang University Department of Architecture 5, 6, 8, 9, 12, 14

teaching-research nexus 214–215, 215

Technical University of Lisbon workshop, 2008 131, 132, 133

'Technologies for Environmental Design and Urban Requalification' course unit 107, 117, 118

Tejo river estuary, Lisbon 131

Telnykh, Evgeniia 106, 108

temporal stages, Arbutus Corridor project 91

temporary architecture 56

Tepotzotlan, Mexico, 2004-5, case study 130

terrain grading 96, 97; *see also* grading

terrain vague 61

Thau, J. 230, 231, 232, 234

"THE design method" 123

"THE planning method" 123

Theatre Island 57, 59, 63, 64, 65

Thinking Eyes course, SLU Alnarp 186, 192–194, 195–196

Third Generation City 4, 8, 9, 10, 14

third nature 140

Thoren, Roxi 2, 3, 30–41

Topion, T. 235

topography, in digital design 70

Touboul, A. 229

tourism: coastal 163; mature coastal tourist destinations 171; sustainable resort development 163

training, French landscape architecture 176, 177–178, 184

transformative agents, interventions as 61

Trappes 177

Treasure Hill, Taipei 4–5, 6, 7, 7–8, 14

Tromp van Holst, Kate 34, 35

Turin 117

Turrell, James 31, 33

UAM (Universidad Autonoma Metropolitana) 130

Université Libre de Bruxelles (Free University of Brussels) 203

University of British Columbia: Arbutus Corridor project 81, 82, 83, 83, 84–85, 86–89, 87, 88, 89, 90, 91–92, 92, 93

University of Copenhagen 189; *Landscape Architecture and Urbanism* research group 56

University of Melbourne 68, 72, 72–73; Master of Landscape Architecture 69, 73

University of Michigan 153

University of Natural Resources and Life Sciences (BOKU) 214, 215, 216; *see also* LArchiv (Austrian Landscape Architecture Archive)

University of the Neighbourhood 56

University of Washington 228–229

Urban Acupuncture 2, 8, 9, 14, 15, 56

urban areas in transition 56

Urban Breakfast Salon 61, 63, 63

urban compost 8

urban design: and acupuncture 14; "adaptive" 104; inclusive 104, 109

urban development, ecologically sustainable 4

urban ecological restoration 4, 14

urban ecology 150, 151

urban energy flows 4

urban farming, organic 5

urban interfaces 61

Urban Intervention Studio 56–58, 58, 59, 59, 60, 61, 62, 63, 63, 64, 65, 66

urban morphology 74

urban nomad settlement 5

Urban Patches 143

urban transformation 56

urban waterfronts 162

USGS national Wildlife Center 91

Uyttenhove, Pieter 201, 202–213

value of bodily experience 28

van Dooren, Noël 81

Vancouver, Canada: Arbutus Corridor project 81, 82, 83, 83, 84–85, 86–89, 87, 88, 89, 90, 91–92, 92, 93

Vansgaard, Laura 64

Vargas-Moreno, Juan Carlos 130–131

Varhegyi, Lajos 29

Varis, Olli 14

Vazzanino, E. 235

Velibeyoğlu, Koray 121, 136–161

Vellinge 23

velocities, Arbutus Corridor project 91

Venice lagoon 130

vernacular landscape 202, 212

Verneuil 230, 231, 232, 234, 235, 236, 237, 243

Versailles 121, 176, 177, 178, 179, 181, 201

vertically integrated studios, RMIT University 70, 72

Vexlard, Gilles 178

Viale Colli Portuensi 113

Vicenzotti, Vera 81

Vienna 221, 223, 224; *see also* University of Natural Resources and Life Sciences (BOKU)

visitor's perception of the place 33

'visual appropriation' of landscape 203

visual assemblage of site photos, Arbutus Corridor project 84–85, 86

visual matrix, Arbutus Corridor project 89

visual representation 69; *see also* representational techniques

Vogt, Günther 187

Wageningen University 177

Wagner, Anne Margrethe 3, 56–67

Waldheim, Charles 81, 176, 181

"walking through the landscape" 16, 17

Walliss, Jillian 2, 3, 68–78

Walsh, Christopher 153

water: in Overlook Field School 34, 37, 39; water cycle, in coastal areas 163, 165; *see also* rainwater management; stormwater management

water percolation 96, 97, 99, 100, 103

water retention 96–97, 99, 100, 103

water-based regional/urban transformation 136, 138, 146

Webb, John S. 24, 25, 26, 29

Werthmann, Christian 131

'wicked problems' 187, 189, 189

Wilson, S. E. 46

Wingren, Carola 2, 16–29

Wladar, Josef Oskar 215, 216, 220, 221, 222, 224

WNS (White-Nose Syndrome), in bats 91

Woess, Friedrich 215, 216, 220

Wück, Roland 201, 214–225

Xindian River, Taipei 4

Yocom, K. 148

Zago, M. 238

Zamberlain, L. 46

Zehrfuss, B. 238

zero nature through fourth nature 18

Ziou He 106, 108

Zona Industriale Padova (ZIP), Italy, 2006-5, case study 130–131

Zonnebeke 205